In the Family Way

IN THE FAMILY WAY

Childbearing in the British Aristocracy, 1760–1860

Judith Schneid Lewis

Rutgers University Press
New Brunswick, New Jersey

Copyright © 1986 by Rutgers,
The State University
All Rights Reserved
Manufactured in the United States of America

Library of Congress Cataloging in Publication Data
Lewis, Judith Schneid, 1950–
In the family way.

Bibliography: p.
Includes index.
1. Motherhood—Great Britain—History. 2. Mothers—
Great Britain—Attitudes—History. 3. Great Britain—
Nobility—History. 4. Childbirth—Great Britain—History.
5. Family—Great Britain—History. I. Title.
HQ759.L49   1986   306.8'743'0941   85–1907
ISBN 0–8135–1116–x

For

my mother

and

my daughter

Contents

Acknowledgments
ix

Introduction: Public Functions, Private Emotions
1

CHAPTER I
Love and Marriage
17

CHAPTER II
The Name of Mother
57

CHAPTER III
The Aristocratic Accoucheur
85

CHAPTER IV
Pregnancy
122

CHAPTER V
The Confinement: Childbirth
153

CHAPTER VI
The Confinement: Recovery
193

Contents

In Conclusion
218

Appendix: Summary of Group Experience
233

Notes
245

Bibliography
291

Index
305

Acknowledgments

THIS book began as a graduate school seminar paper some ten years ago, evolving into a dissertation along the way. My major intellectual debt is owed to David Spring, whose support for the project—at a time when the subject still seemed highly unorthodox—was of critical importance. Thanks also go to other members of the Department of History at Johns Hopkins University whose support for my dissertation should not pass unnoticed. Nor should the contribution of Anthony Wohl of Vassar College, under whose guidance (if not spell) I first decided to become a historian—a decision I have never regretted.

Special thanks go to the Woodrow Wilson Foundation, which provided me with a dissertation fellowship in women's studies. That financial and moral assistance came at a crucial moment in the original manuscript's preparation.

My colleagues at the University of Oklahoma have been enormously helpful by providing an excellent working environment. Robert Griswold, Paul Gilje, and Gary Cohen read early portions of the book, and I have tried to incorporate their always pertinent suggestions. I owe a special debt to William Savage, who, during a very busy period in his own life, took time to read the entire manuscript and offer his own pungent comments. His efforts are especially appreciated. So, too, are those of Martha Penisten, who has cheerfully, intelligently, and expeditiously typed the manuscript. Thanks also go to my students at the University of Oklahoma, particularly those in my Eighteenth-Century England class. Their enthusiasm for the subject was reassuring to a person who fears the public no longer finds history relevant or even interesting; their provocative insights were enormously helpful in the preparation of this book.

England's many archive collections, both private and public, are part of her great national heritage. This book could not have been written without the cooperation of the many owners and keepers of such collections who allowed me the privilege of reading these documents and then gave me permission to quote from them. The following individuals and institutions richly deserve my thanks: the Department of Manuscripts of the British Library; the staff of the Warwickshire County Record Office, and the Marquess of Hertford, for permission to use the Seymour of Ragley MSS; the Hertfordshire County Record Office and the Earl of Verulam, for the Gorhambury MSS; the Kent Archives Office; the Staffordshire Record Office and Lord Hatherton, for the Hatherton MSS; the Public Records Office in London, for the Crown copyright material in its custody; and the Greater London Record Office, including the Middlesex Records. I also appreciate the assistance of His Grace the Duke of Grafton, for permission to quote from the Grafton MSS; the Administrator at Ickworth House, for the Hervey MSS; and Sir William Bunbury, for the Bunbury MSS; all of which are now deposited at the West Suffolk Records Office, Bury St. Edmunds. I also wish to thank the staff of that office for their friendly and efficient service. The Banbury/Knollys papers were used with the permission and assistance of the Hampshire Record Office, whose help was also appreciated. Documents from the collection of the Wellcome Institute were used by courtesy of the Wellcome Trustees. The staff of the Royal Commission on Historical Manuscripts has provided continued assistance. Special thanks must go to Richard Page Croft, Maldwin Drummond, and Richard Hobbs, who, with enthusiasm and graciousness, gave me access to their valuable private collections of family papers—at some risk to the privacy of their respective ancestors.

The jacket photograph is of a portrait of Georgiana, Duchess of Devonshire, and her daughter, by Sir Joshua Reynolds. The painting is part of the Devonshire Collection at Chatsworth and was reproduced by permission of the Chatsworth Settlement Trustees.

I have the permission of the *Journal of Social History* to quote from my article, "Maternal Health in the English Aristocracy, 1790–1840: Myths and Realities," which appeared in the Fall 1983 issue.

Greatest thanks must be reserved for the members of my family. My parents, Ruth and Murray Schneid, have, from my earliest years, had an unflagging, if not always uncritical, confidence in my abilities. Their support has probably been the greatest single factor in whatever success I may achieve; my gratitude toward them is therefore incalculable.

Instead of thanking a nonexistent wife for keeping the kids out of my way, I prefer to use this opportunity to thank my daughter, Laura, for staying *in* my way. She testifies daily, if unwittingly, to the power of the human spirit, reminding me constantly of our enormous capacity for learning and for caring. Most of all, she has provided daily reminders that the pleasures of motherhood, however culturally construed, are nonetheless real. By keeping my life in perspective, she has made me a better historian. I look forward to the day when she is old enough to read this.

Norman, Oklahoma
October 1984

In the Family Way

Introduction: Public Functions, Private Emotions

WHEN the poet Shelley asked, "Can man be free if woman be a slave?" his readers might have understood that the enslavement in question had been imposed as much by the nearly untrammeled fetters of reproductive biology as by the economic and legal arrangements of patriarchal society. That women were more or less enslaved for the best years of their lives by the continuing cycle of pregnancy, childbirth, and lactation was an assumption that Shelley's contemporaries could make. Certainly it has been made by twentieth-century historians of women and the family. The purely physiological burden of motherhood is an important issue for feminists, for—unlike childrearing—childbearing would seem to fall nearly equally on women of all classes. If indeed there is such an entity as women's history, then childbearing must be a unifying theme. Even Queen Victoria, at the very pinnacle of the social world, complained of the burdens imposed by reproductive biology. Childbearing "is indeed too hard and dreadful," she wrote her newly married daughter in 1859. "Men ought to have an adoration for one, and indeed to make up, for what after all, they alone, are the cause of!!!"[1]

In the creation of a history of childbearing, scholarship has come to be dominated by the theme that this critical experience once belonged exclusively to women, but eventually was "stolen" by men. The theft is thought to have taken place at some point during the nineteenth century when the triumph of the professionally trained obstetrician over the traditional midwife was assured.

Historians are also beginning to believe that the nature of marriage and family life changed between the eighteenth and nineteenth centuries. The traditional, non-emotive marriage, in which loyalties and associations were largely directed toward the lineage, came to be replaced by the "companionate" marriage, one in which private emotions, not public functions, predominated. This new form was marked by a primary loyalty to the nuclear family rather than to the larger network of kin.

The relationship between these dual transformations has been interpreted in two general ways. What we might call the orthodox feminist argument sees the development of the nuclear family, with its attendant emphasis on the values of domesticity, as a major aspect of the subordination of women during the nineteenth century. The proper sphere of women became increasingly restricted within the confines of home and family. According to this view the simultaneous rise of the obstetrician represented the advance of male supremacy, the ultimate example of the triumph of Victorian patriarchy.[2] The alternative, or revisionist, explanation, propounded by Lawrence Stone and, most recently, Edward Shorter, views the obstetrician in a more benign light.[3] As a result of the affectionate, or companionate, marriage, husbands were no longer willing to tolerate their wives' suffering as inevitable. Thus the intervention of the medicial profession is seen as an act of caring, not one of domination. According to this interpretation, while the growing cult of domesticity indeed did wean women away from the traditional female culture, the redirection of emotional energy was not necessarily pernicious. The domestic sphere had always belonged to women: the cult of domesticity simply made that sphere more important for the society at large. Women grew stronger, not weaker, as a result.

The significance of the medical profession is central to both arguments. Yet the linkage between medical developments and social history is often difficult to make. Social historians write about the family and speculate on medicine, while medical historians—if they are at all interested in the social history of their discipline—do the reverse. One problem is supplying the linkage has been the perceived difficulty of studying medicine as experienced by the patient. Too many students have relied on the official testimony of doctors, as though this were the whole story. Indeed, we have often been told that it is impossible to get the patients' view.[4] This is particularly true in the history of obstetrics. Anne Oakley has written that what "the sociology of reproduction has lacked" is "a repertoire of first-hand accounts." Childbearing women, she complains, "have been represented as statistics."[5] This lacuna has heretofore rendered nearly impossible the task of understanding the relationship of medicine to family life.

With the study of the British aristocracy, however, the linkage can be made. The leading obstetricians of the day, the ones who wrote the most frequently quoted textbooks and instructed the greatest number of students, were usually the personal attendants of the British aristocracy. And the members of the British aristocracy, male and female alike, wrote, often at great length, about their experiences with these doctors. Their letters and diaries form a rich, though hitherto largely untapped source for studying the role of childbearing in the lives of women in the past.

The story of childbearing is, however, much more than the story of the interaction of the public and its medical advisers. To complete the picture we need to know much more about the values and attitudes with which British families greeted the childbearing experience. To understand how childbearing affected and reflected the patterns of adult life, we must look more closely at those patterns. For this reason the first two chapters of this volume will be devoted in a general way to the families and individuals whose childbearing experiences will later be studied more intensely. The transition to domesticity, I shall argue, was accompanied by a privatization of values that affected every aspect of family life. By rationalizing and deritualizing childbearing, its meaning and the meaning of motherhood were irrevocably altered. The third chapter focuses on the men who delivered obstetric care to the aristocracy—the accoucheurs. Dependent as they were upon their patients for the success of their careers, these men, I argue, lacked the professional autonomy necessary to the imposition of a medical orthodoxy. Instead, medical theory and practice emerged out of the complexity of relationships between accoucheur, patient, and aristocratic family. Having established the social, economic, and ideological context in the first half of the book, the second half explores the actual conduct of childbearing in the aristocratic family which reflects these vital but changing parameters. A chapter is devoted to each of the three major stages of childbearing: pregnancy, birth, and recovery.

This is not the first time that the family life of the aristocracy has been studied, but it is the first time that a small group has been examined so closely. Focusing on fifty women and their families makes it possible for the historian to know that she is making the proper connections between experiences and attitudes—an otherwise impossible task when one confronts massive amounts of data about anonymous people. The close study of a social microcosm provides an alternative to the usual method of social history, in which juicy quotations are used to enliven an otherwise bland mass of data. The quotations are assumed to reflect mass experience, but no one can be sure that they do. By studying this small but important group so closely, I can make connections between attitudes and experiences with confidence.

The English aristocracy constituted perhaps the smallest, wealthiest, and most powerful group of people in Europe during the period under consideration. Traditionally, its wealth and social position were based on the ownership of land. At the time of the New Domesday survey in 1873, over 80 percent of the land of the United Kingdom was owned by fewer than seven thousand persons—less than half of 1 percent of the population.[6] Although the upper class was often referred to as the Upper Ten Thousand, it in fact consisted of a much smaller group of families with vast wealth and influence. To a certain extent, this group can be identified as the peerage.[7]

The peerage itself technically includes only the male bearers of one of five titles: baron, viscount, earl, marquess, and duke, in ascending order of rank. These were the men who were entitled to a seat in the House of Lords. The peerage was tiny, but growing. There were 208 peers in 1784 and 353 in 1840.[8] Unlike Continental peerages, only the head of the English family was a peer: wives and children, including heirs, bore courtesy titles only. Legally they were commoners. Thus the House of Commons was filled with heirs and younger sons of the peerage, and titled men like Lord Althorp could become a major force in the lower house. Women could never be other than commoners and could not sit in Lords. This was true even on those rare occasions when a woman inherited a title of her own. One of the women in the group of fifty was the only surviving child of the eighteenth Earl of Sutherland. As his successor, Elizabeth, Countess of Sutherland (1765–1839), was heiress to his vast estates, but she held the title only as a steward for the next male generation. In keeping with the classification used in the seminal demographic work of T. H. Hollingsworth, I have strictly defined the female aristocracy as a group composed of the wives and daughters of peers and the female members of the royal family.[9]

The fifty women discussed in this book were those whose childbearing experiences could be thoroughly recovered through a search of sources—mainly diaries and correspondence. They were all born between 1731 and 1834 and gave birth between the years 1760 and 1860, a period identified by Hollingsworth as the century of greatest fertility in the entire history of the English aristocracy. To assist the reader, these fifty women are identified, in alphabetical order, in the appendix.

The statistical experience of these fifty women generally parallels that of the aristocracy as a whole, where Hollingsworth's figures are comparable. Their fertility rate, however, appears considerably higher. This does not detract from the value of the study. The fifty women produced a mean of 7.5 children in all marriages, and just over 8 in marriages of completed fertility, as demographers refer to those marriages in which both spouses were still alive at the wife's forty-fifth birthday. Among other factors, this high fertility rate can be explained by the relative absence of childless couples in the study, who Hollingsworth estimated composed nearly 19 percent of all aristocratic marriages. Fertile couples were thus even more fertile than Hollingsworth's figures might lead one to believe. General trends, however, remained the same for the fifty women studied in comparison with the peerage as a whole. Infant mortality rates were similar at approximately 10 percent. The group's stillbirth rates were slightly higher than Hollingsworth's, but this was probably due to my enhanced ability to identify such births, which was also a factor in the group's overall fertility. In both groups, the generation born between 1775 and 1799 achieved the largest completed family size. Interestingly enough, it was among this age group that domestic values first became dominant.[10]

The fifty-woman group is socially and economically a homogeneous one: to be included, a woman had to be part of the great landowning Anglican ascendancy that dominated every aspect of British life. These women were selected from both Tory and Whig families, since the winds of partisanship, as we shall see, even pervaded the rarified air of the lying-in chamber. In selecting the fifty, I attempted to include women from the same families, both within a single generation and over the course of several generations. This was done to identify patterns of mutual assistance and advice, as well as belief systems within families. I also made every effort to include women whose families were in no way related to each other—a difficult task in so inbred a group. This was necessary, however, to distinguish between family idiosyncracies and the habits of a class. More than half the women selected were both the daughters and the wives of peers—a class composed of only a few hundred members in any given year. The lives of women married to younger sons of the peerage differed only slightly from their coroneted sisters.

Queen Victoria and her cousin Princess Charlotte represent the royal family. Both women had an important (if unwitting) influence on the childbearing lives of their contemporaries. They also represent extreme examples of reproductive success and failure. Queen Victoria gave birth to nine children, all of whom survived. She never suffered a miscarriage or stillbirth, and she died at the age of eighty-two. Her older cousin Princess Charlotte—the heir of George IV—died at the age of twenty-one after giving birth in 1817 to a stillborn son. That tragedy led to a reproductive sweepstakes among the brothers of King George IV to ensure the succession; it lasted until the Duke of Kent produced the future Queen Victoria eighteen months after Charlotte's death. The contrasting but related fates of these two women provide a necessary reminder of how much variety there can be in life, even among socially identical people.

If the advantages of studying so small a group are obvious, so too are the disadvantages. Clearly, these women cannot represent anyone other than the aristocracy. The story of the masses of the European population—the overworked and underfed—is important, but it is very different from the one told here. Indubitably there were more of them, and their experiences might seem more "typical" of the period. Yet the aristocracy had an impact on the times far greater than their numbers alone might warrant. That, indeed, is what it means to be an elite group, and the British aristocracy of the years 1760 to 1860 was one of the most successful elites in history.

It is perhaps difficult today to appreciate the overwhelming social impact the aristocracy enjoyed in the absence of any other competing elite group. Very much the celebrities of the day, women of the peerage, like royalty, combined the glamour of present-day Hollywood with the power and prestige of modern political and economic elites. Aristocratic comings and goings, successes and failures, travels and travails, were avidly reported in the English press. If the Duchess of Devonshire's endorsement of a Wedgewood flower pot (bearing her name) guaranteed the worldwide sale of thousands, then her patronage of a physician or her enthusiasm for breast-feeding were similarly influential.[11]

The political confidence and expansiveness of the aristocracy during this period is reflected in family life. It is no mere coincidence that they achieved their greatest fertility during a century of political hegemony, or that the peak of fertility occurred in 1815,[12] the very year of the Battle of Waterloo, when the supremacy of the British political nation—still led by its hereditary aristocracy—was established for all to see. Yet this was also a century that brought with it the Industrial Revolution and the challenge of the middle classes. Childbearing provides a window into the mechanisms by which the aristocracy successfully adapted the forms of family life to meet the new age.

Historians Lawrence Stone and Randolph Trumbach are among those who have identified the aristocracy as the class that led the way to the modern domesticated nuclear family.[13] By studying this small group so closely, we can observe social change under the microscope, as it were. We will learn that transitions happened more slowly than historians have hitherto assumed, and that they caused a considerable amount of conflict within individual families. For that is ultimately the only way in which social change can occur: as perceptions and values change, family members no longer agree on how things ought to be done. They are nevertheless left to cope with one another. I shall argue that the obstetric profession, originating from a relatively weak position, became important as an apparently benign and neutral force often able to mediate differences between family members.

In this very new area of inquiry historians are only beginning to question why the aristocracy should have turned to a new set of values at a time when the old set seemed to have worked so well. In documenting the history of childbirth in America, the Wertzes see the rise in domesticity as exemplifying the privatization of family life.[14] This, too, can be seen with the British aristocracy. The transition was a more complex one for the aristocrats, however, for they had visible "public" identities. It is essential to explore the nature of the public identity and its connection with the traditional orientation of the aristocratic family, before examining the paradox of privatization. For it is a paradox: why should the group with the most to gain from the maintenance of a public identity, and therefore, the most to lose from its eradication, nevertheless seek to subsume that identity into the private sphere? Though we cannot fully answer the question in an essay focusing on childbearing, we can at least suggest that privatization was wonderfully suited to the rising principles of competitiveness and individualism.

The preservation of the landed aristocracy as a small, wealthy, and powerful group had traditionally depended upon the sacrifices of individuals for the good of the family as a whole. The aristocratic family was very much the paradigm for society as envisioned by Edmund Burke in "Reflections on the Revolution in France." The family, too, was a partnership "not only between those who are living, but between those who are living, those who are dead, and those who are to be born."[15] Thus even the inheritance of a great landed estate was itself hedged about with restrictions in the interests of posterity. Estates were usually entailed, so the owner could enjoy the income from his land but could not sell it and thus dissipate the family's inheritance and the source of its power. The head of a family was responsible for passing on the estate (and the traditions that went with it) intact, to his heir. This system of primogeniture and entail thus limited the freedom of heirs as well as that of their siblings. Nevertheless, the eldest son was privileged far above the deserts of his younger brothers. While he inherited title and estate, they usually had to enter one of the few professions considered appropriate for men of their rank—a profession, moreover, usually chosen by the parents. Like daughters, sons were also necessary in making the political and marital alliances that enhanced a family's prestige, wealth, and power. The demands made upon young women, particularly in their childbearing capacity, must be seen in this context.

That the personal wishes of an individual might conflict with his or her designated function within the family was often a fact of life, giving rise to an emphasis on duty that preoccupied this class even before the Victorian era. Behind its glittering and occasionally licentious facade, the British aristocracy, as David Spring has pointed out, "having been so tenacious, so concerned to perpetuate itself and having succeeded for so long in doing so, must inevitably have practiced at least as much prudence as imprudence."[16] This conflict between the personal and public interest provides a dialectical current running throughout the history of the aristocracy during the century 1760 to 1860. Gradually the interest of the individual gained increased legitimacy, as opposed to his or her mere function in a role. Domesticity meant that the private emotional interaction of family members came to be viewed as important a part of family life as were its public functions. But public functions remained; even in 1860 they were too important to be ignored altogether.

That the British aristocracy had a public as well as a private role can be understood simply: they alone, of all social groups, had titles as well as names.[17] Whether family members chose to address each other by name or title is not only a sign of their perceived intimacy, it is also a clue to whether they see that relationship as predominantly a public or private one. It is thus one good index for tracing the growth of domesticity.

Lawrence Stone recognized the importance of modes of address and asserted that by the end of the eighteenth century, aristocratic husbands and wives commonly referred to each other by name rather than by title. My evidence does not support his contention that this was a temporary change and that by 1830 couples had resumed the use of titles in personal discourse.[18] Instead, I believe that the use of informal modes of address continued to grow in popularity from the end of the eighteenth and into the nineteenth centuries, but that this change occurred far more slowly than Stone implied and that it was by no means complete by 1800. Instances of formal usage occurring after 1830 would not indicate the resurgence of an old custom: some families simply had not made the change in the first place.[19]

Among the study group of fifty families, the use of the formal mode of address was more common before 1800. The transition to the informal mode became more acceptable to younger people about that time. In 1792 Lord Gower still referred to his wife appropriately as Lady Sutherland, and in the 1780s and 1790s his parents always referred to each other as Lord and Lady Stafford. Lady Sarah Napier, correctly identified by both Stone and Trumbach as one of the more "domesticated" aristocrats, nevertheless always wrote of her husband formally as Col. Napier—even as late as 1803.[20] It was at about this time that the younger generation—that most prolific of cohorts—began to use first names with greater frequency. The Countess of Morley referred to her husband as "Jack" in her letters to his sister during the first two decades of the nineteenth century; the Earl of Verulam called his wife "Charlotte" or "Char" during the teens and twenties. The Marquess of Anglesey's two wives, whom he married in 1795 and 1810 respectively, were called "Car" and "Char," which may have added to the confusion of his already confused domestic affairs. The Earl of Scarborough referred to his wife, the Countess Frederica, as "dearest Freddy" even in the mid-Victorian year of 1862. Nor were wives too awed by their husbands to refer to them familiarly. In 1835 Lady Susan

Rivers called her husband "George," and in 1842 Lady Cecilia Ridley called hers "Matt." Indeed, the young Blanche Stanley discovered in 1851 to her dismay that she and her fiancé were expected to be on a first-name basis as soon as they had become engaged.[21]

During the early decades of the nineteenth century nicknames and diminutives—some of which have already been mentioned—also began to appear regularly. In 1803 the Duchess of Bedford called her husband "Johnny" to the amazement of her guests, but other families made more imaginative use of nicknames. Two daughters of the Duke of Rutland were called "Katty" and "Bibi" in 1832. Elizabeth, Lady Holland, called her husband "Holly" while their daughter-in-law nicknamed her spouse "Buz." The Duchess of Devonshire's daughters were called "G" and "Hary-O." Hary-O's three children would be called "Dody," "Sukey," and "Gink"—the latter a future foreign secretary—within the family circle.[22]

These informal modes of address were not confined to the nuclear family, but increasingly pervaded all domestic relations—though again, not until after the turn of the century. In 1805 the elderly Duchess of Grafton still referred to her daughter as "Lady F. Churchill," and Lady Sutherland always referred to her mother-in-law as Lady Stafford in their letters of the 1790s. But all this was to change. More and more, grown children tended to refer to their parents and in-laws familiarly, providing a clear indication of affectionate domesticity supplanting the formal respect once due the more traditional parent. Thus Lady Caroline Capel called her mother "dear Mama" as early as 1815. Queen Victoria's eldest daughter referred to her august parent as "dearest Mama."[23] Even in-laws were included under the rubric of domesticity. Sir Galbraith Lowry Cole referred to his mother-in-law as "Mama" rather than as Lady Malmesbury in 1824, and Lady Augusta Fox called her father-in-law "pappy" in 1833.[24]

This switch to informal and even casual modes of address is

significant in two ways. First, it clearly indicates that the individual takes precedence over the rank that he or she holds. This is especially obvious in the use of highly idiosyncratic nicknames, which humorously testify to the triumph of what Stone has called "affective individualism." Second, this verbal transformation identified varying levels of intimacy among people. In a letter of 1807 to her grandmother, Lady Harriet Cavendish refers to three women of her acquaintance in three different ways: one with a nickname, one with a full name, and one with a title. It is important to note that in-laws were often included within this informal mode—cousins much less frequently.[25] Often it has been argued that domesticity separated the nuclear family from the larger network of kin. I will argue that this was not true for the aristocracy. Domesticity, as we will see in the next chapter, simply increased the affective content of relations with in-laws. For this elite group, the family in its largest sense remained important.

That women of the aristocracy continued to have an important public role can be seen by a brief glimpse at the funerals given them, which emphasized their rank above all other considerations. Aside from the royal funerals of Charlotte and Victoria, the most extraordinary funeral of this group was that of Elizabeth, Countess of Sutherland, owner of over one million acres in her own right, the largest landowner north of the Tweed. Her funeral in 1839 indeed bore witness to her feudal inheritance. The Countess's body was shipped by steamer from London, where she had died, to the city of Aberdeen. The remains, which arrived in February, were met at dockside by the Lord Provost and the city magistrates and then placed in a six-horse hearse. The actual burial at ancient Dornoch Castle did not take place until mid-April, when the funeral procession finally arrived at this remote part of the United Kingdom. "An enormous concourse of persons from all parts of the late Duchess-Countess [as she was then styled] of Sutherland's estates attended at the funeral of its lamented proprietrix," read the account in the *Times*. "The procession," it said, "extended to about two miles in length."[26]

Perhaps more typical of the pomp usually accorded the death of a female aristocrat was that attending the obsequies of Frances, Marchioness of Salisbury (1802–1839), mother of the future Prime Minister. "The coronet of the lamented Marchioness was placed on a velvet cushion, borne by a man on horseback, preceded by six other persons on horseback bearing wands," the *Times* informed its readers. "The body was placed on a hearse drawn by six horses, the trappings of which were emblazoned with the arms of the noble family." Her funeral procession was "led by the nobility and gentry of Hertfordshire, and the tenantry of the Marquess of Salisbury." The *Times* did not think it equally noteworthy that the deceased was only thirty-seven years old and left five small children.[27]

As the nineteenth century progressed, the private character of funerals is more frequently referred to by the newspaper accounts, but the public nature of the event remained paramount. Emily, Lady Palmerston (1787–1869), was buried beside her famous second husband in Westminster Abbey. "All funerals in the grand old Abbey partake more or less of a public character, even when they are meant to be most private," noted the *Times*. "This was the case" of Lady Palmerston's funeral, "as ordinary as any funeral in Westminster Abbey can ever well be made to be."[28] Even as late as 1895, the funeral of Henrietta, Lady Stanley of Alderley (1808–1895), a founder of Girton College, testified only to her position as an adjunct of the landowning class. Her procession was led by her husband's tenantry rather than by members of the immediate family or her many noteworthy friends.[29] (Although at least her body had been promptly shipped by rail!)

The major rites of passage, funerals, and, as we shall see in much greater detail, marriages, births, and christenings, incorporated both private and public functions, which were sometimes, though not necessarily, in conflict. More often they were two sides of the same coin. Rites of passage were public institutions for this very public class, much like the vast country houses in which they took place: symbols and instruments of power and authority, but still homes for families to live in. Public ceremonies and country houses could not be abandoned as long as the landed aristocracy remained England's preeminent social group. Nevertheless, these did not exclude the existence of private emotions behind the facade. As we shall see throughout this book, the women of the aristocracy often enjoyed and endured rich emotional lives. The death of Georgiana, Duchess of Devonshire (1757–1806), was very much a public event: she was one of the most celebrated persons of her day. But her death was also very much a private sorrow to her sister, who had nursed her during her final illness. "Anything so horrible, so killing as her three days' agony no human being ever witnessed," wrote the distraught Harriet, Countess of Bessborough (1761–1821), whose grief still seems palpable nearly two centuries later. "I saw it all, held her through all her struggles, saw her expire, and since have again kissed her cold lips and pressed her lifeless body to my heart—and yet I am alive."[30] The public and private faces of an event served two different but often complementary functions, the latter providing emotional reinforcement for the former. And as with death, so too with marriage and birth.

Finally, in studying the aristocracy, we are focusing on the single social group best able to get what it wanted. Aristocratic behavior can reveal far more about values than can the behavior of less powerful groups. If any class of women might have been spared biological enslavement, one would expect it to have been these very women. And, as we shall show, particularly in chapters 4 and 5, pregnancy and childbirth were considerably less restrictive for these women than is often assumed. Their condition was more often a source of pride than of shame, and pregnancy was not an occasion for hibernation. During all the years covered by this study, women maintained a high social profile throughout their many years of pregnancy. They remained publicly—if often frivolously—active even through the ninth month. Their glamorous lives of Grand Tours, Royal Drawing Rooms, masked balls, fox hunting in the country, and salon politicking in town were often conducted while pregnant. For the majority of aristocratic women who were healthy—as indeed the majority were—biological maternity, however uncomfortable, was only rarely confining, much less physically enslaving.[31] It was not specifically the degree of suffering related to reproduction that was so enslaving, it was that women had no choice but to undergo the experience, primarily in the interests of her husband's family, that made it one of servitude.

Nevertheless, the physical reproduction of the species did (and does) involve a considerable amount of suffering, no matter how pampered the mother. It was specifically the pain of childbirth that was thought to give meaning to that experience in aristocratic society. Childbirth had traditionally provided for women an initiation into full adulthood, an important rite of passage. The demystification of childbirth that accompanied the privatization of family life during the century 1760 to 1860, as well as the attendant rationalization of obstetric technique, inevitably altered the meaning of childbirth. Although the process of deritualization had already been underway for some time, it was the application of anesthesia in 1847 that dealt the critical blow to traditional childbirth and its emotional significance. Suffering was, indeed, eliminated, but so too was the remarkable transformation it was thought to accomplish.

Even under the most ideal conditions, however, childbirth could be hazardous. As the case of Princess Charlotte so shockingly reminded the public in 1817, royalty itelf was not spared its dangers. Human biology, as well as human society, established ineluctable parameters. The story of the aristocracy is necessary to identify these fully. The history of women's condition can only be completed by a look at the best the past had to offer.

CHAPTER I

Love and Marriage

Sociologist Anne Oakley has written that women will never truly have control over childbirth as long as childbirth is performed in the service of men.[1] A cruel judgment, perhaps. Yet she acknowledges something that seems to have been ignored in much of the recent historiographical debate over midwives and obstetricians. Childbearing is a social activity and cannot be understood in isolation from the network of social and economic relationships within which it takes place. It is the family setting that is most critical in assessing what childbearing meant to the British aristocracy. Whether or not women "lost control" of birth to the obstetricians becomes a secondary issue when seen in this light. The suggestion that childbirth has been performed "in the service of men" also asserts that women were not serving their own interests as well. The implicit assumption—with which modern Americans might agree but certainly not British aristocrats—is that personal, inner-directed satisfaction is more authentic, and thus greater, than the satisfaction that comes from doing one's duty. Such a "quality of life" assessment is difficult enough to make for one's own self, let alone for others who, moreover, have been dead for two hundred years. The task of examining the emotional lives of the English aristocracy would seem to be insuperably difficult. But the task is as important as it is difficult if historians are to assess the consequences of domesticity for the status of women and if we are to contribute to current discussions on the family. We must seek to understand the patterns of the past.

For the British aristocracy, marriage had both a public and a private face. It served the needs of the family by providing for the production and support of heirs, by maintaining or enhancing the family's position in the community, and by promoting the interests of the two individuals most nearly concerned. One's personal needs, after all, are economic as well as emotional. And whatever else it may have been, marriage was an economic institution. Through the vehicle of the "strict settlement," marriage established the financial futures of all family members. It usually decreed an annual income for the newly established family, most often to come from the estate of the groom or his family. The strict settlement provided the bride with a sum of "pin money" for her own use and an annuity, or jointure, in the event of her widowhood. And, of course, the bride's family normally provided a substantial dowry. Families stood to make considerable gains by a good match: a large dowry acquired by the marriage of a son, social rank, and a secure financial future for one's daughter. For a child to ignore the opportunity of making a grand alliance would have seemed foolhardy. Indeed, as Lawrence Stone has astutely noted, the younger generation was as wont to marry for money as the older generation was to long for such a match.[2]

Nevertheless, parents were equally unlikely to ignore the affective implications of a proposed match. But the nature of the emotional component thought to be requisite appears to have changed during the century 1760 to 1860. Early in that period, a lukewarm respect and regard for a proposed spouse, based on a minimal acquaintance, was thought sufficient. When Lady Harriet Spencer accepted the suit of the future Lord Bessborough in 1780, she wrote to a friend:

> I have a very high opinion of Ld. Duncannon [as her fiancé was then styled] it is impossible one should be very well acquainted with anybody in the intercourse of the world, with him I was less than most people. I had not the least geuss [sic] about it, till the day papa told me. . . . I wish I could have known him a little better first, but my dear papa and mama say that it will make them the happi-

est of creatures, and what would I not do to see them happy. . . . There are many people whose manners and conversation I should like better, as *flirts* only, *car assurément il n'a pas les manières prevenantes*, but when one is to choose a companion for life (what a dreadful sound that has) the inside and not the out is what one ought to look at, & I think from what I have heard of him, & the great attachment he professes to have for me, I have a better chance of being reasonably happy with him than with most people I know.³

If being "reasonably happy" was all that a young girl in 1780 expected of marriage, by 1860 she was in ardent pursuit of romantic love. Whether or not she actually found that more exciting emotion is a different question, one that will be addressed more fully later. I suggest at this point, however, that expectations may have changed more than experiences, and that these changes may have been more rhetorical than real.

The apparent dichotomy between the arranged and the romantic marriage is a false one. At best, these are ideal types, and most marriages fell between the two extremes. First, all betrothals were concluded with an eye toward the instrumental and affective functions of the relationship, whether forged primarily by the parents or primarily by the children. Second, as in any society, adolescents could choose spouses only from among persons to whom they had been introduced. In the case of the British aristocracy, this was likely to be a carefully controlled set, nearly all of whom fit the necessary requirements of rank and fortune. The national marriage markets that developed in London and Bath during the appropriate seasons gave young people the opportunity to meet others of the opposite sex, all of whom might be considered marriageable. The establishment early in the nineteenth century of Almack's, a fashionable private club, is significant. Those deemed socially fit could become members and, for the price of a subscription, were allowed to buy tickets to a series of balls and suppers offered by this "seventh heaven of the fashionable world."[4] Two women from the fifty we shall discuss, Emily, Lady Palmerston (1787–1869), and her contemporary Sarah, Countess of Jersey (1785–1865), were among the original six patronesses of Almack's. Thus they had the power to determine who was worthy of admission to Almack's and, by extension, worthy of admission into the aristocratic class they represented. The Lady Patronesses, as they were named by Almack's and known to contemporaries, were thought to exercise a sort of social despotism. (It was once said that they turned the Duke of Wellington away because he was wearing trousers instead of knee breeches.)[5] One contemporary estimated that only a half-dozen of three hundred officers presenting themselves were "honored with admission to this exclusive temple of the *beau monde*."[6] By providing a carefully controlled social environment, aristocratic parents were willing to relinquish the appearance of arranging marriages without sacrificing the substance.

Finally, the distinction between the arranged and the romantic marriage is not a useful one because the experiences of young women on the marriage market were so different from those of young men. What may have been a romantic choice for the groom might well have seemed to be an arranged marriage for the bride. Two extended examples, drawn from women born a half-century apart, will indicate this disparity and show how analytically useless the dichotomy between the arranged and the romantic marriage can be.

Georgiana, Lady Morpeth (1783–1858), was perhaps the least conspicuous member of an otherwise prominent and glamorous family. Born Lady Georgiana Cavendish, she was the eldest daughter of the fifth Duke of Devonshire, one of the wealthiest men in Britain. He possessed over two hundred thousand well-distributed acres and a series of the most beautiful and architecturally distinguished homes ever owned by a single individual. His country seat, Chatsworth, remains one of the finest examples of the English country house. In addition, he owned two older homes, Hardwick Hall (an Elizabethan masterpiece) and Bolton Abbey, used mainly by the Duke as hunting lodges. Devonshire House in London was a grand urban palace, and Chiswick House provided a comfortable—and exquisite—suburban retreat. Lady Georgiana's mother, the Duchess, was perhaps the most famous woman of her day. Beautiful, charming, and generous, the Duchess was the political intimate of Fox, Sheridan, and the Prince of Wales. The Duke was thought to be the only man in England not in love with her: she had relegated him to being "the husband of the Duchess of Devonshire."[7]

Considering her origins, Lady Georgiana Cavendish lived a relatively uneventful life. She was educated at home (whichever home) by Miss Selina Trimmer, daughter of the Evangelical author. Trimmer had been placed in Devonshire House by the Duchess's mother, the formidable Dowager Countess Spencer, who thought her grandchildren needed an antidote of religion to counteract the effects of their parents' dissipation. The medicine, not too unpalatable, worked, and the Cavendish girls grew up to be the morally upright women their grandmother envisioned when she appointed Miss Trimmer.

Lady Georgiana Cavendish entered society during her seventeenth summer in the year 1800. She was presented at Court for the first time on the King's birthday, June 4—a formal ritual that announced Lady Georgiana's marriageability. On the eve of her seventeenth birthday in July, the Duke and Duchess gave a lavish coming-out party for their daughter. They invited four hundred guests, one of whom, it was hoped, might prove to be Lady Georgiana's eventual husband. Lord Morpeth emerged as her most frequent dancing partner that evening.

George Howard, Lord Morpeth, was the heir of the Earl of Carlisle. Of a family equal in stature, if not in brilliance, to the Devonshire brood, Lord Morpeth seems to have been as personally undistinguished as was Lady Georgiana. Born in 1773, and thus twenty-seven years old when he began this eminently suitable courtship, Lord Morpeth had already made the Grand Tour and kept a mistress. The Devonshires invited him to a large house party at Chatsworth in the autumn of 1800. This gave the family the opportunity to give Morpeth a thorough examination, and George and Georgiana a better chance to get to know each other under adult supervision. The man proved as suitable as his background. Lady Georgiana, ten years younger and lacking any alternative personal experience with men, was criticized by her family for being "too standoffish" with her suitor.[8] The family held its collective breath, but no engagement was immediately forthcoming. The Duke, apparently fearful that his daughter would let a "good catch" slip away, dangled the promise of a £30,000 dowry and the use of Londesborough House should Lady Georgiana decide to accept Morpeth, who left Chatsworth before any decision had been reached.[9]

The campaign was resumed at a Christmas house party at Chatsworth, where twenty-three people reportedly consumed twenty-three sheep and two oxen in a week. The heavy-handed bribery worked, and on December 18 Morpeth proposed and Lady Georgiana accepted. The couple married on March 21.[10] A year after her coming out, Lady Morpeth was pregnant with her first child. She would ultimately produce twelve, an even half-dozen of each sex. Like many another eighteen-year-old mother, Lady Morpeth lived with her husband's parents. Unlike others, however, home for her was Castle Howard, the enormous Baroque pile in Yorkshire.

This marriage was not, strictly speaking, an arranged one. Lord Morpeth had proposed to the girl and not to her father. Lady Georgiana had had the right to reject her suitor. But lacking any alternative, with little experience of the world, and with the full weight of family pressure brought to bear, the freedom of her choise was negligible. It is more difficult to assess Lord Morpeth's motives. It seems unlikely that worldly considerations played no part in his proposal. Yet it also seems unlikely that he would have proposed to a girl for whom he felt no physical attraction whatsoever. He was probably well aware that worldly considerations (or prudence, as Jane Austen would have it) contributed to personal happiness. Whatever the mix of motives in his choice, he clearly enjoyed more personal autonomy in making this critical decision than did his young fiancée, and was perhaps better equipped than she for such a role. Already sexually experienced, Morpeth had for several years enjoyed a cosmopolitan social life quite apart from his parents. His choice, unlike Lady Georgiana's, was freely made.

For later generations, domesticity urged the obligation of love as well as that of marriage. A young girl could be forced to marry. Could she be forced to love as well? By 1850 Blanche Stanley's parents hoped so.

Blanche, later Countess of Airlie (1829–1921), was the second daughter of Lord and Lady Stanley of Alderley. The Stanleys were not as grand as the Devonshires had been, Lord Stanley being simply a baron. But his was an old family with a Cheshire estate and a London home. Blanche's father was an active Liberal politician; her mother, Henrietta Maria, would emerge in her widowhood as a woman's rights activist and founder of Girton College. The Stanleys were more intellectually than socially eminent, and have so remained.[11]

David, Earl of Airlie, was a relatively impoverished nobleman with an ancient castle when he met Blanche Stanley during the London season. Both his parents were dead. Late in the summer of 1851 Lord Airlie visited Blanche at Alderley Park, where the courtship reached its unpromising climax. "I am anxious you should know in what an uncertain state of mind I find Blanche," her mother wrote Lord Stanley, who, as Under Secretary for Foreign Affairs, was busy in London.[12] Blanche's family, even at a distance, was eager to help her make up her mind. In response to his wife's letter, Lord Stanley replied, "I hope the Damsel will not do anything foolish or hasty," by which he meant reject her suitor. Blanche had asserted that she was perfectly happy as she was and had no wish to marry. "She must remember," her father wrote, "that though it may be very pleasant to enjoy herself at Alderley now she is young & gay—it would not always be the same." But then he added in the modern vein, "I of course would not wish her to do anything contrary to her feelings if she really knows what they are, but I do not think she does, and if she was to reject him she would probably repent it before long."[13] Similar advice came from Blanche's grandmother: "I hope Blanche is quite satisfied & will hold on through the week an equal tenor of conduct to meet with her reward at the end [a proposal], if she feels no doubt in her mind whether she can love him perfectly and take him for better or worse."[14] But Blanche did doubt whether she could "love him perfectly," and complained to her mother that "she cares little for him and should so like to be desperately in love."[15] When, despite Blanche's brusque manners, Lord Airlie finally found the courage to propose to her, she replied that "she had no great objection";[16] so the matter was settled to the evident satisfaction of everyone but the bride.

Despite the tepid nature of Blanche's affection, her courtship had all the earmarks of modern, sentimentalized romantic love. On the day of her engagement "she came down with the heath he had gathered in her hair," and later in the week the betrothed pair went into the woods to cut their names on trees. If Blanche was not "desperately in love" with the man, she was indeed attracted to the Scottish Earl. She had set her heart on reaching his home for the wedding night because "it has always been her dream to be carried to a Castle at once."[17] The romantic could thus worship rank as much as could the more cynical traditionalist.

Neither the betrothal nor the subsequent marriage relieved Blanche from the fear that she did not love Airlie sufficiently. Jane Welsh Carlyle, who attended the wedding, thought it sad that "amidst the excitement and rapture of the trousseau she doesn't know whether she loves *the man* or not she hopes well enough for practical purposes."[18]

There it is: love has come to be considered a practical necessity rather than a luxury. Nevertheless, Blanche Stanley seems to have had little more real freedom of choice than had Lady Georgiana Cavendish in making the same decision fifty years earlier. Indeed, the expectation of romantic love was, in Blanche Stanley's case, an additional source of frustration. Expectations aside, her real sentiments appear little different from those of Lady Bessborough toward her husband a century earlier. In both cases, eligible and romantically inclined suitors were aligned with girls' parents: in the face of such pressures, and with few (if any) viable alternatives, the young women submitted. By 1851 expectations that marriage would bring happiness as well as security had developed, but there is little evidence that this either gave more freedom or more romance to young women.

Lord Airlie, like Lord Morpeth a half-century earlier, enjoyed far more personal autonomy than did his younger fiancée. He was free of all paternal authority, had prior experience of love, and was probably capable of making a more socially brilliant match had he so desired. Airlie's decision to propose to Blanche Stanley seems to have been more clearly based on romantic considerations than Morpeth's had been. Airlie admitted to having "loved her from the first" and was unhappy at the prospect of her rejection, which accounted for his hesitation in proposing. This seems to have been more than mere rhetoric (though even such rhetoric was unnecessary earlier). "He never leaves her side for a moment," Lady Stanley reported of Airlie's courtship of her daughter. "They are now . . . sitting on the lawn with a book each, but I can see by the reflection in the window that he is not reading, . . . I never saw any man so completely mesmerized." And finally, she wrote, "Lord Airlie is rather unobservant of natural beauty, at least at present, & a dusty high road with his love in it would do just as well as he never looks at anything else."[19] Indeed, it was the Stanleys' confidence in Airlie's love for their daughter that was decisive in their promotion of the match.

It appears, then, that young men had more freedom than young women in choosing marriage partners throughout the century 1760 to 1860, but that by 1860 men were more likely to make their decisions for romantic reasons than they had been earlier. This impression will be confirmed by a look at two other alliances from the male point of view.

A marriage usually classified as arranged was that between the aforementioned fifth Duke of Devonshire and his Duchess, the former Lady Georgiana Spencer. Although Lady Georgiana had known for some months that she was promised to the Duke—and had even danced with him once—she had virtually no part in the decision that made her a Duchess before her seventeenth birthday. She was simply awakened one morning in 1774 and told she would marry the Duke of Devonshire that day.[20] But for the Duke it was not an arranged marriage. Both his parents had been dead for some time and the decision was very much his own. Nevertheless, the criteria the Duke used in selecting Lady Georgiana to be his bride were very traditional ones. His goals were instrumental, not affective. He was looking for a Duchess rather than a wife and thought more of the position of his family than of his own personal pleasure. The Cavendish and Spencer families were two of the more prominent and tightly knit groups that had formed the Whig ascendency since 1688. It was a match of which he thought his ancestors would approve and by which he assumed his descendents would benefit. The Duke even insisted on marrying Lady Georgiana prior to her seventeenth birthday: both his mother and his sister had married at sixteen.[21] The Countess Spencer feared quite rightly that her daughter was too immature for so great a position in society, but she was loath to lose the opportunity of making her daughter a Duchess. According to common gossip, a compromise was reached whereby the Duke got his young Duchess, but the couple would not "live together" for a year.[22] The Duke, though he had freely chosen his partner, had no romantic designs on her. At the time of his marriage he was keeping a mistress whom he had no intention of sacrificing. If this was an arranged marriage, it was one the groom arranged for himself.

Later generations of young men were more apt to seek companionship, if not romance, in their partners and to enjoy considerable freedom in doing so. John Lord Duncannon's experience is telling. After being rejected by the cousin whom his parents preferred him to marry, he was left to find his own wife. When, in 1805, he decided to marry Lady Maria Fane (1787–1834), daughter of the Earl of Westmoreland, his parents gave him their written consent without having met the young lady. "If Lord Westmoreland consents to the marriage," Lady Bessborough wrote her son, "you know how dear anything you love must be to me." Duncannon's father added, "I assure you I approve, as far as I am acquainted with the circumstances of the match you propose. I never meant to control you in any match you wished to make."[23] The couple was married within six weeks and acted like any other young couple in love shortly thereafter. "She thinks him the greatest wit in the Kingdom and he thinks her the greatest beauty." Romantic love indeed had its rewards for the male of the species. Duncannon's bride "watches him incessantly, obeys him implicitly, and they sit hand in hand."[24]

If the new Lady Duncannon was happy with her callow spouse she was not alone. It would be as incorrect to assert that young women never had any significant input in the selection of their husbands, as it would be to assume that they always did. A few examples will help explore the criteria women used in choosing husbands and explain how they got what they wanted.

The high-spirited and intelligent Lady Harriet Cavendish's (1785–1862) experiences of courtship and marriage were quite different from those of her more docile older sister, Lady Morpeth. However clever, Lady Harriet very much wanted to fall in love before agreeing to marry. She also wanted a husband who could provide stimulating companionship. She had been brought up to believe that she would marry either of her two first cousins, Lord Althorp (the Spencer heir) or Lord Duncannon (the Bessborough heir). Either marriage would have made her a countess eventually. By the age of twenty she had rejected Althorp's attentions out of hand. "How could one speculate upon anything but a weary, tedious existence with a man whose whole soul is engrossed with one most uninteresting pursuit [fox hunting], who never speaks or seems alive but when one subject is mentioned?" she wrote impatiently to her sister.[25] Lady Harriet was more genuinely fond of her cousin Duncannon, but she rejected him eventually too. Although she found him "uncommonly handsome, good-tempered and affectionate," he was also "trifling and inconsequent." "I have been contentedly his cousin so long," she wrote, "that I don't see why I should ever be anything else."[26]

Finally, in November of 1809 at the age of twenty-four, Lady Harriet decided to accept the proposal of Lord Granville Leveson-Gower, then thirty-six. A successful diplomat, Lord Granville was often described as "the handsomest man in England" and "the best whist player in Europe." The French, who knew him well from his many years as the British ambassador in Paris, called him "le Wellington des joueurs."[27] Lady Harriet's feelings for this dashing figure were more than cousinly. "Adored Granville," she wrote as a bride, "who could make a barren desert smile."[28] And yet, though Granville's rank was eminently suitable—he was the second and only younger son of the Marquess of Stafford—he was in one respect the most unsuitable husband Lady Harriet might have found, for he had been for many years the lover of her aunt, Lady Bessborough. When Harriet agreed to marry Granville, she also agreed to raising his two children by her aunt—a daunting prospect, one should think.[29] Thus the plucky Lady Harriet walked off with Lady Bessborough's lover, instead of her son.

There is a substantial difference, however, between rejecting the suitors one's parents have chosen—as Lady Harriet did with her cousins—and finding a suitor to whom one's parents object. Lady Elizabeth Drummond (1800–1886) had the effrontery to do just that. Born Lady Elizabeth Manners, she was the eldest daughter of the fifth Duke of Rutland, one of England's great magnates. Lady Elizabeth could well have married into the highest ranks of the peerage. She chose, instead, to marry Andrew Robert Drummond, scion of a banking family. The Drummonds were indeed related to much of the Scottish nobility, and Andrew's mother was herself the daughter of a peer. Young Drummond was, as he anxiously assured the Rutlands, descended from a family as ancient as theirs, which had suffered only because of its adherence to the Stuart cause. The Rutlands seemed to have had no objections to Andrew personally, but rather to his bank, where he expected to be a working partner—an occupation that was anathema to this High Tory family. The Rutlands asked the young couple to wait two years to see if their affection withstood the test of time. When, in 1822, the young couple still wished to marry, the Duke finally consented, but only after Andrew's father agreed to provide the young couple with a £2,500 annual income and £2,000 on their wedding day.[30]

Similarly, nearly half a century later the Earl of Derby—the great Conservative leader—disapproved of his only daughter's proposed fiancé. Emma had fallen in love with her father's private secretary, W. P. M. Chetwynd Talbot, a son of the Earl of Shrewsbury. His was a family with more breeding than money, little of which seemed likely to reach the pockets of an eighth son. Lord Derby feared the match was an impractical one. Emma had an important ally in her mother, Emma, Countess of Derby (1805–1876). Although Lord Derby initially refused to allow his daughter to marry Talbot, Lady Derby continued to plead on behalf of young Emma's heart. After two years Lady Derby wore her husband down. Her most successful argument was that the Clarendons—also eminent politically and socially, though Liberal—"expressed their willingness to have their daughter marry a poor curate if it would make her happy." Lord Derby relented, apparently wishing to be no less loving a father than others of his milieu. He resigned himself gracefully as well. Shortly after the Talbot-Stanley wedding took place in 1862, the new bride found a check for £5,000 under her breakfast napkin.[31]

The romantic marriages of Lady Elizabeth Drummond and Lady Emma Talbot nevertheless contained a number of traditional elements. Neither young woman, for instance, was willing to marry without her father's permission even after she came of age. They were perhaps too mindful that only their fathers could secure their financial futures and were not themselves too much in love to ignore money. Second, by modern standards, even unacceptable suitors came from a remarkably circumscribed social sphere.[32] Both young women, in fact, met their future husbands through their fathers. This concurs with David Thomas's contention that the British peerage remained remarkably endogamous throughout the eighteenth and nineteenth centuries.[33]

On the other hand, parents appreciated the importance of their daughters' romantic expectations. The delays in approving these marriages came from the need to "prove" their love, not because love was dismissed as irrelevant. Both fathers knew their daughters could have made more socially advantageous matches. In sacrificing that opportunity, fathers wanted to be sure their daughters were getting something in return.

I would conclude, therefore, that it is impossible to claim with any confidence, as does Randolph Trumbach, that by 1784 three-quarters of aristocratic marriages were romantic rather than arranged.[34] Most marriages do not fall neatly into either category. Most, in fact, contained elements of both the traditional alliance, based on the maintenance of a family's social position, and the romantic alliance, based on private considerations. Parents were rarely immune to the emotional needs of their children, and children were just as unlikely to ignore their own material welfare. The traditional marriage was by no means dead in 1784, 1800, or 1850, because traditional concerns had not died out. A variety of individual factors contributed to the consummation of an engagement. Birth order, family size, whether or not one's parents were dead, one's personal character, the parent-child relationship, the degree of "retirement" of one's family, the distance in time between one's coming out and the first reasonable proposal: these were among the many components that created the precise balance struck between private and public concerns in any given marriage.

However, during the century 1760 to 1860 families seem to have changed their perception of the emotions requisite for a successful marriage. Whereas in 1760 a quiet mutual regard based on hearsay and a short acquaintance was thought sufficient, by 1860 one needed to be "perfectly in love." Whether the emotions experienced by a young pair in 1860 were in fact all that different from the emotions experienced by an earlier pair may be open to question. But romantic love rather than companionship was increasingly seen as desirable for the success of a marriage, and therefore came to be viewed as a practical necessity in itself. This presented something of a dilemma, for if an advantageous alliance presented itself, a young woman might well feel obligated to be "in love," since that had come to be expected as necessary for marital success. Thus the romantic ideal may have been more emotionally burdensome for many young women than the less complicated companionate marriage of a century earlier. For young women like Blanche Stanley, love was hardly an emancipating force. It is no mere coincidence that John Stuart Mill's 1869 *The Subjection of Women* was the product of this highly romantic and domesticated society. "Men do not want solely the obedience of women," Mill wrote, comparing the lot of women unfavorably with that of all other subject classes, "they want their sentiments." "All men," he continued, "except the most brutish, desire to have, in the woman most nearly connected with them, not a forced slave, but a willing one."[35] These phrases will come to mind again when we examine the childbearing lives of these women.

Weddings reflected the increasingly sentimentalized view of marriage during the century 1760 to 1860. In the eighteenth century and into the first decades of the nineteenth, a wedding took place as soon as a couple agreed to marry and the settlements were drawn up. Engagements were rarely protracted beyond six weeks.[36] The timing of the wedding was of no great significance. "It is impossible to say when the wedding will be" wrote the guardian of Lady Sarah Lennox (1745–1826) to the clergyman who was to officiate at her forthcoming marriage to Sir Charles Bunbury. "It may be Wednesday, or Thursday, it may be delayed till the next week."[37]

Few people would have been inconvenienced by such a last-minute delay because, until the middle of the ninteenth century, there were essentially no guests at aristocratic weddings. Only a few members of the immediate family would be present to act as witnesses to the ceremony. The Duke and Duchess of Devonshire were married between Sunday services at Wimbledon parish church in 1774. Besides the bride's parents, the only people present were her grandmother and the groom's sister.[38] When their daughter, Lady Harriet, was married in 1809, the only persons present were her father and stepmother (the Duchess Georgiana had died in 1806, and the Duke had married Lady Elizabeth Foster, his mistress of many years, who had actually lived in Devonshire House for all of Lady Harriet's life) and her brother. Her beloved sister, Lady Morpeth, was not present, having given birth the day before.[39] There was no expectation that the wedding should be postponed until Lady Morpeth could attend. The groom's parents were dead, and he was accompanied by his sister.

As marriage became more sentimentalized, weddings themselves took on greater importance. In 1819 two of the bride's younger brothers interrupted their Grand Tour to be present at the marriage of Lady Elizabeth Leveson-Gower to the future Marquess of Westminster. And by 1868 the marriage of Lord

Clarendon's third daughter was postponed until May because her two elder sisters were expecting babies in April.[40] As weddings became increasingly important, they were more likely to become the social extravaganzas so dear to twentieth-century hearts. Blanche Stanley was attended by seven bridesmaids at her 1851 marriage to the Earl of Airlie. Jane Welsh Carlyle was one of the many guests who crowded Alderley park for the event. "I saw a *trousseau* for the first time in my life," she wrote, "about as wonderful a piece of nonsense as the Exhibition of all Nations." "Good heavens," she continued, "how is any one woman to use up all those gowns and cloaks and fine clothes of every denomination? And the profusion of coronets! every stocking, every pockethandkerchief, everything had a coronet on it!"[41]

By the middle of the nineteenth century, weddings at the top of society had become full-fledged social extravaganzas requiring an enormous outlay and considerable planning. *The* social event of 1852 was the marriage of Lady Constance Leveson-Gower, the daughter of the Duke and Duchess of Sutherland, to her first cousin, Hugh Lupus Grosvenor, the future first Duke of Westminster. Queen Victoria graciously invited the couple to marry in the Chapel Royal of St. James's Palace. The celebrations were prolonged. Three days before her wedding Lady Constance visited the Queen. The following day the bride received her future in-laws and attended a party given in her honor by her aunt, the Duchess of Norfolk. On the eve of the wedding, the Grosvenors came to Stafford House to sign the marriage settlements and view the trousseau. Queen Victoria's account of the wedding itself reveals its curious—but thoroughly modern—mixture of opulence and sentimentality.

> The Chapel was full of relations, 120 in number. The lovely bride had a white satin dress on with lace flowers, held by a little chaplet of orange flowers. It reminded me so much of *our* dear marriage.... Constance had eight bridesmaids in white, wearing white bonnets. I had not witnessed a marriage in that spot since our one.[42]

After the ceremony the Sutherlands gave a luncheon for 150 guests at Stafford House, "a table being spread from end to end with an array as magnificent as it was costly," in the words of the *Times*. The bridal pair left the luncheon "in the travelling carriage and four, preceded by outriders, for Cliveden, the Duke of Sutherland's seat near Maidenhead [sic]." The bride's mother, overcome with emotion, "had most difficulty in behaving well and not showing any sign just at the moment of their departure."[43] As though this were not enough, the public role of the marriage was given greater emphasis by the two days of celebrating enjoyed on the Grosvenor estates in Flintshire and Cheshire, where attentions to "all tenants paying rents of £20 and upwards" and "Freemen and voters of Chester" were particularly marked.[44] A year to the day after her marriage, Lady Constance gave birth to a son and heir. In twenty-one years of marriage, she was to bear eleven children.

Whether a young woman approached the altar in modest or lavish fashion, the transfer of a large sum of cash in the form of a dowry preceded her arrival there. Randolph Trumbach estimated that women who married peers usually brought dowries worth £25,000,[45] at a time when only two thousand families in the entire kingdom had annual incomes above £10,000. These fortunes provided an infusion of liquid capital into families whose wealth was often tied up in entailed real estate. However romantically inclined, a young woman would not overlook the attractions of a dowry in securing the husband of her choice. When Hyacinthe Wellesley (1790–1849) decided in 1812 to marry a handsome scion of the gentry (the future Lord Hatherton), she wrote her father to remind him that he had once promised her a dowry of £11,000 and that the time to pay was at hand.[46]

Financial arrangements were often extremely complex. The wealthier the families involved, the larger the sums in question. One of the grandest alliances in this group of fifty women was that between Lady Elizabeth Leveson-Gower and Richard

Grosvenor, Viscount Belgrave, the future Marquess of Westminster. Lady Elizabeth (1797–1891) was the daughter of that Duke of Sutherland whom the diarist Charles Greville called the "Leviathan of wealth . . . the richest individual who ever died."[47] In 1819, the year of her marriage, the Chancellor of the Exchequer declared that her father and her father-in-law were two of the four richest men in England.[48] Lady Elizabeth brought with her a marriage portion of £20,000. Her husband was guaranteed a minimum income of £5,000 a year during his father's lifetime from the revenues of specific estates placed in trust for the young couple. Lady Elizabeth herself was granted, by the terms of the settlement, the additional sum of £600 a year for her personal use. The couple's guaranteed income was also scheduled to rise with any increase in their family. As it turned out, this was substantial: Lady Elizabeth was to have thirteen children.[49]

As seen in the discussion on strategies for marriage formation, highly romantic expectations existed alongside the more mercenary motive. Money hardly precludes affection, Lydia Languish notwithstanding. The combination of personal attraction—Lady Elizabeth met her husband at Almack's —secure financial arrangements, and a common social background often led to happy and emotionally secure marriages in the aristocracy. The romantic expectations were frequently satisfied. Typical of many aristocratic marriages was a mutual esteem and shared regard that grew throughout a couple's years together. Even after ten years of marriage, Elizabeth, Marchioness of Westminster—whose aforementioned nuptials were supported by such wealth—felt that any day without her husband's presence was one of "utter forlorn misery." His continued "perfect good sense, kindness, affection and consideration" were the greatest comfort to her.[50] Similarly, Lady Salisbury, mother of a future prime minister, recorded in her diary on her wedding anniversary that "thirteen years have only added to my attachment and sense of my husband's worth."[51] Most revealing, perhaps, was the constant care spouses gave each other during their many illnesses. "My Dear Much Loved Granville," Susan, Marchioness of Stafford (1731–1805), wrote her only son from her aged husband's sickbed in 1801, more than thirty years after her marriage. "I am sure you would not wish me to forego the little attentions I pay your dear Father; they make him comfortable, and they are the Pleasure and Happiness of my Life. It may be Vanity," she added, "but I fancy that nothing is so well done about him as when I do it, and I rather believe he thinks so too."[52]

For many aristocratic couples, these comfortable domestic unions were also a source of sexual satisfaction. The prolonged childbearing period typical of aristocratic marriage in this century indicates that sexual relationships generally remained vital long after the need to secure an heir had been satisfied. Of the fifty women studied, thirty-five enjoyed marriages of completed fertility, that is, where both partners were still alive at the wife's forty-fifth birthday. These thirty-five women produced an average of more than eight children each. Emily, Duchess of Leinster (1731–1814), was the most prolific woman studied, and her marriage to the Duke was highly charged sexually. In 1762 the Duke wrote his wife that he had provided money to have her dressed appropriately for the coronation of George III, "and would give more than I could name to have the pleasure of undressing you myself, thou loveliest of the sex!"[53] By this time the Leinsters were the parents of eight children, but had only just begun: they would have ten more children in the twelve years remaining before the Duke's premature death in 1774. Yet it was Leinster's younger contemporary, the Duke of Devonshire, who looked for sexual satisfaction outside marriage. Even at the time of his wedding, Devonshire kept a milliner for his pleasure and expected his wife simply to provide an heir and play the duchess—a view of marriage not shared by his wife. Indeed, Leinster's notion of marriage as the preferable source of sexual satisfaction seems to have become the dominant one. In 1835 a twenty-three-year-old bachelor nobleman wanted very much to be married for this reason: "Conceive the delight of having a wife to do this," the future marquess confided to his diary, "instead of being obliged as one now is to go running after every dirty nurserymaid in there *pour passer le tems* [sic]."[54]

Women too, looked to marriage as a source of sexual satisfaction. Evidently the Duchess of Leinster did not find marital sexuality burdensome. Undaunted by the births of eighteen children, she married her sons' tutor six months after the Duke's death and went on to produce three additional children. This second marriage was undertaken for personal satisfaction alone. The Duchess had nothing to gain by it, economically or socially. Even a mid-Victorian aristocrat like Henrietta, Lady Stanley of Alderley (1808–1895), looked to her marriage for sexual satisfaction. Her husband's annual hunting trips to Scotland were an annual source of irritation to her. "My cold is so bad I can do nothing but sneeze and cry," she complained to her husband in 1846, some twenty years after their marriage. "I believe it is all owing to my cold bed, I really cannot keep warm alone."[55]

Twentieth-century cynics often imagine that when marriages in the past were successful, they were so because spouses rarely saw each other. This seems not to have been true. The increasing domesticity of family life, particularly after 1800, provided a far different social imperative. Married men and women were expected to spend their time together. By extension, social life was less sexually segregated than it had ever been before. To an elderly memoirist writing in the 1860s, this was one of the most remarkable changes he had witnessed in the fifty previous years. "Drinking and play were more universally indulged in then than at the present time," wrote Captain Gronow of the Regency,

> Indeed female society amongst the upper classes was most notoriously neglected [presumably by the males]; except perhaps, by romantic foreigners, who were the heroes of many a fashionable adventure that fed the clubs with ever present scandal. How could it be otherwise, when husbands spent the days in the hunting-fields,

or were entirely preoccupied with politics, and always away from home during the day.[56]

Men, of course, were not always pleased by the new social order. When Lord Stanley of Alderley violated it, he incurred his wife's displeasure. At other times men submitted. When, in 1843, Charles Richard Fox contemplated a solitary journey to Egypt, his aunt dissuaded him. "Unnecessary and voluntary separations, when people are married, seem to indicate that husband and wife no longer feel themselves necessary to each other's happiness," she reprimanded him, "and that the passion of love has not been succeeded by that close confidence and habitual communication which frequent and uncalled-for separations must tend to loosen."[57] Not surprisingly, Fox stayed home, though perhaps his wanderlust remained unsatisfied. Like his contemporary Blanche Stanley (though in a somewhat different context), Fox had discovered that domesticity could be frustrating as well as enriching. And, like her, he discovered that domesticity required that public behavior bear witness to the intimacy of married life, whether or not that intimacy was a reality.

Nevertheless, in some marriages the failure of intimacy was impossible to contain. Adultery and, less frequently, divorce were occasionally the result. The only recognized ground for divorce was the adultery of the wife. The divorce rate, though infinitesimal by modern standards, appeared to be rising dramatically from the third quarter of the eighteenth century onward, precisely when domesticity was becoming important.[58] Contemporaries feared, as George III put it, "that bad conduct among the ladies" was on the rise.[59] In retrospect, it appears more likely that romantic marriages were less able to contain a wife's adultery—the sole ground for divorce—than arranged ones had been. Moreover, adultery was private business; divorce was public. As we have seen, domesticity demanded a greater congruence between private and public lives.

The traditional attitude toward divorce held that it was in the worst possible taste. It was thought to be an extreme reaction to adultery, and the eighteenth-century aristocrat preferred moderation. As long as adultery did not interfere with anything important, such as the inheritance of property, private joys and sorrows were better kept private. The issue was perceived as economic, not moral. Dr. Johnson once said that the criminality of adultery lay in the "confusion of progeny which might result. All the property in the world," he wrote, "depended on female chastity."[60] According to this view women were thought to owe their husbands one real heir. The marriage of Lord and Lady Melbourne is often taken to typify this cynical approach.[61] Born Elizabeth Milbanke (1751–1821), the only daughter of a baronet, she married the wealthy Peniston Lamb in 1769. Within a year a son was born to the couple and Lamb had taken a mistress. Elizabeth's seven subsequent children, born after an interval of seven years, were generally thought to be the results of affairs with the Earl of Egremont and the Prince of Wales. Far from wishing to divorce his wife, Lamb was elevated to the peerage on the basis of his wife's favor with the Prince. Lady Melbourne's conduct was not thought unusual. Even as late as 1792 the Countess of Sutherland believed it was common practice for English women brazenly to pass their children off as legitimate when in fact they were not.[62] The Duchess of Devonshire believed that women disappeared into Switzerland and Italy "when in scrapes."[63]

A considerable amount of delicacy and finesse was required to keep adultery within the family, that is, to avoid the public break of a divorce. One never embarrassed one's husband in public. One of the better practitioners of this art was Harriet, Lady Bessborough. As we have seen, her marriage in 1780 had been more or less arranged, and her affection for her husband was more or less lukewarm. The great passion of her life was Lord Granville Leveson-Gower, whom she met in Italy in 1794. At the time Lady Bessborough was thirty-three, Lord Granville twenty-one. Their long affair was a "well-known secret" in London society. Lady Bessborough's all-too-discerning niece, who was later to marry Granville, described the continued progress of the affair in 1807:

> Lord Granville has not yet arrived. My aunt is, of course, anxious to be in Town when he is, and if she would be so, with less *detour* and prevarication I should not blame her for it; but there is so much of representing poor yielding Lord B. as a Tyrant from whose Commands there is no way of escaping, and herself as a Victim to him, that it is really distressing to hear her. I do not know how she contrives to manage him as completely as she does.[64]

Like many other husbands of his time, the Earl of Bessborough preferred "not to know" as long as his wife did not force the unpleasant truth upon him.

But a new morality was developing by the end of the eighteenth century, a morality in which vice refused to disguise itself as virtue. The private had to be made public. When Lady Sarah Bunbury eloped with a lover in 1769, the censorious Lady Mary Coke reported with gleeful indignation: "The saying her conscience would not allow her to impose a child upon her husband was quite new."[65] This new morality represented less a flaunting of community standards than an internalization of them. Yet a woman who chose, like Lady Sarah, to admit her love openly ran the grave risk of being divorced. And while a divorce procedure would publicly brand her husband a cuckold, Lady Sarah was to suffer even more. For a woman, divorce meant loss of status, reputation, economic security, and, perhaps worst of all, loss of her children.

Divorce was a procedure that legally embodied both the sexual double standard and the property value of female chastity. Only men could seek the remedy of divorce: women could not divorce their husbands for adultery. Prior to 1857 when divorce courts were first instituted, divorce was an unpleasant, arduous, expensive, time-consuming, and irregular legal procedure. A husband like Sir Charles Bunbury, wishing to divorce his wife, was first compelled to sue her lover for damages in an action for "criminal conversation." He therein sought pecuniary compensation for the loss of his wife's chastity. The wife was not a party to the case. Following that verdict, the husband took his case to the Ecclesiastical Court, which could provide for a separation agreement. Only Parliament, however, had the authority to make a divorce final through the passage of a private bill to that effect. Each divorce, therefore, required a separate piece of legislation. The terms of a divorce varied. Specific clauses, for instance, had to be introduced to enable the divorced woman to remarry. Moreover, since a divorce overturned the property settlements made at the time of the marriage, Parliament was obligated to provide for the redistribution of that property. The sexual offense of an upper-class woman was a sufficient threat to society to warrant Parliament's attention. Parliamentary divorce was so expensive that it was realistically available only to men of wealth. But that too was appropriate: only a rich woman's chastity had much value.

Aristocratic society punished divorced women in a variety of ways. After all, by voluntarily relinquishing the honor of matrimony, she had committed an affront that society could not afford to tolerate. A major method of punishment was social exclusion. Social recognition of a woman necessitated acknowledging her position in society, and a divorced woman had sacrificed hers. Nearly twenty years after her divorce and remarriage, the Marchioness of Anglesey found her social acceptability remained problematical. When her second husband was appointed Lord Lieutenant of Ireland in 1828, Lady Anglesey discovered his Under Secretary's wife would not receive her.[66] Similarly, the famous Coke of Norfolk refused to invite Lady Holland to Holkham, even after she had become something of a social lioness despite her divorce and subsequent remarriage. Coke nevertheless continued to invite Lord Holland, who always declined on his wife's account. For their part the Hollands regularly invited the Great Commoner to dine at Holland House, and he occasionally did so. "When I do so," he once explained,

> I am as attentive as I ought to be to Lady Holland, and there is no kind of flattery she does not apply to me, but it won't do! She is not a woman I approve of at all. I am only surprised that so many people have been bullied by her to letting her into their houses. For myself, I have always made up my mind that she should never enter mine.[67]

Even family members were likely to ostracize a woman who had the effrontery to be divorced. Anne Wellesley (1788–1875), first the wife of Sir William Abdy, gave birth to four children in less than four years after her elopement, divorce, and subsequent remarriage to Lord Charles Bentick. The loneliness caused by "the neglect of the world" made Lady Anne quite miserable, particularly as she was often confined to bed.[68] Only her sister was compassionate enough to visit Lady Anne. Neither of their parents, the Marquess and Marchioness Wellesley (who had not married until after the births of their children), saw or communicated with Lady Anne on the occasions of her divorce and remarriage, and Lady Wellesley excluded her erring daughter from her will.[69]

Divorced women were expected to atone for their sin by spending the rest of their lives in seclusion. It was probably Lady Holland's unrepentant attitude that so irritated Coke of Norfolk. Similarly, Lady Sarah Bunbury discovered that even eleven years' repentance was not thought sufficient. Lady Sarah, a daughter of the second Duke of Richmond, had been married to Sir Charles Bunbury. After six childless years of marriage she gave birth in 1768 to a child by Lord William Gordon and eloped with her lover a year later, unwilling, as we have seen, to disguise any longer her child's paternity. Sir Charles did not secure a divorce until 1776, by which time the affair with Gordon had ended. Lady Sarah retired with her daughter to the Goodwood estate of her brother, the third Duke, where she lived as his pensioner in seclusion. Her decision to remarry in 1781, at the age of thirty-six, came as unwelcome news to her family and remaining friends. Her closest friend, Lady Sarah O'Brien (who had herself made a misalliance with an actor), explained the opposition to Lady Sarah's remarriage.

> There was a propriety in yr. retreat, & a dignity annex'd to the idea of *one great passion*, tho' unfortunately placed, that gratified your friends & silenced your enemies. I have so often heard you praised and admired for not marrying again and giving up your time to your daughter, that I grieve that you sh^d change a plan, the only one in the world that perhaps could thoroughly reinstate you in the good opinion & esteem of every body.[70]

The loss of reputation, freedom, and friends engendered by a divorce was accompanied by a loss perhaps most keenly felt of all—the loss of one's children. Parliamentary divorces always awarded the children to their father. The threat of losing one's children probably deterred many women from openly breaking with their husbands. Elizabeth, Lady Webster, acted desperately after she eloped in Italy with the young Lord Holland. She and her lover lived together openly in Florence with her three Webster children while her husband, Sir Godfrey Webster, returned to England to initiate divorce proceedings against her. While Sir Godfrey was gone, she falsely announced that her infant, Harriet Webster, had died. A mock funeral was held. "The certainty of losing all my children was agonizing," she later recorded in her journal, "and I resolved to keep one in my possession, and I chose that one who from her age and sex required the tenderness of a mother." After three years of anxious subterfuge Lady Holland (as she had become) finally decided to surrender the child to Sir Godfrey.[71] Lady Holland did not see her daughter again until she was grown and married.

Women were not only isolated from their legitimate children but from their illegitimate children as well. Unlike men, women could not acknowledge their "natural" children without risking their social positions. Eliza Courtney, the Duchess of Devonshire's daughter by Charles Grey, was brought up by the elder Greys in Northumberland, far from the Duchess's anxious eyes.[72] Lady Bessborough's two children by Lord Granville were raised by their father and ultimately by his wife, Lady Bessborough's niece, "with the same care" as the legitimate Granvilles received.[73]

Men, as the Granville episode indicates, were able, if they so chose, to develop strong affectional ties with their illegitimate offspring. In contrast to the treatment accorded the Duchess of Devonshire, who rarely saw Eliza Courtney, her husband had three illegitimate children (one by a milliner and two by Lady Elizabeth Foster) brought up in the Devonshire household along with the legitimate children. The Duke gave his daughter by Lady Elizabeth the extraordinary marriage portion of £30,000 to enable her to marry the man of her choice.[74]

Thus aristocratic women contemplating adultery risked enormous losses, far greater than the potential deprivations their husbands might suffer. Patriarchal society had an enormous range of controls of female sexual behavior, both formal and informal. These restraints were used both to deter adultery initially and to contain its consequences once it had occurred.

Still, if the new morality of domesticity made it psychologically more difficult to tolerate adultery within marriage, it also rendered impossible the toleration of loveless but chaste marriages. Loveless marriages were seen increasingly as immoral, mercenary arrangements. Lady Holland described a friend of hers in 1794 as having had the opportunity of marrying Lord Grandison, "but she preferred a handsome young lover to the worse prostitution of marrying a disgusting old man."[75] Randolph Trumbach is right in suggesting that divorce, while originating as the means of protecting male property rights, also became the means of ending an unhappy marriage to begin a new life.[76] To that end, divorce became the vehicle for the eighteenth-century pursuit of happiness. The stories of Lady Sarah Bunbury and her niece by marriage, Lady Holland, illustrate this point.

Legend has it that the young George III wished to marry Lady Sarah Lennox, the fourth daughter of the Duke and Duchess of Richmond, but was prevented from doing so by reason of state. A few months after the King's marriage in 1762, Lady Sarah, aged seventeen, was herself married to Sir Charles Bunbury, a Suffolk baronet and patron of the Turf. It was thought to be a love match "of her own making,"[77] but it was evident even before the marriage that the love was more on Lady Sarah's part. Her brother-in-law, the uxorious Duke of Leinster, thought that "neither she nor Mr. Bunbury seem to be much in love according to my notion of being in love." He continued, "She seems to me to court him more than he does her in a free way (but I would not have you say so to anybody)."[78] After the wedding it was thought that Sir Charles neglected his wife in favor of his horses (he was the owner of Diomed, the first Derby winner). As we have seen, the unsatisfied Lady Sarah was to elope with a lover.

Like Lady Sarah, Elizabeth, Lady Webster, could not accept a loveless marriage. Born Elizabeth Vassall (1771–1845), she was the heiress of a fabulously wealthy West India planter. She was married at the age of fifteen to a man many years her senior, Sir Godfrey Webster, owner of Battle Abbey. It was a union in which breeding and money complemented each other nicely; unfortunately their personalities did not. Within two weeks of the marriage, Sir Godfrey threatened suicide. After several years of overt and covert hostility and the births of several Webster children, she refused to sleep with her husband any longer. She had never thought this was an acceptable marriage; her disappointment and frustration were intense. "My heart felt the want of some object to open itself unto, for in spite of my cold, hard maxims of solitary comfort, I often detect my wishes wandering to some imaginary happiness," she recorded in her diary in 1794 in her usual florid style. "The want of Passion in my constitution will always save me from the calamity of letting my heart run away with my reason."[79] Within two years, however, she would meet and elope with Lord Holland, two years her junior. Like Lady Sarah Bunbury, Lady Holland was a woman of romantic expectations married to a man of more traditional concerns. Neither woman was willing to tolerate "arrangements" like those of the Melbournes or Bessboroughs. They believed, quite simply, in risking all for love. For Lady Holland, the revelation of her passion and consequent divorce had been well worth the sacrifices she endured. She was much happier in her second marriage. "I am a better Person and a more useful member of Society than I was in my years of Misery," she concluded.[80] For her, romance had indeed been an emancipating force.

Yet as in other aspects of family life, romance was something of a double-edged sword. If an emphasis on the affective functions of marriage led to an increased divorce rate, it also made divorce a more painful experience. It was not only the traditional doctrines of aristocratic patriarchy that stood ready to condemn the woman who openly left her husband for another. Women left marriages they had made for love, as well as those they had made for money or position. The psychological constraints against leaving a husband one had married for love might indeed be greater. Moreover, society did not look benignly on one for whom romantic love appeared to be only an ephemeral passion rather than a solid foundation upon which a great family was raised. In the past, the seduction of a married woman was often simply seen as an injury to her family's honor, appropriately avenged by a duel. Romanticism transformed the social meaning of adultery: it came to be seen as less a public than a private crime. As such, it could not be so easily expiated. The sentimentalization of chastity was a view shared by the adultress. A pariah from society, she was likely to be alienated from herself as well. The case of Lady Charlotte Wellesley perfectly illustrates the transformation of adultery from a public to a private crime in which the victim became an instrument of her own punishment. In 1809 Lady Charlotte, the Duke of Wellington's sister-in-law, eloped with the commander of his cavalry, Lord Paget. Lady Charlotte's husband and brother consciously decided not to challenge Paget to the traditional duel, believing that Lady Charlotte, referred to by an intermediary as a "stinking pole cat," was not worth "shedding blood."[81] Lady Charlotte, sadly enough, internalized this view of herself. Upon a request that she return to her husband and children, she declared that she never could "after the Iniquitous Act she had been guilty of with Lord Paget."[82] This transformation of adultery from public crime to private iniquity was one witnessed by the perceptive, if cranky, Lady Mary Coke, as early as 1771. Now "that virtue must be its own reward, I'm afraid people will grow cooler in its cause," she wrote.[83]

Lady Mary was correct in her diagnosis, if not in her prediction. Society was indeed becoming increasingly inner directed, as we would say today—a thoroughly appropriate response in an age of affective individualism. If virtue was to be its own reward, then guilt was likewise its own punishment. People were to become warmer, not cooler, in the defense of virtue. A reputation for chastity was no longer a cloak of respectability one could put on when going out of an evening with one's husband and remove as soon as one arrived home with one's lover, as in the days of Lady Melbourne and Lady Bessborough. A sinful nature stayed with a woman wherever she went.

Chastity had lost its largely mercantilist connotations. While it continued to have a property value in this landowning class, chastity became sentimentalized as well. This change has already been identified in the increasing attention given the marriage ceremony as a sentimental celebration of a couple's love and the birth of a new emotional unit—as opposed to a minor celebration of property arrangements. The reasons for this change will become more apparent in the next chapter. The delicacy of the age viewed with increasing distaste the notion of property in chastity, however sexual relations functioned in fact. As part of its 1857 reform of divorce, Parliament ended the procedure of criminal conversation for just this reason. Lord Lansdowne objected to treating the loss of a wife's chastity like the lost of ordinary chattel, while Lyndhurst agreed with Erskine that "any man who could be satisfied with pecuniary compensation for such an injury deserved no award of damages at all."[84]

However important the personal component of romantic love, marriage necessarily remained an economic and social institution. The continued interest of Parliament in such personal matters as marriage and divorce is indicative of the continued public functions that marriage performed even as late as 1857. Ultimately, a successful aristocratic marriage required the production of an authentic heir to perpetuate the family and its class. This child, of course, was not merely the heir of his parents: he was the heir of countless generations of his family, the progenitor of countless more. Since the economic support for all family members came from the same estate, the interests of all family members—horizontally as well as vertically—were related. The cult of domesticity, one may argue, did not isolate the aristocratic nuclear family from its larger network of kin.

Instead, domesticity had two major consequences for the relations of a married couple and their extended family. First, it tended to increase the affective content of interactions between family members. The extended family might become more, rather than less, important. Second, the component of affective individualism provided a person with more freedom to choose between family members. This often resulted in a reorientation of interactions in the direction of the wife's family.

As with marriage formation, the strategies used in determining the components of kin relations varied enormously. Several factors determined how a couple interacted with its relations. Some families simply modernized faster than others. In many families, the question of whose parents were alive directed the course of family relations. And as always, the relation of a husband to the head of his family accounted for a great deal. Men who were already the heads of their families had the most independence. Younger sons, because they counted for less, were often (though not always) more independent of their parents than were heirs. Nevertheless, even with this variety of factors in mind, we can examine, in turn, ways in which domesticity transformed relations between extended kin. As with other areas of family life affected by domesticity, differences in value systems existed simultaneously, occasionally leading to conflict or, at best, dissatisfaction.

The Carlisles of Castle Howard retained the traditions of formal patriarchy longer than did many other aristocratic families. When Lady Georgiana Cavendish married George, Lord Morpeth, in 1801 and moved to his home, Castle Howard, she immediately encountered this clash of values. Castle Howard, she discovered, enclosed a world in which parents were treated with awe and respect, and where honest affection, of the kind Lady Georgiana had enjoyed since childhood, was virtually unknown. Lady Morpeth's bleak situation was relieved by the occasional visits of her younger sister, who was shocked by the cold patriarchal formality that reigned at Castle Howard. Lady Harriet Cavendish's contrasting modernity can be gauged by the degree of her indignation. "Lord Carlisle certainly keeps his children in great awe of him," she wrote her grandmother familiarly. "They are in their behavior to each other more like a Prince with his followers, or a General with his aide de Camp, than a Father. . . . Those who will not submit their opinion entirely to his direction have no alternative but silence," she concluded.[85] In another letter, this time to her mother, Lady Harriet provided an impeccable description of formal social life, usually thought by historians to have died decades before 1804:

> Lord C.[arlisle] is in better spirits and better *humeur* than he has been for some days, and of course, so are we, for he is *par force* the

mainspring of every smile and every frown that *publickly* appear upon our faces. This, I think, the great inconvenience of the system here. *Il regne en despote*; his gloom or gaiety, are not, as in other individuals, *en particulier*, and one is, of course, almost always stifling a laugh or forcing one. His sons, at least Wm. & Frederick, are at times perfectly mute, and conversation is *managed* too much to be agreeable or even easy. Charles Bagot once told me that he went to a dinner and found a most formal circle established round the room, from which the lady of the house advanced and said to him, "The subject is Lord George Gordon," which method of conversation is a little in the style of ours here, and without being very impudent, I am almost the only person here who does not blush at the sound of my own voice.[86]

There was not much room for affective individualism at Castle Howard. Unfortunately for Lady Morpeth, her domineering father-in-law would live until 1825—by which time she would be a grandmother. Lady Holland, who had traded the stultification of a traditional marriage for a union of passion (and affective individualism), was appalled by the formality of social life at Castle Howard. She thought Lady Morpeth a perfect angel for coping as well as she did with her difficult and old-fashioned in-laws. "If you did not feel the faults of his character and the *weariness* of hers you would have no merit in bearing with them," she commented. "The pinnacle of merit *ici bas* is to have the feelings of a mortal and the endurance of an angel."[87]

Social change could also work to the advantage of a young woman. For someone marrying into a more affectionate and informal family, the change was a refreshing one. Maria, Lady Duncannon (1787–1834), told the Duchess of Devonshire the day before her marriage to the woman's nephew that "having lost her mother and seeing nothing of her father she had already experienced more kindness from D.'s [Duncannon's] family than from anybody else."[88] The affection between family members (apparent, for instance in the letters between Lady Granville and her sister, Lady Morpeth) was a fact of life that will be continually manifest throughout these pages. We have also seen it reflected in the adoption of informal modes of address. Yet perhaps the complaints made by family members against each other provide us with the best sense of the replacement of formal filial duty by affective individualism. Lady Cecilia Ridley (1819–1845) summed it up in complaining to her mother about her mother-in-law: "What a bore she is!"[89]

Even as late as the end of the eighteenth century, childbirth still took place most often under the paternal roof. Hester, Lady Mahon (whose husband was Earl Stanhope's heir), was extremely ill after the birth of her third daughter in 1780. From the home of her husband's parents, where she was confined, Lady Mahon expressed relief and satisfaction when finally allowed to write to her mother, more than two months after this difficult delivery.

> It is unnecessary to tell you, my dearest mother, my joy in at last being able to write to you how much I feel your affectionate goodness to me. I do assure you during the whole course of my illness, the anxiety you suffered upon my account was a most distressing circumstance to me. I know the sight of my handwriting is the best assurance I can give you of how much I am recovered; and I hope you really are at ease about me, for indeed I begin to feel very comfortable again, and I am as you may imagine very truly thankful to find myself once more writing to my dear Mother, and well enough to have been able to have ventured here after this long illness. How much I owe Lady Stanhope I could not tell you if I was allowed to write a very much longer letter than for the first time I may, for nothing could equal her affectionate care of me, more than the kind attention of all about me.[90]

Did Lady Chatham feel any jealousy because another woman was nursing her daughter, for whom Lady Chatham retained very strong ties of affection? We have no way of knowing, nor do we know whether she ever saw her daughter again. Less than two months after writing this letter, Lady Mahon was dead.

The diaries of Elizabeth, Duchess of Grafton, also reveal the dominance of the paternal tie even into the early years of the new century. While the Duchess spent a good deal of time nursing her son's wife, and even her stepson's wife, through their confinements,[91] she was estranged from the childbearing experiences of her own daughters. The first to marry was Lady Frances (1780–1866). In 1801 she wed the third son of the Duke of Marlborough, later created Baron Churchill in his own right. The fifth of Lady Churchill's children, like so many of the others, was born at the Marlborough home in London. The Duchess of Grafton, though living nearby, did not visit her daughter's lying-in chamber until the tenth day after the birth. The Duchess was treated like any other visitor. After seeing her daughter briefly, she "had some cold meat with the Duke and Duchess, then went."[92] The births of many of the Churchill children are not even recorded in their maternal grandmother's diary.

By the middle of the nineteenth century, as much if not more time and emotional energy were directed toward the maternal family. As Lady Morpeth's experiences at Castle Howard indicate, patrilocality was not necessarily an indication of the direction of emotional ties. As domesticity advanced and formal patriarchy receded, young women were increasingly able to make those domestic arrangements that reflected their continued emotional dependence on mothers and sisters. Childbirth more and more frequently took place in the presence of maternal rather than, or in addition to, paternal relations. As with the previously discussed changes in family life, this change took place slowly over the course of many years. As early as 1772 Lady Stafford's sister came to be with her for her confinement; Lady Horatia Seymour-Conway was attended by a sister and a friend in 1793.[93] The transformation in orientation is clearly seen in the case of Lady Caroline Lamb (1785–1828). Married to an heir, she spent most of her married life under the roof of her hostile in-laws, the Melbournes. But she remained emotionally closer to her mother, Lady Bessborough. When Lady Caroline gave birth in 1809, it was Lady Bessborough rather than Lady Melbourne who attended her. Lady Bessborough reported staying up all night with her laboring daughter, who finally gave birth to a child who died in the morning, on its grandmother's lap.[94]

By the third decade of the nineteenth century, childbirth in the presence of the maternal family had become the norm. When Blanche, Countess of Burlington (1812–1840), gave birth to her first child in 1831, she was attended by her mother and two sisters, both of whom forwarded an account of the event to an absent sister.[95] When Constance, Duchess of Westminster, gave birth in 1853, it was her father who forwarded the news to her husband's family, the pattern a reverse of what it had been a century earlier.[96] This shift acknowledged the ascendancy of the private, emotional meaning of birth. This ascendancy was not yet achieved at the royal level, where public duty still took precedence over private emotion. But the maternal norm was recognized by the middle of the century. Queen Victoria resented her own inability to attend the birth of a first child to her daughter, the Crown Princess of Prussia, in 1858. "I feel it bitterly," the Queen wrote, "that I have to forgo my natural right and duty to be with my dear Child in her hour of trial, as every other Mother does."[97] Yet a hundred years earlier, there had been no such "natural right" in existence.

Under the sway of domesticity, however, a young woman's relations with her in-laws were not universally cooler than those she enjoyed with her own parents. As we saw with Maria, Lady Duncannon, relations with in-laws might even be warmer than with one's family of origin. Lady Elizabeth Drummond found this to be true too. Her mother, a daughter of that domestic tyrant, the fifth Earl of Carlisle, maintained the patriarchal traditions of Castle Howard. As the Duchess of Rutland, she was known as "the proudest woman in England."[98] She was very cool in congratulating her daughter on the birth of a second child to the Drummonds in 1824, and felt no desire or obligation to visit Lady Elizabeth during her confinement in London, although the Duke planned to go.[99] Not surprisingly, during the course of her married life, Elizabeth usually turned for advice and comfort to her mother-in-law.[100] So, too, did Lady Augusta Coventry (1812–1889) after her marriage to Henry Fox, the Hollands' heir.

Lady Augusta's parents had separated when she was a small child. She had grown up in Italy with her mother, the Countess of Coventry, isolated from the rest of her family. Henry Fox was astonished at what little interest Lady Coventry took in her daughter's welfare and how poorly his fiancée was dressed—"worse than Cinderella," as he wrote his mother.[101] Only a few months after her marriage in 1833, Lady Augusta shared secrets with Lady Holland rather than with her own mother.[102] A few years later she admitted that her mother had been "inexorably averse to female friendships."[103]

For most families, however, an increase in the affective content of family life meant that young women remained emotionally tied to their families of birth even years after they had married. If Lady Augusta Fox shared secrets with her mother-in-law, then many more young women of her generation asked their mothers or sisters for help in coping with their mothers-in-law.[104] But perhaps increasingly typical was a relationship between mother-in-law and daughter-in-law that simply replicated the close affectionate ties each had formed with her biological family. For women like Henrietta, Lady Stanley of Alderley, warm personal relationships with her family of origin continued even as ties deepened with her husband's family. Indeed, for both generations, intensely affective relations with one's own parents or children provided a model and a training ground for the newer relationship with in-laws. "Dearest Hen," the Dowager Lady Stanley wrote her daughter-in-law in 1851, "Of all the comforts I can receive, now or ever, the greatest is that of feeling that you are as truly a daughter in all your sympathies and interests and all your recollections as one of my own born ones—and as anxious to give me pleasure in telling me all you know I care for."[105]

Domesticity did not isolate the nuclear family from its kin, but the function of the extended family changed somewhat during the century 1760 to 1860. While the family never ceased being an economic support and an instrument of power, the extended family also became an increasingly important source of emotional satisfaction to its members. That aristocrats after 1800 increasingly preferred to use names and nicknames rather than titles in their personal discourse provided us with one tangible sign of this change. These new family relationships were more often achieved than ascribed. Individuals selected others from the network of kin to be their intimates. Relations between sisters were often particularly intense. So, too, for some, was the mother-daughter dyad. Relationships between married women and their in-laws often remained important, but they had changed in tone. When women and their mothers-in-law became especially intimate, it was often because the younger women sought mother substitutes. Whatever the reason for the closeness, these relationships were often intimate and informal, which was very different from the patriarchal relationship of in-laws of a century earlier. It seems clear that most aristocrats grew to expect continued intimacy with their kin. Accordingly, the emotional range of their life experiences gained breadth as well as depth.

The British aristocracy in the century 1760 to 1860 incorporated a variety of experiences during the course of their domestic lives. Individuals employed diverse strategies in the formation of marriages. Once married, they encountered a range of emotional opportunities. Nevertheless, overall social change in the shape of an increasing emphasis on domesticity had an impact on the members of this class, though at different times for different families. The variable rate of change was itself a major source of stress in many families. This seems to have been especially true around the turn of the century, when old norms had by no means yet been thoroughly replaced by the new. Domesticity did not become fully normative until the second or even third decade of the nineteenth century.

The public function of the family in this elite group was not, however, thoroughly eradicated. For many, the public sphere was simply subsumed within the growing realm of private emotion. Even the so-called romantic marriage, for instance, was likely to have been endogamous and based on a firm foundation of wealth. Parents, in-laws, and spouses ceased being remote figures of authority and came to be emotionally significant individuals, whether for good or ill.

Yet domesticity, if offering the promise of a richer emotional existence, also carried with it the greater threat of emotional failure. Social norms were more likely to become part of an internalized value structure. The sentimentalization of marriage brought with it a heavy burden of guilt for those unable or unwilling to live in accordance with the new code of behavior. Men, like women, occasionally found domesticity inhibiting as well as emancipating. In many cases, domesticity may have changed expressed values more than it changed actual patterns of behavior. Emotions may have changed less than the interpretation of them.

However one perceived marriage during the years 1760 to 1860, that institution was regarded as a necessary fact of life. The choice was not *whether* to marry, but *whom* to marry.[106] And marriage almost inevitably brought with it the joys and burdens of motherhood. For whatever else aristocratic women did with their lives, there was only one function for which they were regarded as indispensable: childbearing.

CHAPTER II

The Name of Mother

For the British aristocracy during the century 1760 to 1860 the essential emotional and biological ingredient in childbirth was suffering. That, indeed, was the meaning of Eve's curse. Referring to his wife, Katherine, Countess Jermyn (1809–1848), a young aristocrat wrote in 1832:

> She had nourished with her life blood and brought forth that little being into the world, at an expense of solicitude and of suffering of which we Husbands can probably form but an imperfect conception. She is younger and more tender-hearted and of a weaker frame and constitution than I am; & in short, I believe that under the name of "Mother" there lies a charm by which emotions more exquisitely tender than any known to humanity are called into existence.[1]

In this perfectly mundane piece of family correspondence, Lord Jermyn summed up much that his contemporaries felt about childbirth. It was not, after all, merely the production of a child that commanded the sentimental worship of a husband, but the maternal suffering that accompanied it. It was suffering that defined "Mother" and removed her (albeit, supposedly to a higher plane) from the company of mere humanity. And we shall see, it was maternal suffering that reinforced the notion of the inferiority of women in English aristocratic society. Yet paradoxically, it was also in this essential role of mother that women both demanded and won the respect often denied them in their other capacities. The attitude toward maternal suffering was therefore extraordinarily complex and further complicated by the rise of domesticity during the century 1760 to 1860. It was also during this century that anesthesia was first administered to obstetric patients. That event took place in 1847 and represented more than a technological breakthrough. The potential of laughing gas to eliminate pain had been known for nearly half a century. But it was only with the advent of domestic values that the use of anesthesia to eliminate pain in childbirth became acceptable and even desirable in aristocratic families.

Domesticity transformed family life and altered the meaning children had for their parents. The eldest male retained his role as heir. But children came to be desired as more than "walking sperm-banks," to use Lawrence Stone's phrase.[2] Children also came to be thought of as the products and objects of their parents' love: a "pledge of affection," as the Duke of Rutland referred to his first grandchild in 1822.[3] Children were increasingly perceived as emotional resources, particularly for their mothers. The public function of heirs came to be superseded—though by no means obliterated—by the private function of children as their parents' darlings, loved for themselves as much as for the contributions they could make to the family's power and influence. This private function demanded a greater emphasis on each child's individuality—a change reflected in the aristocracy's increasing emotional receptivity to female infants and in the patterns used in naming children of either sex. This greater emphasis on the individual personal development of each child also transformed the ideal of motherhood. As children were thought to require more attention than they had been given hitherto, the primary function of motherhood shifted from an emphasis on the biological function of childbearing to an emphasis on the nurturant function of childrearing.

This transformation could hardly have occurred without altering the meaning of childbirth itself. A later chapter will examine how aristocratic families actually organized the conduct of a birth. For the present we will limit ourselves to the exploration of the meaning that childbirth had in the lives of adult women.

Because that meaning had always been identified with the pains of labor, a woman's suffering had come to be considered the core of her existence. Eve's curse was thought to be both cause and consequence of the subordinate status of women in society. Once motherhood came to be perceived as a lifelong pursuit centered around the rearing of children, maternal suffering became less identified with the contractions of labor. Indeed, Eve's curse may be said to have progressed from an acute to a chronic condition: from one of physically intense, but finite pain, to a less intense but limitless state of "exquisitely tender" emotional vulnerability.

As with other areas of family life, the transformation in the meaning of motherhood was slow and uneven. For some families the transition has already begun by 1760; for others it was not yet complete even by 1860. The most tangible watershed was 1839—the year that Parliament passed the Infant Custody Act, which for the first time gave women the right, in the event of a legal separation, to the custody of their children under the age of seven. (Paternal authority remained absolute for older children.) In so doing, Parliament recognized the importance of the "maternal instinct" for both mothers and children. There was much opposition to the act: one popular pamphleteer denounced it for bringing about the "destruction of the family."[4] And in a sense, it did, because for the first time Parliament denied the principle of the absolute authority of the father. The act is also significant because it provided the first recognition that married women had a legal existence independent of their husbands. For our purposes, it is important to emphasize that this bill, often considered the first example of feminist legislation, addressed itself to women's rights as mothers. Caroline Norton, who had campaigned for the Infant Custody Act, believed that none of the legal liabilities that women then suffered weighed as heavily upon them as the ability of a husband to deprive his wife of her children.[5] Historians who affirm the supremacy of domesticity as early as 1775 ought to ponder the prevailing situation in which even a nursing infant could be taken from its mother's breast if its father so desired.[6] Until 1839, therefore, women had no right to their children whatsoever. Husbands did not even need to prove their wives "unfit." Legally (if not often in reality), women enjoyed the company of their children on the sufferance of the father.

As long as traditional social and economic concerns remained, traditional forms of family life could not be easily overthrown. It will be useful at this point to establish what is meant by the traditional attitude toward children. Primarily, their significance (as attested by their pre-1839 legal status) was as paternal heirs. This is illustrated by the correspondence of our fifty families. In 1772, for instance, General Pitt congratulated his friend Lady Stafford on the news that she intended making her husband "a present of a son."[7] The child proved to be a girl. Lady Mary Coke recorded in her diary in September that Lady Stafford had been "in the greatest danger, and for no better purpose than to bring her Lord a sixth daughter, which he certainly did not desire."[8] During her pregnancy in 1789, the Duchess of Devonshire promised to dedicate all her time to "quiet of body and mind, that I may not lose the advantage of giving the Duke a son."[9]

The need for heirs remained of paramount importance. Even as late as 1895, the American Consuelo Vanderbilt, recently married to the ninth Duke of Marlborough, discovered that her primary function (presumably after the payment of a huge dowry) was to provide an heir to Blenheim. Her first meeting with the Dowager Duchess began with "an embarrassing inspection of my person." Then the formidable Dowager, according to Consuelo's account, told the young bride "Your first duty is to have a child and it must be a son, because it was intolerable to have that little upstart Winston become Duke [sic]. Are you in the family way?"[10]

Thus a young woman's most personal secrets were considered

part of the family business. She could be left in no doubt that her primary duty in life was to produce an heir. All the young women in the study group of fifty felt this pressure. The Duchess of Devonshire complained to her mother in 1783 that her husband's relatives "abuse" the nursing of her daughter because of "their impatience for a son and their fancying I shan't so soon if I suckle."[11] Sarah, Lady Jersey, was so anxious to become pregnant that her health was visibly affected. Only ten months after her marriage in 1804 it was reported that she "is alter'd not to be known it is thought she frets herself at not being *grosse*, and quacks herself."[12]

It is hardly surprising to learn that women were often relieved to find themselves pregnant even after only a few weeks of marriage,[13] or that they felt considerable pride upon the birth of a son. "Certainly the moment when I found myself the mother of a boy was the happiest I ever experienced before or since," wrote Frances Anne, Marchioness of Londonderry (1800–1865).[14] A friend of Lady Stanley's told her that "life will be a blank" if her 1859 pregnancy did not result in the birth of a boy.[15]

The birth of a son was a service a wife owed a husband and his family. Women often received extravagant presents upon the birth of a first son. In 1821, for instance, Lord Londonderry gave his wife a set of pearls worth £10,000 on that occasion.[16] In the case of the Devonshires, it is clear that there was payment for services rendered. According to the Duchess's biographer, the Duke could have paid off his wife's debts if he so chose. "But he wanted value for money," Arthur Calder-Marshall has written. The Duchess understood the bargain. Early in her third pregnancy she assured one of her creditors that she would inform the Duke of all her debts if she gave birth to a son. In May of 1790 she did give birth to a boy, and six days later the gratified Duke deposited £13,000 in her bank account.[17]

Although childbearing would come to be much more than a service women performed in the interests of the paternal line, that function remained. Would that service have seemed as great had it not been accompanied by suffering and the risk of death? It will be useful to keep this question in mind.

Under the traditional patriarchal regime, the responsibilities of women toward their children—like their rights—scarcely existed beyond the cutting of the umbilical cord. The Countess of Sutherland's attitude was perhaps typical. She gave birth to her first child in 1786 and departed for Europe in the company of her husband about six weeks later, leaving the tiny heir in England in the care of servants.[18] Her mission had been accomplished.

All this was to change. The medical profession during the century in question actively promoted the idea that maternal responsibilities did indeed last beyond the child's birth. In his influential book *Domestic Medicine*, first published in 1769, William Buchan warned that she "who abandons the fruit of her love, as soon as he is born, to the care of her nurse, must forever forfeit the name of mother."[19] That the medical profession continued to inveigh against what it regarded as maternal neglect may well indicate that the public was slow to respond. The work of an influential German physician, Christian Struve, was translated and published in England in 1801. He hammered home the same message. Women who entrusted the care of their children entirely to servants were guilty of "a criminal species of indulgence," Struve wrote, and were therefore "unworthy of the sacred name of mother."[20]

Motherhood, one might say, had once been an ascribed function. It was becoming an achieved status. Women may have been attracted to the new, domestic ideal of motherhood for precisely that reason. The new motherhood required that women make use of emotional, intellectual, and moral talents that they were traditionally thought to lack. Those deserving of "the name of mother" were theoretically, at least, to be accorded an honored status that was otherwise unavailable to them. "The greatest charms and dignity of a woman are derived from her maternal office," Struve wrote, and "a good mother equally deserves the affection of her husband and the esteem of the world."[21] Lay authors were no less active in promoting the attractiveness of motherhood. "But great as the influence of the maiden and wife, it seems to fade away when placed by that of the mother. It is the mother who is to make the citizens for earth," claimed an article in an 1847 issue of *The Ladies' Cabinet*, one of the fashionable new Victorian periodicals for women.[22]

The new sense of maternal responsibility did not eliminate a need for servants. On the contrary. Servants were more than ever necessary to perform those menial tasks required by the presence of small children. Menial tasks, after all, could not be considered honorable by the aristocracy. In order to be worthy, motherhood had to be limited to those genteel, rational, and moral tasks that elevated childrearing. Indeed, one Victorian advice manual (1855) emphasized how very critical a sufficiency of servants was to the adequate performance of a mother's duty.

> But how can she be adequate to this if the whole attention to the personal comfort of several young children devolves upon her? If she is to make and mend their articles of dress, bear them in her arms during their period of helplessness, and exhaust herself by toils throughout the day and watchings by night, how can she have leisure to study their various shades of disposition, and adapt to each the fitting mode of discipline, as the skillful gardener suits the seed to the soil. . . . The remedy is for the mother to provide herself with competent assistance in the spheres of manual labour, that she may be enabled to become the constant directress of her children, and have leisure to be happy in their companionship.[23]

Central to these arguments about maternal responsibility was the belief in each child's uniqueness. Each child was to be carefully nurtured so that his or her capacities could be most fully developed. In this way, the growth of affective individualism would seem to have functioned, if unwittingly, as an adaptive mechanism, preparing aristocratic children for the new age of competitive meritocracy.

Perceptions of change in family life are notoriously difficult to pin down. One useful exponent of change in this regard is in naming patterns. In the fifty families under study the slow triumph of affective individualism can be seen easily. Gradually, children's given names came to reflect their parents' personal taste rather than the weight of family tradition. Thus, children in 1860 were far more likely to bear a novel name than those in 1760, who more often bore the names of parents or other immediate family members, living or dead, or traditional Hanoverian names. These traditional names bespoke no more individuality than a generic label. By 1860 children were also less likely to bear the names of their contemporaries, as parents chose names from an increasingly larger pool. The plethora of Charlottes, Carolines, and Georgianas that dominated the second half of the eighteenth century was replaced in the mid-nineteenth century by highly idiosyncratic names like Sibell, Algitha, and Theodora, fashionable French names like Blanche and Constance, and "olde English" names like Alice and Maud. Boys' names underwent the same transformation, but more slowly. In 1760 all the fathers in the families studied had sons named for themselves. By the middle of the nineteenth century, only a minority did so. As in so many instances, heirs were distinguished from their brethren by their greater likelihood to bear a traditional family name. Continuing to hold a public function, heirs fitted into a "prearranged" slot, bearing the same name as countless ancestors. Younger brothers, like their sisters, were more likely to be given spanking new names like Algernon, names that seemed to imply that the young bearer had no place in history, merely a personality that would last only as long as he did.

One additional sign of the increasing individuation of children was the decline in the practice of giving newborns the same name as elder siblings, deceased or not. In the eighteenth century the Duchess of Leinster (1731–1814) had been quite shameless about the practice, though one might forgive a mother of twenty-one for running out of new names. She had two Georges, two Carolines, and two surviving Emilys: the Emilys had different fathers, however. Emily was her own name as well. In the next generation Lady Holland (1771–1845) and Lady Elizabeth Foster (1757–1824) each gave two surviving sons of different fathers the same first name. The paucity of available names can easily be seen in Lady Elizabeth's case: two of her three sons were named Augustus.[24] Although the practice had earlier been a common one, only one mother born after 1775 used the same name twice.

Another signpost of the slow growth of domesticity was an increasing appreciation of girl children. As the fruit of love rather than merely the fruit of a "suitable marriage," children came to play an emotionally important role for their parents. The moral education of a girl—a potential future mother—was an important task that her own mother was best able to undertake. Moreover, as companions for their mothers' leisure, girls were perhaps even better suited than their brothers. Not surprisingly women often viewed daughters as the more desired sex. Lady Sarah Napier expressed the wish in 1790 to have another daughter "to comfort me in my old age, when my boys are gone to school."[25] Frances, Countess of Morley, (1782–1857) desperately wanted a daughter. Even in her first pregnancy she assumed she was carrying a girl; she gave birth, however, to a boy. Two subsequent miscarriages were lamented primarily because they deprived her of the chance of a daughter.[26]

Yet the needs of patriarchy had not really changed. In the eighteenth century people could be quite brazen about their preference for a boy; by the nineteenth century they were more likely to feel obligated to apologize for that predilection. Gerald Wellesley neatly expressed this ambivalence in a letter he wrote his expectant sister in 1815. "You should not be anticipating boys" he wisely warned, "because you subject yourself to disappointment and the poor little girl does not meet with a fair reception." Children, after all, were now supposed to be appreciated for themselves, not just for their potential contribution to the family fortunes. Nevertheless, Wellesley could not subscribe wholeheartedly to this ideal. "Not withstanding this wise advice," he added, "I hope to hear of an heir."[27]

The responsibilities of raising these valuable little paragons of both sexes were increasingly weighty. Lady Sutherland, as we have seen, felt little of that sense of duty toward rearing her children. They were of such minimal importance to her that it is difficult to tell from her correspondence how many children she had at any given time. Her contemporary, Lady Sarah Napier, felt that sense of responsibility but found living up to it difficult. She is perhaps representative of a generation in transition, as she seems somewhat confused about her maternal role. "It is a very healthy strong child, and promises very well to make its way in the world as well as his neighbors," she wrote of her month-old son, Charles, the future conqueror of the Scinde. Louisa, her fourteen-year-old daughter, Lady Sarah reported, was very helpful. "I am not one of those who know how to nurse and make a fuss with a little child, she [Louisa] is always pressing me to attend more to it, & wondering how I can be so little taken up with it."[28]

Later generations of women seemed more secure in the primacy of the maternal role. They were more commonly able to summon up the enormous reserves of perseverance and stamina necessary to nurture carefully the many sprigs they had produced, or to think that they should. Joining her sister for the children's lessons at Castle Howard, Lady Harriet Cavendish wrote in 1807 that

> George's reading goes on prosperously and Georgiana is the quickest little creature that ever was met with, but Caroline remains on my knee sometimes (to the credit both of aunt and niece) with a 'ba be' before us, till I hardly know them better than she

does, and my sister [Lady Morpeth] who is their great instructress, must have great talents for teaching if she makes anything of her.[29]

Lady Morpeth's task was one that would occupy much of her adult life. At the time of this letter, the maligned Caroline was barely four years old, while Georgiana and George were three and five respectively. Lady Morpeth also had two more children in the nursery, too young as yet for lessons, and she was pregnant with a sixth child. She was to bear six more children. She would become a grandmother before she had ceased bearing children of her own and long before she was free of the responsibilities of the nursery and schoolroom.

Under traditional patriarchy fathers and mothers alike were relatively indifferent to the rearing of their children, but domesticity created a significant difference in their respective responsibilities. Wives, in every respect, certainly bore the brunt of the large families produced by aristocratic couples. Lawrence Stone has pointed out that domesticity created more role conflict for women than for men.[30] Women were often torn between the duties of wife and mother, while men continued to suit themselves, perhaps finding less emotional resonance in family life. Indeed, the continued inveighing of the medical profession against paternal indifference bears witness to its reality. "Men generally keep at such a distance from even the smallest acquaintance with the affairs of the nursery," wrote Buchan, that

> many would reckon it an affront, were they supposed to know any of them. Not so, however, with the kennel or the stables. A gentleman of the first rank is not ashamed to give directions concerning the management of his dogs or horses, yet would blush were he surprised in performing the same office for that being who derived its existence from himself, who is heir of his fortunes, and the hope of his country.[31]

The Duchess of Devonshire provides a good example of this emotional conflict and the personal hardship it engendered. Arising early to have time to be with her small children, she also tried to stay up late to have time alone with her husband. Their tête-à-tête supper, she wrote her mother, had been very comfortable, "What is not so comfortable is that it is between 2 and 3" in the morning. Then the harried Duchess admitted the inadmissable: "*cette chienne de vie me tue* [this bitch of a life is killing me]."[32] At a time when husbands and wives were expected to spend more time together and enjoy each other's companionship, their interests frequently diverged. This created a considerable amount of stress, particularly for the women. Half a century after the Duchess's letter, Lady Stanley of Alderley, isolated in Cheshire with eight small children, wrote resentfully to her husband:

> People who have only to amuse and be amused have great advantages over unfortunate women who have as many children to see after as I have—all the same I shall be very happy to see you and it will be eight weeks since we have met.[33]

Lord Stanley did return home shortly thereafter and once again impregnated his wife.

Less emotionally involved with their children, husbands often could not sympathize with their wives' maternal preoccupations. Although most husbands believed, at least theoretically, in the supremacy of the maternal role, in reality they preferred to occupy the center of their wives' attention. That was the masculine idea of domesticity. Men were also dismayed by maternal duties that diverted wives from their public responsibilities.

Even Queen Victoria believed that public affairs distracted her from the more important tasks of raising her nine children. Albert, like so many other husbands, failed to understand the importance of child nurturance. "Tomorrow Papa insists on our going to Town for no earthly reason but that tiresome horticultural garden," she wrote in 1861, "and we have to leave poor little sick Leopold [her hemophiliac eight-year-old son] behind here in his bed which makes me sadly anxious and adds to my low spirits! . . . I own I think it both cruel and wrong to leave a sick child behind, when I have nothing to do till the 19th. I am very much annoyed and distressed at being forced to leave him by the very person [Albert] who ought to wish me to stay. But men have not the sympathy and anxiety of women. Oh! No!"[34]

The conflict between public and private duty was a continuing source of tension in marriages at lower ranks in society too. Charlotte, Countess of Verulam (1783–1863), became very anxious in 1820 when her eight-year-old son developed measles. Her husband, irritated by her concern, convinced her to go with him to a party at Hatfield House. She spent the evening "fidgetting about Edward," Lord Verulam recorded in his diary. One of the noble guests "made an enemy of Lady V.," continued the disgusted husband, "by joking about the Meazles which he thinks nothing of. Lady V. sillily violent afterwards with me."[35]

If childrearing was at times burdensome, it nevertheless also provided much gratification. Mary Wollstonecraft's dictum that "the most neglected wives make the best mothers" may have been true in many cases. Young women who had been raised with sentimental notions were probably disappointed in their husbands who, having been sufficiently romantic during courtship, went their own way once married. As we saw in the previous chapter, more romantic expectations sometimes led to increasing frustration. Expecting to find emotional satisfaction in private life, women as different as the Duchess of Devonshire, Lady Stanley of Alderley, and Lady Verulam turned to their children to provide it. Most women would have agreed with Lady Hatherton's estimate of her sister's marriage. The husband, "though *very stupid*," had undoubtedly made her a mother. "Having children to occupy her," Lady Hatherton wrote in 1818, "is the greatest point for a married woman to ensure her domestic happiness."[36]

There can indeed be little doubt that, for women bearing children after the turn of the century, offspring were an intense source of emotional happiness. Child worship became increasingly common among successive generations of aristocratic women. Lady Morley expressed "boundless adoration" of her "most darling and extraordinary child," the long-awaited daughter.[37] Queen Victoria's eldest, the Princess of Prussia, admitted to worshipping her first child, the future Kaiser.[38] One indication of the focus on children as a source of pleasure can be seen in the transmission of childish bons mots, which occupy increasing portions of letters. In 1804, for instance, Lady Harriet Cavendish visited her married sister at Castle Howard and enthusiastically reported the cute sayings of her two-and-one-half-year-old nephew. "He is rather conceited," the doting aunt admitted. The little heir called himself "a *little tiny* romp" and said of himself, "George Howard is a very beautiful boy, a very good boy, and a very *clean* boy." He also told his "Aunt Hary-O" that he wanted to kiss "Danmamma Dutchess with his lips," referring to the Duchess of Devonshire.[39] Daughters were often more child centered than their mothers had been. "I certainly do not feel anxious for any great addition to my family," Lady Frances Cole wrote her mother in 1824 on the occasion of the birth of her sixth child, "but I cannot agree in considering as an evil that from which I derive my greatest interest and comfort in life."[40]

If childbirth had traditionally been the occasion for providing paternal heirs, it had now become, under the sway of domesticity, the ordinary mechanism for elevating a woman into a Mother. This too, is reflected in the statements of the fifty families under study, particularly from the second decade of the nineteenth century onward. Lord Wellesley told his son-in-law in 1813 "how anxiously I partake" of his daughter's "happiness in becoming a Mother." In 1833 Lady Augusta Fox, married only a few weeks, wrote her mother-in-law, "I am anxious, so anxious to be a mother, if you could but guess my joy at the possibility of it even you would forgive me annoying you with so many details."[41] As it turned out, Lady Augusta never did bear a surviving child. Her thirst for maternity however, remained unquenched, and in 1851 she and her husband took the novel step of adopting a child. In this way she became a Mother, although her husband did not acquire an heir. An appropriate female infant was found in Paris by the Foxes' physician, and after a sojourn with a wet nurse, little Marie came to live with the Foxes at Holland House. She remained unaware of her adoptive status until her own marriage.[42] A century earlier, biological maternity had been sufficient to warrant the status of motherhood. Now it was not even necessary.

Lady Augusta's experience dramatically illustrates a point that requires elucidation in the remainder of this chapter: the new notion of motherhood not only altered the significance that childbirth had for English aristocratic families, it also diminished the significance of childbirth in the lives of adult women. When childbirth was primarily a mechanism for the production of heirs, it was something of an end in itself. However, when childbirth became a means for attaining the status of motherhood, childbirth represented only the beginning of a process that could last nearly a lifetime. Moreover, the carnal associations of traditional childbirth seemed less appropriate for the new motherhood. As we have seen, the "name of mother" signified rational and moral virtues. There was little room here for the physical and menial aspects of biological maternity. Could one really earn the sacred name of mother through blood, sweat, and tears? Dr. Struve thought not. "The full period of pregnancy having arrived, the woman is seized with the pains of labor"—thus begins what is surely one of the most astonishing descriptions of childbirth ever to appear in medical literature. Dr. Struve continues, "Scarcely has a minute elapsed when, to her utmost astonishment and extacy, she perceives that delivery is accomplished. She beholds in her lap a lovely full-sized infant, fresh as the morning dew."[43]

For the English upper class, changes in language usage also reflected an increasing aversion to physical reality. The change was evident as early as 1791, when an article appeared on the subject in the *Gentleman's Magazine*: "All our mothers and grandmothers, used in due course of time to become *with child* or as Shakespeare has it, *roundwombed* . . . but it is very well known that no female, above the degree of chambermaid or laundress, has been with child these ten years past . . . nor is she ever *brought to bed*, or *delivered*, but merely at the end of nine months, has an accouchement; antecedent to which she informs her friends that at a certain time she will be *confined*."[44] Similarly, an elderly friend of Lady Sarah Napier recounted in 1818 the linguistic changes she had witnessed since 1760. "No one can say 'breeding' or 'with child' or 'lying-in' without being thought indelicate," she wrote. "'In the family way' and 'confinement' have taken their place."[45] Usage by the fifty women under study confirms these accounts. *Breeding*, the most commonly used word to describe pregnancy in the 1760s and 1770s, was last used in 1817, during the very decade of domesticity's triumph. French euphemisms increasingly displaced honest English expressions after that, so by 1860 a woman most commonly became *enceinte* (or endured a *grossesse*), after which she either had a *fausse couche* or an *accouchement*.

The unifying theme here is the obliteration of the carnal element in childbirth. It was indeed this element that Queen Victoria found most repellent about childbirth. "What you say of the pride of giving life to an immortal soul is all very fine, dear," she wrote her eldest daughter in 1858, "but I own I cannot enter into that; I think much more of our being like a cow or a dog at such moments; when our poor nature becomes so animal and unecstatic."[46] If the carnal element interfered with the vision of Mother as a supremely spiritual being, then it was the physiological experience, not the vision, that had to be eliminated. This would seem to be an impossible task—but not so for the earnest Victorians. Anesthesia, first applied during childbirth by the Scottish physician James Simpson in 1847, provided the necessary means. Thus, for the first time in history, childbirth in reality could approach Struve's passive and painless idealization. On the conceptual front, advice literature of the Victorian period simply ignored childbirth—or sex, for that matter. Sarah Stickney Ellis's famous series of manuals on the responsibilities of women during the various stages of their lives—as daughter, sister, wife, and mother—consistently ignored biological reality. In neither *Wives of England* nor *Mothers of England*, both of which were first published in 1843, does she ever discuss how a woman becomes a mother. Childbirth is never mentioned. The experience of motherhood presumably began only after the child's birth—precisely when it was thought to have ended a century earlier.

Yet physical suffering had been, and remained, the critical element in defining women's nature—aristocratic or otherwise—under domesticity. However, suffering became disassociated from childbirth. We have emphasized that according to the traditional dictates of patriarchy, childbirth was consciously perceived as a service women performed for men. It seems unlikely that the service would be so great, were it not performed at the cost of great suffering and even at the risk of death. Without the element of suffering, after all, where is the sacrifice? Surely the comparison with war heroes is useful and informed the patriarchal view of birth. The most decorated heroes, traditionally, are those who served their country by placing their own lives in jeopardy. Men who hunger for the "glory" of heroism cannot play it safe. Even in modern times, men who fight a war from behind a desk are considered cowardly by comparison with the much-touted soldiers at the front lines.

For women, the lying-in chamber was "the front." The pain of childbirth was thought by the tradition-minded English aristocracy to be the penultimate experience that both forged and reflected character. (This notion will be even more apparent in the chapter on childbirth.) Sacrificial pain defined woman's character and was her eternal punishment for introducing sin into Eden. More universal than suckling, more dramatic than sex, more dangerous than marriage, childbirth had been the ideal occasion for the transformation of a girl into a woman. As such, a veteran of the reproductive wars became qualified to move in the company of adult women as an equal. A first birth was therefore of critical importance.

"I cannot tell you how much I felt leaving Blanche with the prospect of the first time before her," Harriet, Duchess of Sutherland (1806–1868), wrote in 1831 concerning her expectant youngest sister, Lady Burlington. "It is an epoch that never returns, and I cannot cease to regret not being with her."[47] Literature of the period provides examples of a personal and sometimes religious conversion wrought by the sufferings of childbirth. In Emily Brontë's 1847 novel *Wuthering Heights*, for instance, there is a passionate and even violent love scene between Catherine Earnshaw and her lover Heathcliff. A few hours later she dies in childbirth, transformed from the previous scene of dark passions. The early morning light now "suffused the couch" and the dead Catherine "with a mellow glow." Her husband, Brontë wrote, was full of anguish, but Catherine was finally at peace. "No angel in heaven could be more beautiful than she appeared; and I partook of the infinite calm in which she lay," continued the story's narrator. "My mind was never in a holier frame, than when I gazed on that untroubled image of Divine rest."[48] In typical Victorian fashion however, Brontë avoided discussion of the fatal childbirth scene. We see the purification wrought by pain, but not the pain itself. Indeed physical pain, in this scene, is associated with Catherine's unholy passion for Heathcliff: dead, she is relieved of both.

It was, of course, the proximity to death that, along with the element of suffering, brought parturient women closer to God. In expectation of childbirth, many aristocratic women prepared new wills.[49] Others, like the effusive Lady Jersey, wrote farewells to their husbands. In January of 1810—for the third time in as many years—she wrote just such a letter: "I have not my dearest Love, courage to bid you adieu, to speak such words would be impossible, but I cannot think I may soon be called from you without leaving some *first* expressions of the love I have borne you."[50] As it turned out, Lady Jersey would live to the age of eighty-two.

For women like Lady Jersey who returned repeatedly from the precipice, the knowledge of suffering enabled them to cross the threshold and join the company of similar veterans. This brought them much closer to their own mothers than they had been before, closing the gap between generations. We saw in the last chapter that aristocratic mothers were increasingly likely to be present at a daughter's *accouchement* and that Queen Victoria resented her inability to be with her eldest daughter. Princess Victoria felt the injustice well. Shortly after Prince William's birth, she wrote, "It is hard indeed to be separated from one's own mother when she has only just learnt *what* one owes her!"[51] From this time on, the Princess remained the lonely Queen's closest confidante, a closeness that would be intensified with Albert's death a few years hence. Even so, there was a bonding between adult women—as this mother and daughter experienced—that excluded even that best of husbands. In reply to her daughter's letter, the Queen wrote "I know that God has willed it so and that these are the trials which we poor women must go through; no father, no man can feel this! Papa [Prince Albert] never would enter into it at all."[52]

Maternal pain provided a major element of bonding between women, all of whom had been initiated into adulthood through childbirth. This element probably accounts for the frequency with which experienced mothers intimidated the uninitiated by telling obstetric horror stories, thus emphasizing the chasm between the two, very much like older men recounting their battlefield heroics to young boys going off to war for the first time. Lady Holland "gave a little specimen of her kind-hearted considerate nature when we females were in the Drawing Room after dinner," Lady Morley, pregnant for the first time, recounted in 1810.

Some one asked her when I was to be confined, which turned the conversation on that subject, & she went on I suppose for half an hour describing all the horrors, miseries, terrors, etc. which always assailed her on such occasions—how much worse the whole business was than any one c^d imagine, & some more of the same consolatory hints—I am not very apt to have fancies. But it really was enough to make any one feel not very agreeably—poor Lady Harriet [Granville, the former "Hary-O" Cavendish] too is in the same predicament and it must have been equally pleasant to her.[53]

Women who escaped the crucible of childbirth were deprived of the transformation it accomplished and were left in a kind of limbo status. This would contribute to the desperation expressed by young women who, like Lady Augusta Fox, did not become pregnant easily. The failure to be fruitful and multiply was thought to leave a harsh and indelible stain on one's character. "I think she was originally soured by not having children," the statesman Lord Clarendon wrote of an acquaintance in 1860, "and I have often observed that women who don't fulfill their vocation in that way like old maids and *bossus* are in a state of chronic hostility to all those who they think have been better treated by nature than themselves."[54] Childless women not only failed to do their duty to the aristocratic class, they failed also to provide themselves with the real emotional satisfactions of motherhood, and were further punished by fate's granting of a permanent character defect that could be eradicated only through childbirth. The failure to suffer, as it were, meant that one remained incomplete as a woman. As with other values examined in the previous chapter, the value of maternity became internalized and therefore strengthened as a consequence of domesticity.

One woman in the study group failed to be transformed by the childbirth experience. In the consternation of her contemporaries, the historian can witness their expectation that this transformation was supposed to take place. This woman was Lady

Caroline Lamb, well known to historians and literary scholars alike for her difficult marriage with the future Lord Melbourne and her passionate affair with Lord Byron. Even early in her marriage, Lady Caroline's defiance of convention and fey appearance indicated that she was not designed for motherhood—certainly not that glorified masochism envisioned by Lord Jermyn in the quote that opened this chapter. A few months after her marriage Lady Caroline had a miscarriage, and her sister-in-law (a future mother of fifteen) was not surprised at Caro's failure to become a mother. "It is quite impossible she should ever have a child," Maria, Lady Duncannon, asserted. "It will be a little thing with wings that will fly away as soon as it is born and nobody will be able to catch it."[55] Two years later, Lady Caroline did give birth to a child—albeit one who would prove mentally deficient—but she remained incorrigible.[56] "Her child has not cured her of her absurdities," her perplexed cousin wrote. "She went to the play the other night tête-à-tête with her Page."[57] While considerable overall behavioral variety exists among the fifty women in the study, Lady Caroline Lamb was the only one to "go beyond the pale" and suffer exclusion from aristocratic society as a result.

As long as physical suffering remained an essential aspect of childbirth—until the use of anesthesia became widespread—it continued to have this transforming and purifying significance for the English aristocracy. But as motherhood came to mean more than the physical act of bearing a child, so too did maternal suffering come to be extended into the entire period of childrearing. Sarah Stickney Ellis's famous dictum (which has since become notorious among modern feminists) was that "so often a woman's highest duty is to suffer and be still."[58] Although women were well equipped to endure suffering because of their capacity to bear children, their talent could be put to lifetime use. "God's curse on Eve had never covered such a long stretch of time as it came to in the minds of nineteenth-century Christians," a French feminist scholar has written. "Since giving birth was now considered as applicable to the entire period of the child's growth, from fetus to adult, maternal suffering was prolonged."[59] Indeed, as an achieved status, motherhood came to be more dependent on what one had achieved: that is, the quality of one's mothering could not be fully assessed until one's children had grown up. It was heroism and self-sacrifice during the period of childrearing, and not merely at birth, that were now necessary to be a good mother. Thus childbirth pain began to seem rather pointless. Moreover, as childbirth gradually lost its primary function as an act performed merely in the service of men, childbirth pain lost an additional rationale. Childbirth was something that women, so anxious to be mothers, were doing for themselves.

The reduced need for the sacrificial transformation of childbirth, inconvenient as its carnal associations were to the Victorians, can be traced in the attitudes of aristocratic women and their families. We saw in the last chapter that the marriage ceremony became more important as a social rite of passage during the first half of the nineteenth century. Simultaneously, the notion that female suffering began with marriage itself (and not with childbirth) became increasingly common among the fifty women studied here. "I think nothing is so melancholy as a marriage, particularly that of a young girl one has looked on more as a child than as a woman," Lady Caroline Lascelles wrote in 1827, remarkably enough, upon the marriage of a beautiful and wealthy young girl to a handsome and wealthy young man.[60] "It is sadly vexatious that marriage should so have disagreed with me," Lady Augusta Fox wrote in 1835, "for as a girl I never knew what it was to suffer, and my constitution was described as an iron one."[61] Queen Victoria was quite effusive on the subject. "Yes, dearest," she wrote her daughter in 1859,

> It is an awful moment to have to give one's innocent child up to a man, be he ever so kind and good—and to think of all that she must go through—(indeed I have not quite got over it yet) and that

last night when we took you to your room, and you cried so much, I said to Papa as we came back, "after all, it is like taking a poor lamb to be sacrificed." You now know—what I meant, dear. . . . It really makes me shudder when I look around at all your sweet, happy unconscious sisters—and think that I must give them up too—one by one!"[62]

This horror of marriage might seem problematic in view of the Victorian domestic ideal; and in some ways it is—as we shall see. But, paradoxically, the Queen also reiterates certain themes that we have identified as peculiar to the cult of domesticity. One was the notion of childhood as a separate stage of life, characterized not merely by "innocence" but also by "unconsciousness"—presumably of sexuality, though Victoria could not bring herself to say so.[63] This ignorance inevitably was ruptured at marriage, which must therefore have become the experience that transformed a girl into a woman. Seen in this way, the introduction of the white bridal gown and the ceremony of the veil, the orange blossoms, and the virginal bridesmaids, make sense. All the paraphernalia of the Victorian wedding testifies to its new significance as marking a loss of virginity.[64] This Victorian repugnance toward marriage reflects its greater sexualization concomitant with domesticity. Marriage was no longer perceived as primarily an economic or political bond, but as a romantic or sexual one, even for royalty. Even though Victoria complained, as she once did, that women were "bodily and morally" the slaves of their husbands, the sexual element in her own marriage had been very important to her.[65] "How am I alive after witnessing what I have done?" she grieved four days after Albert's premature death in 1861. "I who felt, when in those blessed arms clasped and held tight in the sacred hours of night, when the world seemed only to be ourselves, that nothing could part us. I felt so very secure. . . . Oh! It is too too weary! The day—the night (above all the night) is too sad and weary."[66] The bond that united husband and wife had become an extraordinarily intense one, much more so than it had been a century earlier.

The inevitability of female suffering was explained—if not justified—by the notion of women's natural inferiority. Even in this relatively pampered group of aristocrats and royals, women were very conscious of their subordination, which they regarded with a combination of resentment and resignation. A lively and intelligent woman like Lady Bessborough, two generations older than Queen Victoria and of a vastly different personality, had a surprisingly similar view of women's condition. "Being married is a state of great sufferance to a Girl in every way," she wrote her lover in 1805. "I do think it very hard that men should always have *beau jeu* on all occasions, and that all pain, Moral and Physique, should be reserved for us."[67] Suffering was the instrument of subordination. Even the extraordinary Lady Charlotte Guest, a contemporary of Queen Victoria's, was frequently reminded of the need for self-submission.

Lady Charlotte Guest (1812–1895) was probably the most individually remarkable of the fifty women under study. A daughter of the Earl of Lindsay, Lady Charlotte married Sir John Guest, the great Welsh ironmaster, who was many years her senior. She took an active interest in the Dowlais ironworks, conducting business meetings, doing the accounts, and acting as her husband's secretary. She wrote several highly technical articles on the iron-making process. She also taught herself Welsh and translated the epic tale of King Arthur—the *Mabinogion*—from a medieval Welsh text into English. Her translation was the basis of Tennyson's *Idylls of the King*, and she and the poet laureate were good friends for many years. During this productive period of her life she also managed to bear and raise ten children. Nevertheless, this apparently self-confident, intellectual, and socially ambitious woman had strong feelings of inferiority. She discussed a business meeting she had had in 1838 with the Quaker, Mr. Lucy, who "seemed at first rather surprised at seeing me," she recorded, "but we soon began discussing questions of freight, interest, etc., as comfortably as if I had not the mortification of being of weaker sex and intellect than himself." A week later, with the sort of resignation common to women of her class and time, she wrote, "Everything is for the best, and all these little mortifications are good for one who as a woman must expect suffering and humiliation."[68]

The doctrine of the inevitability of female suffering was not simply a socially approved form of masochism. Nor was it merely a social construct designed to assure the supremacy of the male, though it may at times have functioned in that way. Instead, it was a means of making the best of a bad, albeit an inevitable, situation. As suggested earlier, domesticity made the notion of female suffering problematic, particularly for the generations born after 1775, who were most likely to be affected by the new emotive trend of affective individualism. One critical factor was the increasing intensity of the relationship of young married women with their families of origin, particularly with their mothers and sisters, which we have traced to the onset of domesticity. The maternal family, likely to be keenly concerned with a daughter's health, also had a smaller interest in the mass production of paternal descendents than did her husband's family. The childbearing capacity of a young woman, after all, was a capital resource placed at the disposal of her husband's family. At one time, a woman's suffering in chiildbirth was normally dismissed simply as "as well as can be expected," a phrase that was something of an eighteenth-century cliché. By the middle of the nineteenth century, maternal relatives demanded greater specificity. "We are most anxious to know how long Dearest Emma was ill," Lady Derby's brother inquired of her husband in 1841, "and whether her sufferings were the same as in the last occasion, or lesser, which we hope was the case."[69] While young women were expected to do their family duty, their mothers, having known considerable parturient pain themselves, were not inclined to wish the same on their daughters. Both Lady Caroline Capel (1773–1847) and Lady Frances Cole (1784–1847) had to apologize to their mothers for becoming pregnant again. "I must, in spite of incurring your Ladyship's indignation," Lady Frances wrote in 1826, "acknowledge to you that my hopes of not surpassing the half dozen are at an end, and that I expect to add to it the beginning of next October."[70]

Under the influence of domesticity, husbands were increasingly likely to recognize that their visions of aristocratic expansiveness often clashed with the well-being of their wives. It had not always been so. When Lady Sarah Napier became pregnant shortly after her second marriage at the age of thirty-six, her sister sent her condolences. "I am very sorry my dear Sal that you have begun fulfilling my prophecy so soon," Lady Louisa Connelly wrote in 1782, "Mr. Napier I dare say is delighted, as all men are upon these occasions."[71] Subsequent generations of aristocratic men were not, however, universally delighted upon such occasions as a first pregnancy. In 1809 Lord Morley told his sister that his bride of two months, already pregnant, "suffers a good deal from headaches and sicknesses." "It requires a great deal of logick indeed," he wrote, "to persuade me that it is a good thing."[72] It took even more "logick" to approve of maternal suffering when there were already a sufficiency of heirs. The Earl of Verulam kept a careful record of his wife's menstrual periods (identified as X) in his diaries, and became extremely anxious when she was as few as two days overdue. These notations testify to the couple's intimacy. In 1819 Lady Verulam expected the arrival of X on November 25, while she was nursing her seventh child. On December 1, her husband recorded in his diary, "I sadly fear my dear Charlotte is again in a family way as X is not yet arrived," and on December 13, the pregnancy by now fairly certain, Lord Verulam "took a cold walk and felt very uncomfortable at the idea of Charlotte's situation."[73] Her eighth child would be born in July of 1820. The ninth child was born in 1822. Shortly after that pregnancy was established, Lord Verulam wrote in his diary, "My poor dear Charlotte feels her present situation sadly, and sleeps ill, I pray God to alleviate her sufferings."[74] During the intervening year of 1821 she had also endured a pregnancy "scare" when her menstrual period was delayed by more than two weeks. "To my infinite delight Charlotte woke me to say that X was arrived," Lord Verulam wrote. "Thank God for this and all His mercies."[75]

The aristocratic attitude toward maternal suffering was clearly more complicated than it might seem at first glance. Domesticity imposed some conflicting values that at once enhanced maternity and yet made the inevitable suffering intolerable. The disassociation of the conceptualization of female suffering from childbirth was helpful, but only partly so: the process of giving birth remained terribly painful. The true significance of the transformation in attitudes toward childbirth lay in its diminution as a critical rite of passage and its replacement by marriage. Once this had occurred, aristocratic families were prepared to accept the obliteration of consciousness during childbirth in return for the elimination of pain.

Domesticity was not, therefore, a sham. Female suffering was honored only in the absence of any apparent alternative. When the option of obstetric anesthesia became available, aristocratic women clamored to be free of unnecessary pain. "Obstetricians may oppose it, but I believe our patients themselves will force the use of it upon the profession," Sir James Young Simpson, who first applied anesthesia in obstetric cases, declared.[76]

Queen Victoria, who, as we have seen, viewed childbirth as something of a Christian martyrdom, assured the respectability of anesthesia when she used chloroform during the birth of Prince Leopold in 1853. "The effect was soothing, quieting and delightful beyond measure," she recorded in her journal.[77] Two hundred and fifty years earlier, her ancestor, James VI of Scotland, had ordered a woman publicly burned at the stake because she had asked a midwife to give her something to relieve the pains of childbirth.[78] Queen Victoria returned the favor to Simpson, the seventh son of a Scottish baker, by awarding him a baronetcy for that "blessed chloroform," as she called it. She agreed with Simpson that, as he wrote in his memoirs, "a new era in the destiny of women was inaugurated: she was absolved from the curse which is said to have been pronounced on Eve, and upon her daughters to the end of time; pain was subordinated to volition. She can now look forward to the pleasures of maternity unmixed with sorrow."[79]

The application of anesthesia represented only the most dramatic development in the partnership of aristocratic patient and accoucheur, a partnership that had begun nearly a century earlier. For aristocratic families, the conflict between the desire for progeny and the concern for women's health was an intensifying one. Thanks to domesticity, abstinence or adultery were no longer acceptable solutions. Birth control was not yet acceptable, for reasons that will become increasingly apparent. No, this enormously self-confident and optimistic aristocracy wanted both large families and healthy womenfolk. From the end of the eighteenth century, aristocratic families were willing to devote their time and money to finding an answer to this dilemma. And the growing medical profession was increasingly prepared to offer one.

CHAPTER III

The Aristocratic Accoucheur

At the opening of the nineteenth century, a young medical student named William Knighton resolved to continue his education at the University of Edinburgh, rather than embark immediately in private practice. In explaining his decision to his wife, he wrote, "I know that everything that is valuable must have its price." Sacrifices must be expected, he told her, since he aimed to gain "that which of all things is most desirable—pre-eminence in that profession which one has chosen." "Nothing shall ever make me relinquish the object I have in view," he told his wife. "I am in pursuit, I know, of fame and fortune, and virtue and industry must obtain them."[1]

Knighton eventually achieved a success that exceeded his youthful visions. In an unparalleled career he rose from the position of one of London's leading accoucheurs, with a large practice in the nobility, to the position of Keeper of the Privy Purse to George IV. At the height of his medical career, Knighton had a practice worth £10,000 per annum,[2] an income achieved by fewer than two thousand families in the entire kingdom at the time.[3]

Our picture of aristocratic childbearing would be incomplete without a portrait of the men who delivered obstetric care to the peerage. These were men who, like Knighton, reached the top—but not without encountering obstacles on the way. One of these obstacles was the ambiguous position of obstetrics in the structure of the British medical profession. Since midwifery traditionally had been performed by females, it was not a specialty recognized by the corporate bodies that represented British medical men of the time. These were, most notably, the Royal College of Physicians, the Company of Surgeons (which, after 1800, became the College of Surgeons), and the Society of Apothecaries.

The rise of the man-midwife, as he was called, at the expense of the female midwife, occurred gradually during the seventeenth and eighteenth centuries. Originally called in only to assist female midwives during an emergency, men gradually increased their presence at births, until, by the end of the eighteenth century, their participation in lyings-in was commonplace among the classes able to afford their services. While many general practitioners came to rely on midwifery as a staple of business (and the means of gaining entrée to a family), by 1760 increasing numbers of men, called accoucheurs, were able to limit their practice entirely to this field. As their success became more evident, so too did opposition grow to the practice of male midwifery. One pamphleteer in 1779, denouncing the "Profligacy of our Women," related the increasing popularity of accoucheurs to the rising divorce rate and the moral deterioration of society which "gave the enemy direct access to the very citadel of female virtue." More typical were the criticisms that saw male midwifery as evidence of a "slavish desire" among aristocratic women to follow an expensive French fashion and of negligent husbands who allowed their wives to do so.[4] The respectability of the eighteenth-century man-midwife and that of his nineteenth-century counterpart, the accoucheur, was always suspect by large portions of the community.

Accoucheurs were placed in a somewhat anomalous position. While, as Sir George Clark has described it, they "might grow rich in this vocation, might hold a hospital appointment and a court appointment, might write good books and scientific papers," nevertheless, they would have "no contact with any professional corporation, let alone membership in it."[5] Because there was no corporate recognition for midwifery, there could be no control over its practice. Anyone who wished to could, theoretically, establish herself or himself in practice as a midwife or man-midwife. The position of obstetrics within British medicine was not regularized until the General Medical Act of 1858, which provided for the registration and licensing of medical practitioners in each of three fields: medicine, surgery, and midwifery.

While many medical men welcomed the accoucheurs as equal partners, others were hostile to them. The majority of general practitioners, who delivered most of the country's medical care, opposed incorporating the accoucheurs because they feared the removal of midwifery from their own purview. The higher order of practitioners, represented by the College of Physicians, was even more hostile to the elevation of man-midwives to professional rank. In 1827, in response to the professional claims of the newly formed Obstetric Society, Sir Anthony Carlisle, a prominent surgeon, described midwifery as a "humiliating office" and therefore suitable only to women.[6] In a similar response to the Obstetric Society, Sir Henry Halford, who for many years was president of the Royal College of Physicians, said that the practice of midwifery, being a "manual profession," was "foreign to the habits of gentlemen."[7] This issue of "gentlemanliness" is the key to an understanding of the position of the aristocratic accoucheur.

The opposition of men such as Carlisle and Halford was, however, something like the cry of the Luddite, once his battle against the future was lost. For if some within the medical profession who, out of motives of self-interest or prejudice, condemned man-midwifery, other medical men and medical students were anxious to accept midwifery as a scientific pursuit worthy of study. The public, too, was ready for the practice of male midwifery.

Public honors are one measure of popular acceptance of the new obstetrics. The first men knighted for their contributions to midwifery were David Hamilton and Richard Manningham, in 1708 and 1721 respectively.[8] There followed similar honors for

Fielding Ould, Charles Mansfield Clarke, Charles Locock, James Simpson, and others. Significantly, these first awards were contemporaneous with the first knighthoods in other branches of medicine.[9] Distinguished men like Manningham, a Cambridge graduate and the son of the Bishop of Chichester, helped make man-midwives acceptable to the upper classes.

Many factors encouraged the entry of men into the fashionable lying-in chamber. By the end of the eighteenth century, the aristocracy was no longer willing to accept the inevitability of suffering and death in childbirth.[10] They were eager, as we have seen, to augment their family size while, at the same time, anxious to preserve the health and comfort of their wives and daughters. Students of the Enlightenment that many of them were, they were prepared to trust the claims of science, over those of tradition, to secure their wishes. Moreover, tradition, embodied in the persons of lower-class midwives, seemed far less attractive than the pretensions of science as embodied by ambitious men of gentlemanlike manners such as William Knighton. Politically and financially, the aristocracy was in an excellent position to advance the cause of scientific, albeit male, midwifery. They did so, not only through extensive financial support of the lying-in institutions, but also through the patronage of individual man-midwives as well.[11]

Interest in and support for scientific midwifery led to an enormous growth in the body of obstetric knowledge and to the development of a new obstetric technology. The most visible symbol of the new scientific midwifery was the forceps. While not without danger in the hands of the unskilled, forceps were an improvement over traditional obstetric practice, which used various kinds of hooks and crotchets to kill a baby that was otherwise undeliverable. Forceps, developed in England by the Chamberlen family in the seventeenth century, were kept as a family secret until the middle of the eighteenth century. After the "secret" had been sold for profit too many times, knowledge of the forceps began to leak out, finally being published and made available to all.[12] In France, Ambroise Paré had revived the ancient art of version, or turning a malpositioned infant while still in its mother's womb. Englishmen continued to refine this practice. Bernard Pugh was the first to describe the use of the hand externally, on the mother's abdomen, to effect a change in fetal position.[13] The Scot William Smellie, perhaps the greatest exponent of scientific obstetrics in the mid-eighteenth century, designed the curved forceps that still bear his name.[14]

Meanwhile, other students of obstetrics concentrated on acquiring greater knowledge of the anatomy of normal deliveries. William Hunter pioneered the study of the soft tissues, the gravid uterus, and the placenta, while Smellie initiated the study of pelvic measurements. Thomas Denman was the first to describe the spontaneous evolution of the fetus in utero. Charles White and John Clarke made enormous contributions to the improvement of the hygiene of delivery,[15] which may have had the most immediate impact on maternal care of any innovation.[16] Other measures included the induction of premature labor, pioneered by Denman, and the episiotomy, developed by Fielding Ould, the eminent Irish practitioner who brought the future Duke of Wellington into the world.[17]

Medical education also had to modernize to keep up with these new developments. Eighteenth-century lying-in hospitals were established not only to care for the health of the poor, but also to provide a clinical basis for the teaching of obstetrics. Sir Richard Manningham established a lying-in ward at St. James Infirmary for this purpose. During his formal lectures he used a mannequin to demonstrate the mechanisms of labor to his students, and on which they could practice before treating living patients in the hospital.[18] The foundation of a private, autonomous medical school in Great Windmill Street by William and John Hunter in 1768, dedicated to the study of anatomy, was another major innovation in medical education. Significantly, obstetric anatomy was given paramount importance by William Hunter.[19]

Sadly, these exciting developments in the history of obstetrics came at the expense of traditional midwives. Excluded both formally and informally from a scientific medical education, they were doomed to fall further and further behind as obstetric knowledge increased and obstetric technology developed.[20] Indeed, the male pioneers of obstetrics generally believed that women did not have the physical or mental competence to handle the subject properly. And certainly the inclusion of women on the same basis as men would have made it even more difficult for obstetrics to win public acceptance as a respectable, scientific branch of medicine.

The advance of obstetrics as a whole, however, did not ensure that any ambitious young man could achieve success in the field. In fact, the informal obstacles to such achievement were formidable. At the time when obstetrical education was not widespread (confined in Britain to Edinburgh and London), men had to be both highly dedicated and willing and able to undertake the serious commitment of time and money that made study possible. The traditional apprenticeship, useful as it remained, no longer provided sufficient preparation for a career in obstetrics. Mastery of anatomy, both general and obstetric, required study of a more formal nature. The first chair in obstetrics had been established in Edinburgh in 1726, and Edinburgh remained the center of formal education in midwifery.[21] Hospital attendance in particular was essential for anyone wishing to excel in obstetrics. Unlike other specialities in which every patient seen was diseased, the majority of obstetric patients were healthy and delivered normally. In order to gain experience in difficult deliveries—where the need for obstetric expertise was greatest—a young practitioner had to be exposed to a very large number of cases. Thus, apprenticeships, attendance at lectures, anatomical dissections, and hospital rounds were all necessary for a would-be accoucheur as ambitious as young William Knighton.

Having served an apprenticeship to his uncle in Tavistock, Knighton went to London in 1796 to further his education. Soon he was keeping his Devonshire friends informed of his busy schedule. "I attend four lectures on anatomy, two on surgery, three on midwifery, and two on the practice of physic," the young man wrote. "To this must be added dissections and attendance at hospitals."[22] He recognized that all this education was not essential to the practice of a country surgeon, but as we have seen, he aimed higher.[23] It was not until 1806 that Knighton, by then a licentiate of the Royal College of Physicians, was able to establish a London practice, much to the chagrin of friends and relations who had for years urged him to come back and settle in Devonshire, where a secure, if modest, future could be assured.[24]

Of course, these commitments of time and money were not confined to the student of obstetrics. As one historian of the medical profession has noted, any ambitious physician or surgeon needed financial support from relatives and friends to see him through training and the early years of practice.[25]

A further obstacle to a career such as Knighton's was the need to be accepted as a gentleman. To be sure, here was a pressure felt by all ambitious medical men with an eye to fashionable clientele. But with the criticism they received from prominent medical men like Halford and journalists like Foster and Thicknesse, accoucheurs were especially sensitive to the question of gentlemanliness. So too were their clients, who were all too aware of the intimate nature of the assistance accoucheurs rendered.

The peculiarly English status of "gentleman" was not a new concept. But by the end of the eighteenth century it was undergoing a redefinition. By older standards, a gentleman was one who did not need to work for money and was thereby rendered "independent"—traditionally a matter purely of birth, of hereditary privilege. Increasingly, however, men felt capable of rising to the status of gentleman on their own merits, whatever their birth. Quoting an article of Sir Richard Steele, the young Knighton wrote—in the modern vein—that "It would certainly be difficult to prove that a man of business, or a profession, ought not to be what we call a gentleman."[26] Education was viewed as one of the main channels to the status of gentleman for those who had not been born to it. Knighton believed that the "study of the ideas and work of these learned men" in which he so assiduously engaged, would "fit me for companionship to all ranks and degrees, from the highest to that of the clown."[27]

The need to be accepted as gentlemen worked to the financial disadvantage of ambitious young practitioners in two ways. First, they had to support the rank by living in the style of gentlemen, though often before they could afford to do so. Thomas Denman (1733–1815), who gained fame as a teacher, writer, and practitioner of midwifery, recalled this problem in his memoir, written in 1779. "I only wanted a Chariot for the appearance to the world," he recorded of his early years of practice, "who are taught by custom to estimate the abilities and merit of every medical man, by this very expensive appendage."[28] His son-in-law, Richard Croft (1762–1818), the leading aristocratic accoucheur of the next generation, experienced the same problem when he attended the pregnant Duchess of Devonshire on her Continental travels in 1790. Croft, then only twenty-eight years old, had already spent £25 on linen for the Croft household, when he received a £20 fee from the Devonshires. He "trembled to think of the expenses of this journey," he told the Denmans.[29] Yet Croft was unwilling to cut back on these expenditures. His wife, Margaret, and her twin, Sophia Denman, who were with Croft, had to share in the pretense of affluence. The ladies were not pleased at their invitation to the elaborate christening of the newborn Marquess of Hartington, Croft told the elder Denmans, because the event would oblige them "to be at considerable expense to dress themselves."[30] Believing such expenses were a necessary investment in his career, Croft insisted that they attend.

The other way in which the need for gentlemanly status worked to the disadvantage of young practitioners was that it deprived them of control over the fees they collected from their patients. It was simply not considered appropriate for one gentleman to pay another for services rendered. The direct transfer of money from one hand to another was especially frowned upon. As a result, fees usually were not discussed.[31] This reticence makes the subject a particularly murky one for historians, and surprisingly little is known about medical fees. However, it does appear that during the earliest years of a man's career, a doctor was very much at the financial mercy of his patients. This was true not only of accoucheurs. Sir Astley Cooper, who became the richest and most successful surgeon of his day, had this problem when he started his career in private practice. He began by moving into the home previously occupied by his mentor, the surgeon Henry Cline. Cooper wrote that soon after moving into the new premises, a patient came and gave him a half-guinea, saying "I gave Mr. Cline a guinea, but as you were his apprentice, I suppose a half-a-guinea will do for you." Since, according to Cooper, Cline always took whatever was offered him, Cooper felt obliged to do the same.[32]

Similarly, when Croft attended the Devonshires in 1790, he discovered that the recovery of his fees was beyond his control. On May 22, the day after delivering the Duchess of her long-awaited son, Croft wrote plaintively, "Most heartily do I wish his Grace would either give me something or let me know what I am to expect."[33] As it turned out, Croft's financial affairs were to be handled through the indirect medium of the Dowager Countess Spencer, the Duchess's mother. On one occasion Lady Spencer asked Croft quite bluntly if he needed money, but without making him a definite offer.[34] For a young practitioner like Croft, there were few standards that he could apply to his own salary expectations. Like Cooper, he had to take what was offered, even when it barely covered his expenses.[35]

Yet once a medical man had an established reputation among the nobility, the gentlemanly reticence about payment no longer worked against him. Although, according to his nephew and biographer, Sir Astley Cooper never once mentioned a fee in all his years of practice, Sir Astley nevertheless became the most well-paid medical man of his generation, earning over £20,000 in 1815.[36]

Large fortunes were there to be made. For this reason, as well as for more disinterested ones, the number of men entering the field was large, and the competition, even among accoucheurs, was keen. As early as 1752 several hundred man-midwives were practicing in London.[37] Their numbers were increasing rapidly. William Smellie supposed that he had instructed over nine hundred pupils in midwifery during the course of his career.[38] It has been estimated that Thomas Denman and his partner William Osborne, who taught jointly, instructed over one thousand two-hundred midwifery students during a thirty-year span.[39] Competition between medical men increased tremendously after 1815, owing both to the passage of the Apothecaries' Act in that year and to the release of army and navy doctors after Waterloo. Overcrowding of the medical profession became a serious problem.[40]

Very few of these men would have the opportunity of attending the aristocracy. During the one hundred years this study covers, only ten men were named as attendants by the women in our group, when they gave birth in England. Knighton was one; of the others, Thomas Denman, Richard Croft, Charles Mansfield Clarke, and Charles Locock had the largest share of the practice. Just as the peerage represented the elite of British society, these few medical men who established large practices in the peerage were very much the elite of their profession. If the rewards of an aristocratic accoucheur were great, they could be tasted by only a few. The extraordinary success achieved by these aristocratic accoucheurs therefore demands clarification.

Thomas Denman, Sir Richard Croft, Sir William Knighton, Sir Charles Mansfield Clarke, and Sir Charles Locock were among the most noteworthy accoucheurs of their age.[41] Of the five, four were born into medical families. The fifth, Croft, married Denman's daughter. Thomas Denman (1733–1815) was the second son of a country apothecary from Bakewell, Derbyshire, near the great Cavendish estate of Chatsworth. Sir William Knighton's grandfather was of the lesser gentry in Devonshire, but Knighton's father had been disinherited and, dying young, left his young family poorly provided. Knighton's ambition can perhaps be explained by his desire to regain the gentlemanly status his reckless father had lost. Knighton's situation was not a promising one, and he was apprenticed at an early age to an uncle who was a surgeon-apothecary in Devonshire. Sir Charles Mansfield Clarke (1782–1857) was the son of a Chancery Lane surgeon and the brother of John Clarke, twenty years his senior, who also had a distinguished career in midwifery. The senior Clarke has already been mentioned with regard to his emphasis on obstetric hygiene. Charles Mansfield adopted midwifery as a profession on his brother's advice, and joined John in giving lectures on that subject at St. Bartholomew's Hospital between 1804 and 1815. Sir Charles Locock (1799–1875) was the son of a Northampton physician. Sir Richard Croft was the only one of these five accoucheurs who was born into a nonmedical family. His baronetcy, unlike those of his colleagues, was an inherited one—but as a youngster, succession to that title was only a remote possibility. Croft, too, was apprenticed to an apothecary at an early age.

Not satisfied with serving apprenticeships, all five sought an academic education, and all studied with the greatest teachers of their age. Denman was an Edinburgh pupil of Smellie's, while Croft studied at the Great Windmill Street School under William Hunter. Knighton studied under Henry Cline and Astley Cooper in London and later took a medical degree at Edinburgh.[42] Clarke studied surgery and midwifery under his brother, while Locock was a private pupil of the eminent physician Sir Benjamin Brodie and was later an obstetric student at Edinburgh. All five received exceptionally fine educations for their generation. But only the family constellations into which these men had been born—and the medical connections they made while studying—enabled them to rise to the top of their profession. For indeed, it was a man's ability to exploit a system of patronage that could turn a merely successful career into a brilliant one.

This system of patronage, which then dominated English society, explains, in part, the growing preference of the upper classes for accoucheurs rather than midwives. Harold Perkin has described English society at the end of the eighteenth century—the old society that spawned the Industrial Revolution—as a society "firmly based on the twin principles of property and patronage." "Government patronage was no isolated phenomenon," he has written,

> but the visible top growth of a plant whose roots and branches ramified throughout society, the political aspect of a personal system of recruitment which operated at every level and served to articulate the rigidities of a structure based on property.... At all levels, patronage, the system of personal selection from amongst one's kinsmen and connections, was the instrument by which property influenced recruitment to those positions in society which were not determined by property alone ... patronage brings us very close to the inner structure of the old society.[43]

The system of patronage provided for the upward mobility of individuals while at the same time securing the position of old elite groups. The medical profession was one small strand in this seamless web. And accoucheurs, like other medical men, could not rise without access to patronage.

Thomas Denman was particularly fortunate, for he belonged to a family that had previous connections with the Cavendishes, the family of the Dukes of Devonshire. With the influence of the Cavendish family, Denman was made a naval surgeon in 1757 and served aboard ship until the Peace of Paris in 1763. Upon his release, Lord George Cavendish arranged to have Denman named surgeon to the royal yacht, a sinecure worth £70. This freed Denman, who had determined to specialize in midwifery, to continue his education under Smellie. Finally Denman, along with medical school friend William Osborne (who had also studied with Levret in Paris), purchased the practice of a retiring man-midwife. The purchase included instructional mannequins, skeletons, and obstetric instruments. Denman's success as a teacher and practitioner helped him win nomination as physician-accoucheur to the Middlesex Hospital in 1769, a position that put him into contact with the hospital's upper-class patrons.

Denman's private practice grew under these favorable circumstances. As early as 1774 he attended Georgiana, Duchess of Devonshire. By the 1780s Denman had become William Hunter's major rival in obstetrics. At Hunter's suggestion (because he wished to retire), Denman was chosen to accompany the pregnant Duchess of Newcastle to Portugal, where she hoped both to give birth and restore her health. On their return to England in 1783, Hunter died. The Duchess, who had been pleased by Denman, used her considerable influence to secure Hunter's practice for him. Thus, by 1783 Denman had become the most popular aristocratic accoucheur in England. But he was already fifty years old. Denman may well be the doctor to whom Knighton referred in a letter of 1796: "The present Dr. D., who is now at the head of his profession and worth ninety thousand pounds had no practice whatever until he passed the age of forty."[44] Knighton believed this indicated that patience was necessary to achieve so large a reward. In fact, his rise and that of other accoucheurs through the maze of patronage would be far swifter than Denman's had been.

Having been formerly in the position of receiving patronage, Denman had risen to the happier position of dispensing it. He gradually relinquished his private practice in order to devote himself more fully to writing. In 1790 Denman suggested that Richard Croft attend the Duchess of Devonshire on the Continent, where she hoped to give birth to her husband's heir. Richard Croft had lodged with Denman while studying at Hunter's Windmill Street School. In 1789 he married Denman's daughter, Margaret. A few years later, Croft's friend Matthew

Baillie, who had also lodged with Denman, married Margaret's twin sister. Baillie, who would become a renowned anatomist (and be awarded a baronetcy) was Hunter's nephew, a circumstance that drew the network of relationships even tighter.

The success of Croft's 1790 mission to the Devonshires helped him achieve great success at the early age of twenty-eight. The Cavendish family took an interest in his professional future, much as they had in that of his father-in-law. It was the Duchess's mother, Lady Spencer, who convinced Croft to confine his practice to midwifery.[45]

The achievement of so lofty a connection at so early an age proved a great boon to Croft. For the rest of his life—nearly three decades—he enjoyed the largest fashionable obstetric practice in England. The Devonshire House set remained loyal and kept him busy for years. Among his many clients, he delivered the Duchess's two daughters and at least two of her nieces.[46] Croft, too, was able to help young practitioners. His wife's cousin, Benjamin Brodie, who was to become one of the foremost physicians of his day, recalled that Croft had recommended him to his patients "for those smaller services for which they might reasonably apply to a young practitioner."[47]

Knighton, Clarke, and Locock also made youthful climbs to fortune with the help of patrons. At the suggestion of a senior physician, Knighton, age twenty-one, was appointed assistant-surgeon to the Royal Naval Hospital at Plymouth, where he made the acquaintance of Moll Raffles, the mistress of the Marquess Wellesley. Perhaps he made the acquaintance of the Marquess himself at that time.[48] Later appointed the Marquess's domestic physician, Knighton accompanied Wellesley on his embassy to Spain in 1809. In the process, Knighton gained his Lordship's esteem and confidence.

The private correspondence of Richard Croft and that of Charles Locock demonstrate the processes by which senior medical men acted as intermediaries between bright young protégés and the social elite of the nation. The Duchess of Devonshire had become pregnant at Spa during the early autumn of 1789, and, rather than risk a channel crossing, she sent for Thomas Denman to attend her at a Continental birth. Denman, who then was gradually relinquishing his private practice, used the occasion to send Richard Croft in his stead. Croft, his pupil and lodger, had just become Denman's son-in-law as well. As we have seen, Croft assumed this position with the Devonshire household without any prior agreement as to the fee he would receive for his services. It was access to the upper-class patient that made this a desirable career opportunity. "Yesterday morning I was called to the Lady of Sir Willm Jerningham," Croft wrote his new mother-in-law from Brussels in April 1790. "It's most likely that whatever English happen to be ill here if connected with the Dutchess, will become my patients."[49]

The recently published correspondence of Charles Locock, who gained international acclaim as Queen Victoria's obstetrician, also sheds light on how a bright and attractive young man became successful. Locock was initially the protégé of Benjamin Brodie, a cousin of Margaret Denman Croft. As early as 1818 Locock was on intimate terms with Brodie, who first encouraged the young man to specialize in midwifery. Within a few years Locock had also attracted the support of Robert Gooch, then a reigning authority on midwifery. In June of 1823 the twenty-four-year-old Locock wrote a medical school chum:

> I do not know whether you chanced to see an advertisment in the papers about ten days ago which announced me as a Candidate to succeed Dr. Gooch as Physician-Accoucheur to the Westminster Lying-in Hospital, which he has resigned in my favour—The *same* hospital where last year I was a house pupil. The election takes place July 10th, and as I have the support of all the Medical Officers of the Committee and of the late Physician and as besides I have *no* opponent I think I may reckon myself decently sure of success—so I take no trouble about it—I have sent some printed circulars to each of the governors, to let them be aware there is

such a chap in the world as myself. I have advertised once in the papers to let the world know that there is a candidate, else someone might otherwise be tempted to put in their noses.[50]

In the same letter, Locock told his friend of Gooch's critical assistance in introducing him to an upper-class clientele.

> I have been busy lately rather more with Dr. Gooch's patients than my own, consequently have had to do more with Ladyships and Right Honorables than with cobblers' wives and bakers' daughters. These serve as famous introductions to families and Gooch has often sent me where there has been little or no occasion for it, merely as a medium for getting me known.[51]

By 1832, still only thirty-three years old, Locock had attracted the attention of the Duchess of Sutherland, who was quite ill after the birth of her sixth child. Locock, however, was such a find that the Duchess declared "she did not grudge" her illness.[52] Fortunately for Locock, the Duchess was yet to have five more children. No doubt her social eminence helped Locock achieve what was described by the *Times* as "the largest practice ever made by an obstetric physician."[53]

The brilliant aristocratic careers achieved by Croft, Clarke, Knighton, and Locock boosted them to the even more eminent position of royal favor. For Croft, success proved to be his undoing. He reached the pinnacle of his career when, in 1817, he was named Physician-Accoucheur to the royal heir, the twenty-one-year-old Princess Charlotte. In November, following a difficult pregnancy and a labor lasting over fifty hours, the Princess at last gave birth to a dead son, dying herself a few hours later. In the wake of the shock caused by the deaths, the public outrage that ensued, and further attacks on his reputation, Croft committed suicide. Croft's story, an important one to which we shall return, dramatically illustrates the disadvantages of even the most successful obstetric career.

The royal connections of the other accoucheurs proved happier. The Marquess Wellesley introduced Knighton to the Prince Regent, who appointed him as his physician and raised him to a baronetcy in 1813. In 1818 the Prince Regent named Knighton auditor to the duchy of Cornwall, which position he fulfilled so successfully that in 1822 the Prince, by then King George IV, selected Knighton as his unofficial private secretary and made him Keeper of the Privy Purse. Knighton gave up his medical career and devoted himself fully to the King's service. Both critics and admirers of Knighton admit that his role went far beyond that of his official title. He became the King's closest adviser and confidante, playing a not inconsiderable role in the policies of His Majesty's reign. Professor A. Aspinall, an expert on the reign of George IV, quoted Princess Lieven in 1824 as saying that Knighton was the real Prime Minister. "It would be truer to say," Aspinall wrote, "that he was the real sovereign."[54]

Knighton retired from his public duties after the King's death in 1830. Other accoucheurs, however, were to be honored by succeeding monarchs. On the accession of William IV, Clarke was named physician to Queen Adelaide, a distinction followed a year later by the award of a baronetcy. Charles Locock, the leading accoucheur of the next generation, was fortunately placed in that position on the accession of a young female monarch in 1837. Locock's satisfied patient, the Duchess of Sutherland, became Queen Victoria's close friend and served as her Mistress of the Robes. The Duchess probably influenced Her Majesty's choice of Locock upon her first pregnancy in 1840. Locock eventually delivered the Queen of all nine of her babies. She rewarded him with a baronetcy.

The degree to which personal qualities rather than obstetric skill contributed to the success of an accoucheur was a matter of some debate among medical men. The question was a sensitive one, for, as accoucheurs and other medical men sought full professionalization, their continued dependence on aristocratic standards of success reflected their own lack of professional autonomy. No one could deny that social finesse was an asset. Knighton, however, attributed more importance to the social graces than did his colleagues. "I need not tell you," he once wrote, "how little depends on learning in recommending you to the fashionable world as a physician. . . . It is our behavior and address upon all occasions that prejudice people in our favour or to our disadvantage . . . as our learning and industry, cannot possibly appear but to few."[55] Others were quick to criticize Knighton on this very score, a point on which he remained sensitive throughout his life. On his first meeting with the Prince Regent, Knighton was praised by His Royal Highness as being the "best-mannered medical man he had ever seen." "This," Knighton recalled, "did me no good, as it excited the jealousy of my medical brethren, who had already supposed that my practice was beyond my deserts, and that at any rate, it came too rapidly."[56]

As we have seen, however, Knighton was hardly an unctuous quack, as his critics may have wished; he was, in fact, a well-trained, well-educated, hard-working physician who also paid careful attention to his manners. Most responsible and successful physicians, however, played down the role of the personality in a medical man's success. "There may be," Sir Benjamin Brodie wrote, "among physicians, as well as in other professions, some individuals who acquire a reputation to which they have no claim, but my experience justifies me in asserting that no physician acquires a *large* reputation, or retains what may be called an extensive practice, who is really unworthy of it. The public are, on the whole, pretty good judges in a matter in which they are so much interested."[57]

But how did the aristocratic public perceive its own best interest? Of course they were necessarily—and increasingly—concerned with their own physical well-being. But it is no contradiction to say that the aristocracy believed that a gentleman was most likely to deliver quality health care, or that the patronage system was the best way of screening potential medical attendants. Jeanne Peterson has suggested that "family connection" in the Victorian medical community provided a "strong basis for the honorable, reputable behavior in the young practitioner."[58] This would explain the alacrity with which the Devonshires accepted the services of the untried Richard Croft in 1790 for the Duchess's critical pregnancy. Similarly, the sudden death of Dr. Andrew Thynne in 1813 dismayed some of his patients, particularly when they discovered he had left his family in distress. "I like Lady Chichester's object in employing young Thynne," Lady Morley wrote with approval.[59]

If in the twentieth century skill has come to be the guarantor of honor, then in the century 1760 to 1860 it was honor that guaranteed skill. And it was gentlemanly conduct as well as reputable connections that assured patients that one was, indeed, an honorable man. Thus we return once again to that issue of "gentlemanliness" which was so important to the aristocratic patient and which was, at times, such a burden to her accoucheur. Like other medical historians of the period,[60] Jeanne Peterson has concluded that "a liberal and classical education" served as a "basis for a claim to genteel status." Thus the "medical man" became a "medical gentleman" and as such, was a "sought-after representative and leader of the profession."[61] Similarly, S. E. D. Shortt has observed that, until the mid-nineteenth century, the medical elite "espoused the liberal learning and gentlemanlike deportment" valued by the very social group on whom they were most dependent.[62]

As in any stable social structure, the aristocratic value system that then dominated England was self-reinforcing. Senior medical men, happily in a position to dispense the patronage they had once received, were likely to make use of the same social criteria that had enabled them to rise in life. This could lead to extremism in defense of gentility. The career of Sir Walter Farquhar (1738–1819) provides a good example.

Farquhar was best known as the physician to the Prince of

Wales, later George IV. Farquhar's success was reportedly due to the support he had received from the Tory Duchess of Gordon and from William Pitt,[63] but he was also a favorite of the Whig Duchess of Devonshire, whose perspicacious daughter had complained in 1802 that Farquhar "comes to make us sick when we are well."[64] In 1816 Elizabeth, Lady Bristol, asked the aging physician to recommend a doctor to accompany her family on a forthcoming trip to Spa. Farquhar, she wrote her husband, suggested

> Dr. Jones and Dr. Holland, both men of *decided talent*. Dr. Holland has travelled in Greece and is the author of a work upon Albania very highly rated, a man of remarkably pleasing manners and considerable information, and competent to anything we might want in the medical way. Dr. Jones has also travelled, is a man of talent, is about 40, 4 or 5 years older than Dr. Holland and has had the most experience and practice of the two—he says he had the entire case of Lord Carlisle and all his family—he likewise was physician to poor Fish Crawford—but what I could collect, he thought Dr. Holland was the more *accomplished* gentleman of the two, such a man as my Lord would think an acquisition at his table or in his family, & perhaps as I understand him, a more *brilliant* member of society.[65]

Careers like those of Holland and Farquhar exemplify how medical patronage reinforced the gentlemanly values of the upper class. A medical career was therefore a political matter as well as a personal one. The young Astley Cooper was told in 1800 that his adherence to radical politics stood in the way of his nomination to a hospital appointment. He promptly changed his opinions. "These unsettled, discontented views," he concluded, "can never improve us in our profession, nor advance us on its practice. We had better have done with them."[66]

The political content of a major medical career was also important because of the need to integrate socially mobile families into the established hierarchy. The insistence on gentlemanly behavior was of course, a method of ensuring social homogeneity among the elite—new as well as old. A brilliant medical career could also lead to success in other endeavors—and of this Knighton's case is the supreme example. The Denman-Croft-Brodie-Locock network owed its success to the support these men received from the Whig grandees. Denman's daughters remained part of this nexus through their marriages to Croft and Baillie. Denman's son entered a legal career, but remained part of the same network of patronage. The younger Denman's spirited (if not always competent) defense of Queen Caroline in 1820 endeared him to the highly partisan Whigs of that era.[67] When Denman was appointed Lord Chief Justice by the Whig administration of 1832, Lord Holland was happy to take some of the credit. "It tickles me to find that the Recorder I appointed at Nottingham, and a member of the Fox Club should become Lord Chief Justice of England," Holland wrote.[68] Moreover, Brodie's sister (Denman's cousin) had married Holland's tutor. Thus the reciprocal ties between families and connections remained mutually beneficial over several generations. If Englishwomen and their families slavishly followed fashion by using male accoucheurs over female midwives, they did not do so either blindly or negligently. They were simply extending the uses of patronage to include a newly mobile class.

The relationship of the aristocratic accoucheur with his patient differed from that of other types of medical men in three important ways. First, because until 1858 obstetricians lacked even the corporate unity represented by the royal colleges, and because their very line of endeavor was considered indecent by some, they were perhaps even more dependent upon their patients for the maintenance of their reputations than were "pure" surgeons and physicians. Second, the accoucheur's contact with a patient and her family was often far more prolonged than that between most doctors and patients. Many accoucheurs spent weeks or even months at a patient's home to supervise the pregnancy properly and to be there the moment her ladyship went into labor. While this prolonged intimacy may have provided the accoucheur with an opportunity to display his talents and make himself indispensable, it also provided the aristocratic family with ample opportunity to manipulate and toy with this dependent. Finally, the necessarily intimate relationship an accoucheur formed with his "interesting and susceptible patients,"[69] as the *Lancet* referred to Clarke's clientele in 1830, could only exacerbate the need for gentlemanly conduct on the part of the accoucheur.

The 1790 episode in which the young Richard Croft attended the Duchess of Devonshire will provide a useful illustration of these features of the aristocrat-accoucheur relationship. From April to August of that year, Croft and his wife and sister-in-law lived in the Devonshire household. Croft was evidently starstruck by the glamorous aristocrats. On May 9 he wrote, "Don't forget that Dr. Croft, I mean the Gentleman who received a twenty pound fee the other day, goes in the same coach with Her Grace and Lady Spencer."[70] "I was this day in company with three Dutchesses, two Ladys, a Duke and a Marquis," he wrote to Mrs. Denman a few weeks later. "Still my greatest pleasure is to write about my own little family in the cottage," he added unconvincingly.[71] In the same letter Croft recorded the awkward and unsatisfactory conversation he had had with the Duchess's mother, Lady Spencer, concerning fees. Clearly he worked at some disadvantage. Further intimacy with the Devonshires made it clear that Croft, however awed, disapproved of them. When he wrote his mother-in-law that "on my part, nothing shall be spent unnecessarily,"[72] he may have had in mind the fabled Devonshire lavishness. But shortly after Croft took on this assignment, he would have become aware of an even more disconcerting feature of the Devonshire household: In addition to the Duke and Duchess, their children, and her mother, the ducal suite included the enigmatic figure of Lady Elizabeth Foster, the Duke's mistress, who appeared to be on perfectly friendly terms with the Duchess. The younger generation included Caro St. Jules, supposedly Lady Elizabeth's French protégée (later she was alleged to be the child of émigrés), but who in fact was her illegitimate daughter by the Duke. News of this unconventional arrangement may have reached Mrs. Denman, for Croft wrote to assure her that "Your heart may be perfectly at ease, as to any bad habits I am likely to contract from this family."[73] Unfortunately for Croft, nearly thirty years later his reputation would be ruined by his proximity to this eighteenth-century scandal.

On their side, the Duchess and her family were evidently delighted with the ingenuous young Crofts. The Duchess's mother, Lady Spencer, was especially happy to take the Crofts under her wing. She read a sermon every day to Margaret Croft, who wrote her mother that Lady Spencer considered her "as one of her children."[74] Lady Spencer told Richard Croft that she felt free to tell him anything she thought would "tend" to his "improvement."[75]

Far from being offended by her Ladyship's condescending manner, Croft was flattered by her interest in him. "Lady Spencer talks to me just in the manner the Doc^r [Denman] does," Croft wrote his mother-in-law,

> and wishes as much as he does to see me a polished Gentleman, she will not even suffer me to set [?] or with my arms on the table. Though she is, when we are by ourselves, constantly telling me of some little thing of that nature, still its done in such a manner that really it makes one love her, because its clear she can have only one reason for doing it. In short, I am on all sides paid so many Compt.s that you must not be surprised to see me return to you a consummate coxecomb.[76]

Despite the compliments, it was clear that the Crofts were not on a social par with his noble clients. Occasionally Croft—and, less frequently, Margaret and Sophia—were invited to dine with the Duke and Duchess. Croft carefully measured every word or glance thrown in their direction. Lady Spencer's flattery "surpassed even his most sanguine expectation," while Croft strove to assure Mrs. Denman that she could be proud of her twins' behavior in this trying situation. "Your Daughters conducted themselves with the utmost propriety and ease, and talked just as they do in general to people that they have seen two or three times," he wrote after a visit from Her pregnant Grace.[77] The Duke knew full well how to manipulate this impressionable young man. On April 25 the Duke had offered to lend Croft a horse, an offer Croft described as "a great stretch of civility, I mean as to the thinking, . . . for where anything of that nature occurs to him, no man can possibly be more happy to seize the opportunity of obliging."[78] In this case, however, the phlegmatic Duke was in no hurry. A month passed, the birth of the heir ensued, and no horse had yet appeared.[79] In this small incident we witness much of the helplessness that Croft must have felt.

It is not yet clear what remuneration Croft did eventually receive for his four-month treatment of the Devonshire household, which included about one hundred people. Arthur Calder-Marshall, the biographer of the Devonshire triangle, believes that Croft ultimately got his horse. He also notes that Lady Elizabeth presented Croft with a ring made of a stone from the Bastille.[80] The grateful Duchess rewarded Croft with a handsome Sèvres cup and saucer.[81] His reputation was made.

Still, for all the fulsome flattery, Croft basically had been hired to bring the Duchess's pregnancy to a happy conclusion and to take care of the medical needs of the rest of the family. It was in the successful performance of these duties that Croft earned the gratitude of the Devonshires and so established his own reputation. Their physical well-being and Croft's reputation were inextricably entwined. Croft was, not surprisingly, somewhat intimidated by these responsibilities. The illness of the seven-year-old Lady Georgiana while the Duchess was recovering proved to be a particularly difficult case for Croft, and his anxiety was intense. "True, my good Sir," he wrote Denman on June 9, "had these illnesses not happened, the family might not have known the service I could have been to them, but still was the business to come over again, I should beg to be without them, for even now should any of the family die, I should certainly suffer in my character, for which reason I must wish to get home."[82]

Aristocratic accoucheurs often took on additional responsibilities that went beyond their strictly medical duties. This was perhaps inevitable in a situation where the doctor found himself in a subservient position but was nevertheless trusted by the family with whom he lived on terms of relative intimacy. Contemporary notions of health care, as described in the next chapter, contributed to the doctor's concern for the "total environment"—physical and emotional—in which his patient lived. Thus, doctors like Croft assumed many duties that would appear to us to be of a managerial or secretarial nature. It was Croft, for instance, who secured a house for the important Devonshire confinement in Paris in 1790. More commonly, accoucheurs arranged the hiring of other childbirth attendants and controlled the flow of visitors to the lying-in chamber.[83] These duties required the exercise of a fair amount of tact.

The accoucheur's ability to appear both honest and reassuring, in letters as well as in person, was essential to his good standing with the entire aristocratic circle surrounding the patient. This was perhaps more important by the end of the eighteenth century, as maternal relatives became more concerned with a woman's parturient condition. Lady Bessborough in 1790, for instance, engaged Croft to write to her weekly on the condition of her sister, "as she cannot depend on what she hears from other people." Croft was flattered by her request."[84] Similarly, half a century later, Locock's epistolary abilities contributed to his great popularity. In attendance upon Emma, Countess of Derby, in her 1841 confinement, Locock sent letters announcing the birth to friends and relatives. Lady Clanwilliam was delighted with the letter she received. "I must not omit mentioning," she wrote in her congratulatory letter to her friend, Lady Derby, "what a very nice letter that good little man [Locock] wrote to me announcing the event." "I wish I had kept it for you," Lady Clanwilliam explained, "but I was so pleased with it I sent it to Mamma. It was so very nice about you, with so much kind and proper feeling, evidently he was, when he wrote it, rejoicing with you most sincerely."[85]

The ability to write a good letter expressing polished sympathies for the ladies under one's care was invaluable to an accoucheur seeking to gain or keep a patient's loyalty. Locock's popularity among the nobility and royalty was attributed in part to his ability to keep these lying-in chambers "in a happy titter" with his racy jokes. Queen Victoria liked her doctors to provide good company without being unctuous.[86] And readers of Locock's recently published correspondence would certainly agree that the man was entertaining. Charles Mansfield Clarke's social presence contributed to making him a desirable attendant, and he eventually became a habitué at Holkham Hall, the home of the famous Coke of Norfolk, whose estate was near his own.[87] And as noted earlier, Knighton's character and social prowess ultimately became more important than his therapeutic abilities.

There was yet another aspect of obstetric practice that tended to exaggerate the need for gentlemanly manners in its practitioners above that of other medical men—the necessarily intimate relationship the accoucheur formed with his female patient. Because of the very nature of obstetrics, a woman and her husband had to be assured that the accoucheur was, in every respect, a gentleman. The accoucheur was to be trusted with some of his patient's most intimate secrets and was one of the few persons with whom she discussed her sexual functions. Lady Augusta Fox's accoucheur determined when she and her husband could engage in intercourse. Princess Charlotte's letters to Croft during her pregnancy were completely frank and unrestrained in their detailed descriptions of her bodily symptoms.[88] If Francis Place, the Benthamite social reformer, is to be believed, some patients discussed contraception with their accoucheur. In one of his handbills recommending the "sponge method" of contraception, Place noted delicately that "accoucheurs of the first respectability and surgeons of great eminence have in some peculiar cases recommended it."[89] In his lectures to his medical students, Charles Mansfield Clarke advised using wooden pessaries for the treatment of a prolapsed uterus and discussed the relative benefits of those that did not interfere with intercourse and could therefore remain a secret from the husband. We may surmise, then, that this was a subject Clarke had discussed, and expected to discuss, with some of his patients.[90]

The need for discretion in an accoucheur was, of course, a paramount concern of any patient. Knighton's ability to keep a secret was the first quality that attracted the notice of the Prince Regent. That we know so little about what, exactly, Knighton did for the Wellesley household testifies to his discretion. Similarly, it was Croft who attended Lady Webster when she was delivered of a son by Lord Holland in 1796, a few months before the lovers married. That fact would have remained a secret had not Lady Webster asked Croft to testify to the child's birth at the criminal conversation trial that eventually led to her divorce and marriage to Lord Holland.[91]

The successful accoucheur often had to overcome his patient's modesty and win her trust completely in order to care effectively for her. The verbal and diplomatic skills necessary to accomplish these goals were necessities, not luxuries. Those accoucheurs most successful in establishing a large aristocratic clientele were able to cultivate a relationship that would encourage such intimacy. They were probably unusually sympathetic to their patient's problems—or at least they gave the impression of being so. Denman, for instance, warned his medical students that it was important to listen to, and take seriously, all of a woman's complaints. He emphasized that it could be dangerous to slight, ridicule, or dismiss her complaints merely as a "lowness of spirits," because these were often an index of real physical disturbance. Both Charles Mansfield Clarke and Andrew Thynne, another teacher of midwifery with an aristocratic practice, devoted a portion of their medical lectures to ways of approaching difficult questions with their patients.[92] The reassurance that doctors gave their patients and the tolerance and patience with which accoucheurs like Denman listened to them were undoubtedly among the components that contributed to their popularity.

Historians have generally assumed that women of the past were too modest to undergo pelvic examinations. "Ladies were expected, even by their doctors, to object to medical examination, to prefer modesty to health," Ann Douglas Wood has written.[93] According to Regina Morantz, "middle- and upper-class women of the nineteenth century often declined to consult physicians for gynecologic problems," and when they finally mustered the courage to do so, they were too embarrassed to discuss fully their own bodies.[94] None of this is confirmed by the fifty women studied here, who assiduously sought out medical attention. Most would have agreed with Sophia Curzon (1758–1782) when she decided in 1782 that she would allow her doctor to make "a *certain enquirie.*" "I considered that through modesty I was not to give up my life," she concluded rationally enough, though she was to die six months later anyway.[95] Even Queen Victoria herself was none too "Victorian." After his first meeting with the Queen, Charles Locock reported that

> every Medical observation which he made, & which might perhaps bear two significations, was invariably considered by Her Majesty in the least delicate sense. She had not the slightest reserve & was always ready to express herself, in Respect to her present situation, in the very plainest terms possible.[96]

It was the accoucheurs, after all, and not the patients, who needed to display their carefully acquired refined sensibilities. The doctors, therefore, seem to have been more concerned with the modesty issue than the patients were. "Never propose an examination per vaginum but as a matter of absolute necessity," Thomas Denman warned in his popular *Introduction to the Practice of Midwifery*. He emphasized that the examination should always be performed in the presence of a third party "with the utmost care and tenderness, and the strictest regard to decency." "Unimportant as the operation in itself really is, an opinion is formed by the manner of doing it, of the skill and humanity of the practitioner, and the propriety of his conduct," he added.[97] Locock admitted to his friend Lady Mahon (who told Mr. Arbuthnot, who told the Duke of Wellington), that he felt "shy and embarrassed" at his first interview with the pregnant Queen in 1840, but that she "very soon put him at his ease."[98]

The intimate interaction between accoucheur and patient may have become easier as an accoucheur's success grew and his income and stature increased proportionately. Where once an accoucheur, treating a person of rank, felt that he was honored to do so (and therefore had to accept a small fee), an accoucheur of stature and reputation might well be considered to be honoring a patient with his attention—and therefore the fee would increase substantially. As we said earlier, it is difficult to learn much about the fee structure of obstetrics during the century under consideration. It appears likely, however, that fees for the upper classes were the last to become standardized.[99] According to one account, the accoucheur who brought Princess Charlotte into the world in 1796 would have been paid £700 had she been a boy. Presumably Underwood was paid less than that figure because of the infant's sex, though it is unclear what fee he did receive.[100] According to Prince Albert, Locock received £1,000 for the birth of the Queen's first child—a girl—in 1840.[101] If nothing else, this indicates that fees were going up for the very highest class of patients.

When Knighton accepted the invitation of the Marquess Wellesley to act as domestic physician to the Wellesley household during his embassy to Spain in 1809, the Marquess agreed to pay Knighton a £5,000 retainer for his services for two years, since this was what Knighton estimated his income would have been had he maintained his London practice during that time.¹⁰² While £5,000 was an extraordinary amount for a single fee, it was not an unusually large income for two years. Yet Knighton had only been in private practice in London for three years at that time. Had the Marquess needed similar services a few years later, he would probably have had to pay even more. At the time of his retirement from medicine in 1822, Knighton had a private practice worth £10,000—an income that placed him in the very wealthiest ranks of society.¹⁰³

The most successful medical men—accoucheurs no less than physicians and surgeons—were financially able to emulate the luxurious way of life of their aristocratic patients. At the time of Denman's retirement in 1790, for instance, he maintained a Grosvenor Square town house and a country seat in suburban Middlesex. His son, who was given a gentleman's education at Eton and Cambridge, was raised to the peerage as Lord Denman. Similarly, Charles Clarke had bought a country seat in Norfolk, living there as a country gentleman.¹⁰⁴ Locock, too, was able to buy a country seat. His efforts to go into politics, however, were less successful than Knighton's: Locock won the Conservative nomination for the Isle of Wight constituency in 1865, but lost the election and retired from politics. His third son, however, was to become a British ambassador.¹⁰⁵

The career of the surgeon Sir Astley Cooper, who was the most highly paid medical man of the time, is instructive. He always refrained from mentioning a fee, even when none was forthcoming.¹⁰⁶ A better investment, he believed, was in the patient's goodwill. One patient, for instance, in 1804 sent Cooper a very large check, enclosing with it the following explanation:

When I first had the pleasure of seeing you, you requested, as a favour, I would consider you as a friend. I now sir, request you will return the compliment by accepting the enclosed draft as an act of friendship *on my part* . . . I must particularly desire and beg, when next I have the pleasure of seeing you, that you will avoid mentioning the subject, but only consider it as a very small token of gratitude for the kindness shown.[107]

Cooper's gentlemanly restraint resulted in feelings of friendship and respect between doctor and patient: service to the one and profit to the other. Similarly, when Charles Locock first attended upper-class patients referred to him by Dr. Gooch, he often got "nothing but thanks." When offered money, he often refused it—indeed he did so in about half these cases. Two years later his gentlemanly reticence was beginning to pay off. "My practice is increasing most wonderfully," he wrote his friend Dicky Jones in 1825, "I am now making new connections every day, and all amongst the better class of society, where they give good fees and kind words—whereas in the second rate sort of practice they usually give one or the other, but never both." By the end of that year, Locock was earning £800 per annum and could afford to marry.[108] In order to make money, Cooper and Locock had been forced to behave as if they had no need of it.

If only unconsciously, the successful accoucheurs of the period probably echoed Cooper's advice to his grandnephew. "You can never prosper," he told the young man on his departure for India, "unless your industriously perform the duties of the situation in which you may be placed." He added significantly, "You will never succeed, if you are not humble to your superiors, friendly with your equals, and kind and generous to those who are beneath you."[109]

Some strains were inevitable during the course of a fashionable accoucheur's career. Many men never completely recovered from the difficulties of their earlier years. "Mine has been a life of great anxiety," Knighton wrote during the latter years of his career. "Those who pass into the world without money or friends can never, of course, calculate on consequences. This was my case, and hence have I been in a state of feverish anxiety from morning to night."[110] Accoucheurs were not the only ones who had to make their own way in the world. Sir Benjamin Brodie, the prominent physician, expressed himself similarly. He felt secure enough to marry only at the age of thirty-three, by which time he was able to own a house and keep a carriage. His income that year (1816) was a thoroughly respectable £1,530. His new position in the world, however, brought problems with it. "Marriage," he wrote, occasioned a period "of considerable anxiety," since, for the first time, others were dependent on him for support. Only the increase in his private practice, "kept my anxiety within bounds." He wrote, "still it was considerable and was probably the cause of my having some return of the dyspeptic symptoms under which I had laboured formerly, and which continued to trouble me from time to time, for the 2 or 3 following years."[111]

One continuing source of anxiety was the fear that a patient would die. As a medical man became more successful and grew in stature, so too did the stature and rank of his patients increase; thus this particular anxiety was not likely to diminish. The most tragic example of this problem is Croft's suicide following the death of Princess Charlotte. Croft was described by Sir Benjamin Brodie, who knew him well, as "a man of acute feelings, a thorough gentleman, having a high sense of honour, and of a kind and liberal disposition."[112] Other medical men of Croft's stature sympathized with his plight. "I can easily understand poor Croft's feelings when the Princess Charlotte died," Sir Astley Cooper wrote. "I am certain that if anything happened to the King," on whom Cooper had just operated, "I should leave London and live in retirement."[113] Cooper in fact, though at the top of his profession, had avoided treating the king as long as possible, for fear that the patient would die. "I felt thunderstruck, and giddy at the idea of my fate hanging upon such an event."[114]

An additional problem was the continued ambivalence of the social position of even the most successful medical men. No matter how wealthy or socially prominent they became, they never were considered quite the equals of those who had been born to an exalted station in life. Indeed, social confusion may have increased with any augmentation of an accoucheur's social position. When the starry-eyed young Croft, possessed of neither means nor reputation, dined at the table of the Duke of Devonshire, no one would have confused them as social equals. The relationship of patron and protégé would have seemed perfectly natural, if sometimes oppressive. But years later, if Sir Richard Croft, Bart., possessed of a fortune, a country house, and an international reputation, dined with a titled nobleman, one could indeed argue that they had become members of the same social class. Thus Elizabeth Bennett pled the cause of her social equality with the beloved Darcy in Jane Austen's *Pride and Prejudice* (1813): "He is a gentleman, I am a gentleman's daughter; so far we are equal," she insisted.[115] If gentlemanliness was indeed the social Rubicon, then successful accoucheurs had surely crossed it. And if there were some noblemen—most likely left-wing Whigs like Holland or Egremont,[116] both of whom were concerned with cultivating an intellectual aristocracy—who were able to treat physicians or artists as equals, there were more who could not. Indeed the absence of intermarriage between the peerage and the medical profession is indicative of that lack of equality.[117]

Knighton—by rising the most—probably felt this prejudice most keenly. Mrs. Arbuthnot, Wellington's great friend, was one of those who resented Knighton's rise. While having purely political reasons to dislike Knighton, she always attacked him for his origins as an accoucheur, seeing this as his most vulnerable point. She usually referred to Knighton disparagingly as the man-midwife. She recited the litany of his crimes against society on the occasion of his royal appointment in 1822: "The *friend* to whom the king alludes is Sir William Knighton, whose origin was being a physician's shop boy in Plymouth . . . then became an *accoucheur* in London and now ends by being the King's Privy Purse & most confidential friend," she wrote with horror and dramatic emphases.[118] Lord Liverpool, the Prime Minister, refused to make Knighton a Privy Councillor, despite the King's nomination, on the grounds that Knighton had been "accoucheur to all the ladies in London."[119] Mr. Arbuthnot shared his wife's snobbery. "You have galled him [Knighton] to the very soul," he told Liverpool, "by not allowing him to emerge from the lowness of his former situation."[120]

Knighton, who historians agree did a remarkable job of restoring the king's finances to a sound footing and of convincing the cantankerous old monarch to attend to business, was possibly correct in believing that his own contributions had never been fully appreciated.[121] "Gratitude," he wrote, "is not a commonly existing virtue in the minds of those born high in station. Early affluence seems often to put contemplation aside. Without this," he concluded, "the affections of the heart soon go to sleep."[122]

Croft's life—and, more particularly, his death—are again instructive. The emotional strain of his dependence upon the upper classes remained with him. Success provided little assistance, for it only gave him more to lose. Croft apparently plunged into a deep melancholy after Princess Charlotte's death in 1817, a melancholy exacerbated by a public opinion that held Croft responsible for the Princess's tragic end.[123] (In the chapter on childbirth Croft's management of her case will be evaluated; it will be shown that his professional behavior was very much in agreement with the medical orthodoxy of his time.) Croft must have felt these attacks were unfair. But this was not all he had to endure during the three months between Charlotte's death and his own suicide in February 1818. During that time, rumors surfaced in London concerning Croft's conduct in 1790 in his attendance upon the Duchess of Devonshire. It was said—in stories repeated, though coyly refuted by the *Times* and the *Gentleman's Magazine*—that both the Duchess and Lady Elizabeth had given birth in Paris that May, but that only the Duke's mistress had produced a son.[124] According to the rumor, Croft had been the means of exchanging the babies, thus introducing "spurious issue" into the noble house of Devonshire. At a time when his reputation had already suffered severely, Croft was blamed for his loyal attachment to his Devonshire patrons of nearly thirty years earlier—an attachment that had made his career possible. Poor Croft must surely have felt robbed of all honor by these stories.[125] Six months after his death, the widowed Lady Croft discovered that she had been deserted by her erstwhile friends and patrons. Her request that "a place" in the royal establishment be found for her eldest son, who had distinguished himself at the Battle of Quatre Bras, was soundly, if politely, rejected.[126]

The growing and increasingly affluent middle class would make freedom from the necessity of acquiring aristocratic patronage economically viable. Professionalization would make it possible. The first half of the nineteenth century witnessed the attempts of accoucheurs—and other medical practitioners—to form an independent, self-regulating, publicly acknowledged professional group. Thomas Wakley founded *Lancet* in 1823 to establish professional standards and provide a vehicle for sharing medical information and experiences. Within the decade, several other medical journals were similarly established such as the *London Medical Gazette* and the *Medical Times and Gazette*. Groups of medical practitioners—including accoucheurs—used these pages to establish standards for fees.[127] By joining together to set prices, doctors could avoid "competition" and thus continue to appear gentlemanly, while assuring themselves of a certain income. The prohibition against advertising functioned the same way. Thus professionalizing "new men" continued to make use of genteel standards, while nevertheless trying to free themselves from genteel control. In 1827, as we have seen, the Obstetric Society had been founded to establish professional criteria in the practice of midwifery and to win recognition of their authority to do so. Charles Mansfield Clarke was the first president of this organization, and the young Locock was one of its founding members.[128] Indeed, Clarke and Locock, by their continued devotion to the cause of the medical man, may have forestalled the kind of criticism Knighton and Croft engendered. Charles Mansfield Clarke, for instance, was president of the Society for the Relief of the Widows and Orphans of Medical Men. In his obituary, Clarke was praised. "When carriages thronged his doors in Savile Row, he would make any distant visit to the wife or daughter of a medical gentleman, regardless of the consequences to himself."[129] By so doing, he was of course exhibiting the genteel quality of noblesse oblige, while at the same time endearing himself to the less fortunate of his profession. Upon his retirement in 1857, Locock served as president of the Royal Medical and Chirurgical Society, and as magistrate and deputy-lieutenant for the city of Kent.[130]

It was thus the decade of the 1820s that witnessed the surge of interest in professionalism on the parts of accoucheurs and other medical men. The Medical Act of 1858 was a result of their efforts. Several factors combined to create this ferment in the decades following Waterloo. The overcrowding of the medical profession after 1815 made it difficult for medical men to live up to gentlemanly standards of behavior in the face of ruthless competition. But the desire for "gentlemanliness" had been fostered by the extension of aristocratic patronage to include accoucheurs, as aristocratic patients in the second half of the eighteenth century inexorably substituted accoucheurs for midwives. Patients were important, too, for the support they gave institutionally and personally to proponents of the new, scientific midwifery. As Peterson has said, medical authority increased in the early years of the nineteenth century, not because doctors finally knew what they were doing, but because of the increased "social valuation of the work itself."[131] The eighteenth-century pursuit of happiness and the secularization of life in general had enabled men and women to be more concerned with the physical well-being of their bodies. Domesticity enhanced the trend. The aristocratic ideal was of a large healthy family, and medical expertise was seen as an aid to its achievement. Thus, professionalization was a sign of the strength of the accoucheurs, as well as a recognition of their vulnerability. They knew they were needed. The careers of men like Denman, Croft, Knighton, Clarke, and Locock exemplified the potential strength of the profession while revealing its weaknesses. Sir James Simpson referred to this remaining professional ambiguity in his 1842 speech to the graduates of the Edinburgh medical school, in which he urged the young men to free themselves from the dead hand of patronage. "Owe therefore your whole energies to medicine," he told them. "Place your faith in no extrinsic influences. Let your own professional character be the one great patron to whom you look for your professional advancement."[132]

Medical practice does not occur in a social vacuum. Accoucheurs of the century 1760 to 1860 remained dependent on the continued favor of their aristocratic patients. Their professional sources of income and their reputations were tied to these paternalistic relationships. Status anxiety in an increasingly mobile society remained an acute problem for many aristocratic accoucheurs. If nothing else, aristocratic values were reinforced by the attempts of accoucheurs to imitate the gentlemanly standard of conduct. Accoucheurs prior to the year 1860 were hardly in a position to enforce an unpopular medical orthodoxy on an unwilling patient. Instead, medical procedure would necessarily reflect the demands, desires, and values of the aristocratic patient.

CHAPTER IV

Pregnancy

In 1791, after fifteen years of childless marriage, Lady Judith Milbanke (1751–1822) finally became pregnant. She was forty years old. The spinster aunt who had raised Lady Judith was quick to offer advice. "Use moderate exercise & live as near as you can in your usual way," Mary Noel wrote her niece. "As you are accustom'd to so active a life I fear you will be ill if you are too sedentary."[1] Lady Judith followed her aunt's advice on this point, and in May 1792 she gave birth to a healthy daughter. Mary Noel's philosophy of prenatal care was one that would have met with the approval of most accoucheurs and aristocratic patients at the end of the eighteenth century. United as these two groups were in their desires for healthy maternity, they agreed that living normally during pregnancy was often a good way of achieving their goals. In return for satisfying the enormous reproductive demands placed on them, aristocratic women, it appears, achieved a significant—and increasing—amount of freedom during their many years of pregnancy. As this quotation indicates, pregnant aristocrats sought—and often achieved—a high degree of social integration. This was particularly true for the majority of women who were healthy. But by failing to satisfy family expectations, the minority who experienced reproductive difficulties were more likely to be asked to sacrifice at least some aspect of their usual mode of existence.

Aristocratic women typically were pregnant for many years—perhaps the best years—of their lives. Of the thirty-six women in our group who enjoyed marriages of completed fertility, thirty-one were still giving birth after fifteen years of marriage. Nineteen of them would continue to produce children even after twenty years of marriage. The median childbearing span—from marriage to last birth—for the entire group of fifty, was eighteen years, resulting in the production of about eight children each. The "typical" aristocrat, according to the group's median, married at twenty-one and gave birth to her last child at age thirty-nine. Nearly half the fifty women, or twenty-four, gave birth to their first child within one year of marriage, and 80 percent gave birth within two years of marriage. Second children followed quickly thereafter. Twenty-three women actually succeeded in giving birth to a second child within a year or less of the birth of the first: fully thirty-five (70 percent of the total) gave birth to the second child within two years. Charlotte, Duchess of Beaufort (1771–1854), who managed to give birth to three children within two-and-one-half years of marriage, is an example of an intensely fertile aristocrat. Married in May 1791, the Duchess succeeded in giving birth to two children in 1792—one in February and one in December. The third child, born the following November, was premature and died at six weeks. Charlotte's mother, Susan, Marchioness of Stafford, lamented that having three children in twenty-one months was "too much for the strongest constitution."[2] Lady Stafford spoke from experience. Having married for the first time at the late age of thirty-seven, she had nevertheless produced four children within four years before her childbearing life ended.

For most women, aging brought little respite from reproduction. Fertility normally declines as women get older, and approximately half the fifty women did give birth to their last child more than three years after their previous sibling. These babies might indeed be considered menopausal, upsetting the routine of family life and causing a dusty nursery to be reopened. But then, more surprisingly, half of last babies followed in regular succession behind their nearest sibling. One-third of the women had their last child in less than two years after its nearest sibling. These babies usually came at the end of a long period of intense fertility. The most fecund woman of the group, the Duchess of Leinster, had married at fifteen and a half and had given birth within the year. Her twenty-first and last child was born thirty years later, when the duchess was forty-six; it arrived only twenty-two months after the twentieth had been born. Perhaps less remarkable only by comparison with this achievement was the experience of Maria, Lady Duncannon, whose pleasure as an eighteen-year-old newlywed we recorded earlier. Lady Duncannon gave birth to her fifteenth and last child at the age of forty-two, only fourteen months after the birth of her fourteenth child. Sadly, Lady Duncannon was to die only five years later, her fertility statistically completed. For her and others like her, adult life had been nearly synonymous with pregnancy.

Fortunately for women like Lady Duncannon, at no time during the century 1760 to 1860 does there seem to have been any social taboo against appearing visibly pregnant in public, contrary to popular myth. These aristocratic women remained relatively free of restraint, even during their ninth month of pregnancy. Awaiting the birth of a third child in London in June 1805, Frances, Lady Churchill, for instance, kept up a full round of social life throughout her ninth month of pregnancy. She frequently dined out and went to the opera as late as June 11. She gave birth June 28. Lady Morley attended a wedding in the ninth month of her first pregnancy in 1810. In the ninth month of her ninth pregnancy in 1822, Lady Verulam went for a drive in her phaeton and brought some work for the little girls in her school at nearby St. Alban's.[3]

Or consider the example of Lady Charlotte Guest, who wished to reestablish her family in the social world of peerage. As the opening event in this important campaign, she gave a concert at her home in London on June 13, 1834, despite the fact that she was in the ninth month of her first pregnancy. Little cognizance was taken of her condition. "At the beginning of the evening I attempted to sit down," she wrote, "but I was soon expelled from my seat by the crowd, and obliged to stand at the top of the staircase." The evening was quite a success. "From ten to about one o'clock the house was full," she proudly described the scene to her mother. "All being over as to music, my friends made a grand eating and drinking and left me very tired at about 2 o'clock."[4] Lady Charlotte gave birth only two weeks later. Had there been even the slightest question about the propriety of entertaining when so advanced in pregnancy, she certainly would not have arranged the party for that time.

The ultimate arbiter of morality during this century was the royal court. Women great with child were accepted into the royal presence—and not only that of the freewheeling George IV. The court of his successor, William IV, was conducted with far more propriety and sobriety under the aegis of his German consort. Queen Adelaide, who had banned décolleté gowns from her drawing rooms, was not offended by the sight of pregnant women. In 1831, for instance, Lady Clanwilliam attended the royal drawing room in the ninth month of her first pregnancy.[5] William IV's eponymous successor, Victoria, was not overly delicate about pregnancy either. She welcomed Lady Charlotte Guest, six months pregnant, to a ball at the palace in 1840. On that occasion, Queen Victoria was herself pregnant, although unlike Lady Charlotte, not yet visibly so.[6]

While these women—pregnant or otherwise—were not athletic by the standards of the twentieth century, neither were they thoroughly indolent. During their pregnancies, they maintained a level of physical activity similar to what they had known before. Kate, Lady Amberley, for instance, went ice skating during her first pregnancy in 1865.[7] More commonly, pregnant women continued to pursue that favorite sport of the English aristocracy, riding. Frances, Lady Morley, an avid horsewoman, continued to ride even after she had been thrown from a horse during the early months of her first pregnancy in 1809. The accident caused her to lose consciousness for a few minutes and left her badly bruised. The incident terrified her husband, but Lady Morley took it in stride. She even brought her horse with her when she went to London for the season two months later.[8] During her fifth pregnancy in 1802, Charlotte, Countess of Banbury (1777–1818), also met with a riding accident. Her husband guessed that her weight had been too much for the horse, who "gave way with his hind legs," but the quick-witted and nimble Lady Banbury managed to jump off safely just in time.[9]

Once settled into her Portman Square town house, Lady Morley realized she would not be able to get the horseback riding exercise to which she was accustomed on her Devonshire estate, and so she adapted her desires for exercise to the exigencies of city life:

> I have been trying my agility these last three months in taking a certain number of turns around the Square by which I calculate that I walk abt. two miles at a *breathing* this I believe is reckoned a good thing for all ladies under similar circumstances with myself, & for me I think it is quite necessary, as I have always been so much accustomed to air & exercise all my life, that if I was to be deprived of it like many London ladies I sh^d lose all my faculties mental and Corporal & fall into a state of utter imbecility.[10]

Likewise, pregnancy did not curb the wanderlust of the English aristocracy. Travel remained a popular leisure activity. Lady Holland, for instance, traveled through northern Italy during her 1795 pregnancy, carried about the mountains on a sedan chair. In her sixth month of pregnancy she wrote in her diary:

> I crossed the *Vara* a very deep and rapid torrent no less than three times, the water came over the middle of my men, they waded across the stream with difficulty the whole country to Sarzana remarkable pretty—I might have gone round by Spezia but I was weak enough to be overruled—just before I got to Sarzana I was near meeting with an ugly accident in crossing a branch of the *Magra,* the waters were extremely rapid, roaring down to the Sea with fury, my guides were fatigued, the effort of holding the chair

upon their Shoulders was too much, when they were in the middle of the Stream several men fell, & once the chair did more than totter—I escaped that danger.[11]

Less intrepid explorers than Lady Holland also traveled frequently during their pregnancies. During the last trimester of her first pregnancy in 1810, Harriet, Lady Granville, and her husband toured the country seats of his family members, visiting Sandon Hall and Trentham in Staffordshire, Badminton in Gloucestershire, and Lilleshall in Cheshire.[12] Her niece Harriet, Duchess of Sutherland, went to Paris for a four-month visit in March 1825, although she was expecting a baby in August. In August 1832 during her sixth month of pregnancy, the Duchess of Sutherland took her children up to Dunrobin, the family castle in Scotland. In September the family began a slow journey back to London. They paid leisurely visits to friends and relatives at Chillingham and Alnwick castles, Lilleshall, and Castle Howard on the way.[13] During the fifth month of her seventh pregnancy in 1826, Lady Frances Cole (1784–1847) toured the more "remarkable parts" of the island of Mauritius where she had been living with her husband, the British governor.[14]

When women did refrain from participating in social activities, it was specifically on the grounds of health, rather than impropriety. As a result, women were most likely to stay home during the first trimester of pregnancy, when, though still slender, they were apt to be suffering from nausea, dizziness, and vomiting. In any event, women seem to have determined for themselves what they could or could not do.

Pregnancy was used occasionally as an excuse for avoiding something unpleasant—much as any illness can be. Lady Holland (when still Lady Webster) in 1793 made her "*grossesse* a pretext for staying home in the Evening" so that she would not have to accompany her despised husband on his social rounds.[15] Similarly, during the second month of her fourth pregnancy, while at an international conference in the Italian city of Verona, Lady Londonberry used her condition as an excuse for not going out to dine with her husband. Instead she stayed home and received Czar Alexander privately.[16]

Accoucheurs could be extremely useful allies to women faced with demanding relatives. Their voice of authority could be used to approve or disapprove much that women wanted to do—or to avoid doing. Kate, Lady Amberley, told her father-in-law that her doctor, Mr. Merriman, approved of her ice skating. Her father-in-law was Lord John Russell who, though Prime Minister, had found the time to call Kate "a foolish child" and ask her to be more cautious.[17] Queen Victoria seems to have used Locock to help her get out of public duties that she found obnoxious. During the Queen's third pregnancy, Prince Albert told Prime Minister Peel that Locock had forbidden her to open Parliament in person. Yet it seems likely that Locock would not have made so extraordinary a suggestion had he not been convinced that Victoria wanted to avoid that duty. There is sufficient evidence to support such a conclusion. Years later, of course, Victoria notoriously used her widowhood to get out of performing public duties she despised—such as opening Parliament. She once complained to her daughter that she was miserable during her first two years of marriage when she was constantly pregnant. She hated appearing in public only to be stared at. In the face of Locock's authority, however, the queen could disavow doing her duty and still appear blameless.[18]

Women who used pregnancy too often as a pretext for inactivity, however, were likely to be ridiculed. "Lady Jersey is to be confined in March," Lady Harrowby told her brother in October 1807, and "to secure this," she added, "she does not move off her Couch, nor will she risk the exertion of holding a glass up to her mouth, so that all this is done for her."[19] Such indolence was unusual enough to be thought foolish. But Lady Jersey was one of those women who was particularly anxious about childbearing. As we saw in an earlier chapter, her failure to become pregnant soon after marriage made her very tense and unhappy. Her first pregnancy had not resulted in the birth of a live child.[20] Women like Susan, Countess of Harrowby (1772–1838), who had given birth to her first child in less than a year of marriage and went on to give birth to nine more in quick succession, might well laugh at the Lady Jerseys of the world. But such confidence was a luxury Lady Jersey could hardly afford.

Simply because aristocratic women enjoyed social and physical activity during their pregnancies, we should not infer that they were casual about their condition. Landowning society, as we have seen, demanded the production of healthy heirs. Prenatal care was welcomed as part of the larger effort to secure healthy reproduction, even from the earliest weeks of pregnancy. But accoucheurs shared with their patients the belief that pregnancy was a normal, healthy, even desirable condition. Nature, rather than artifice, was to be the guiding principle of prenatal care. The aristocracy, however, often went, willy-nilly, to great lengths to achieve the natural simplicity their accoucheurs recommended.

The successful accoucheur trusted deeply in the beneficial powers of nature and Divine Providence. Nature, the medical practitioner thought, had designed the human constitution to be balanced harmoniously between its constituent parts, which were still identified as the four humors. Good health was a condition in which the elements composing the physical constitution were perfectly balanced. This theory met with the immediate sympathy of the aristocracy, who delighted in the natural order of their Palladian villas and Adam interiors. The role of the physician, restoring the constitution to a state of balance and natural harmony, was remarkably like that of the landscape architect Capability Brown, who used the same principles in restructuring the family park. The female constitution was also "capable of improvement" (to use the phrase that gave Brown his first name), even when in the best of health.

Medical theories were more complicated, however. Diseases

could not easily be isolated, since various bodily organs (especially the uterus) were thought to have peculiar sympathies with one another. The modern notion of disease as a localized physiological process with a specific etiology had not yet been established to the physicians' satisfaction. The medical approach was a holistic one. An entire constitution, or "habit," needed to be cured, it was thought, rather than a particular ailment. The doctor's knowledge of a patient's constitution, rather than his understanding of a given pathological process, was the guarantor of medical success. Thus the prolonged acquaintance of an accoucheur with his aristocratic patient was an asset in his ability to treat her successfully.[21]

Human constitutions were diagnosed on a continuum ranging from weakness to plethora; good health was the happy medium. In the case of weakness, medical management strove to strengthen a patient through a regimen of cordials, exercise, an ample and nourishing diet, and bathing. Plethoric patients, in contrast to weak ones, were described as being of high color and full of animal spirits. Thought to be a dangerous condition, plethora, or fullness as it was sometimes called, was believed to be caused by an excess of blood flowing to the afflicted part, thus creating pressure and irritability which could result in fever.

Plethora was treated by the lowering system, which specifically aimed at weakening the patient. It was probably quite effective in doing that, if nothing else. Bloodletting by leeching or cupping was only part of the regimen. At the same time, the plethoric patient might be given an "opening" medicine (or laxative) and a purgative to relieve the stomach of its contents. Patients on the lowering system could be expected to stay on a diet that denied them animal foods and anything else that might be construed as stimulating. Factors that affect the entire constitution, such as climate, air, rest, and diet, might also have a large role in establishing one's health.

A woman could not expect a reprieve from such medical onslaughts on the grounds of pregnancy. Only a patient with a healthy and well-balanced constitution could expect to become pregnant. As a result, obstetric care had a rationale for its concern with the apparently healthy woman, as well as its more understandable concern for the woman who suffered specific reproductive problems. Most aristocratic women were familiar with the regimens prescribed for the very condition of pregnancy; a minority of women also became familiar with techniques designed to solve their particular problem. There two areas of prenatal management, the general and the particular, will be examined in turn.

Most pregnant women were thought to be plethoric, which logically resulted in the prescription of the lowering system. Diet was an important part of this system. To counterbalance plethora, accoucheurs prescribed "cooling foods" such as fruits and vegetables, and prohibited "heating foods" such as meat, eggs, and spices. Stimulating beverages, including coffee, tea, and alcohol, were also banned on the grounds of being "heating."[22] Though diets were individualized for each patient, most followed the general rules of blandness and limited animal protein. Most accoucheurs also emphasized the need for roughage to counteract the tendency of many pregnant women toward constipation. Most of the so-called cooling foods fell into this category.

Croft put Lady Morley on the lowering diet, as it was called, during her first pregnancy in 1810, and enforced a strictly meatless regimen. "What do you think is likely to become of me and my daughter?" she complained. "I am now living exactly like a *Horse* on *grass food* & water. . . . Croft tells me I must not indulge too much in the luxuries of the table," she continued, "& that I must practice the virtues of temperance and sobriety."[23] Lady Morley nevertheless admitted that the "starvation system," as she bluntly put it, agreed with her.[24]

The diet Croft assigned Princess Charlotte only a few years later was not nearly as strict as Lady Morley's had been. Although the royal patient could have neither eggs nor animal food for breakfast, for lunch she had her choice of "fruit or sweet meat" with "Bread or Biscuit," and for dinner, "plain dressed Meat . . . that which is most easy of digestion, and not to exceed two glasses of Wine at and after dinner & this to be the only Wine taken in the course of the day."[25] After the Princess's death in childbirth, Croft was criticized for having weakened her through a low diet. In fact, her diet was substantially more nutritious than those of many of her pregnant contemporaries.

Dieting was not the only method by which accoucheurs sought to restore their patient's health. A removal to a more natural situation, away from urban social life, was another aspect of prenatal care. Sea bathing and "taking the waters" at a spa served that purpose as well as the additional one of invigorating the constitution. The growth of English watering places during the late-eighteenth and nineteenth centuries testifies to the emphasis on bathing in medical regimens of the time. Bathing was considered "strengthening" and a good substitute for exercise. Although sea bathing was preferred, a tub of cold water also answered the purpose, according to at least one physician.[26] Sir Archibald Macdonald hoped that the "bracing water" at Tunbridge Wells would completely "establish Lady Louisa's constitution" and "bid defiance to the winter." Charlotte, Countess of Banbury, took the waters at Bath in January 1810, during the sixth month of pregnancy.[27]

Lady Morley, whose country seat Saltram was located near the south coast of Devonshire, found sea water readily available. Her accoucheur, Andrew Thynne, did not, however, expect her to go out bathing in the sea, but to have the sea water brought into her home via the hip bath, which became fashionable at the turn of the century. Under Thynne's orders, Lady Morley used the hip bath with "sea water not quite cold, viz, the chill taken off as to enable me to continue in it some time without giving me a cold."[28] The shower bath was also introduced about this time, and Croft included it as part of Princess Charlotte's regimen in 1817. She was to shower between breakfast and 2:00 P.M. on alternate days, "beginning with the water a little Tepid, but to sponge the loins every morning with Cold Water."[29]

Exercise was also prescribed as part of the lowering plan. As proof that outdoor exercise was good for pregnant women, Dr. Denman pointed to the lower classes, who, he believed, were healthier because they were "obliged to follow labourious occupations in the open air."[30] The aristocracy, he thought, might learn from their example. When an accoucheur prescribed exercise for a patient of rank, however, he expected that it would be taken within the limits of genteel dignity. Denman believed that leisurely travel was an appropriate mode of exercise during pregnancy. Dr. William Moss, surgeon to the Liverpool Lying-in Charity, also recommended travel, which he believed was appropriate anytime before the seventh month of pregnancy.[31] In 1835, Susan, Lady Rivers, told her mother that the doctor urged "a good deal of exercise" and, as a result, she felt herself to be gaining strength every day, though she was in daily expectation of her delivery.[32] The excercise her accoucheur prescribed suited her—and, as we have seen, many other women were eager to seek out exercise.

The prenatal practice of phlebotomy or bloodletting was the most unfortunate aspect of the usual regimen. Traditionally it had been the custom to bleed women almost as soon as their pregnancies were known. The Duchess of Devonshire, who was under Denman's care during her first successful pregnancy in 1783, was phlebotomized because of a cough and a nosebleed. In 1790, when his son-in-law Croft attended the Duchess, he bled her consistently throughout her pregnancy—both at her own behest and because Croft needed to practice his bloodletting skills. During that pregnancy she was not bled for any specific ailment. The last bloodletting took place only two weeks before the Duchess gave birth.[33] Perhaps the condition modern physicians call "edema," a swelling caused by the accumulation of serous fluids in the tissues, common in pregnant women, was diagnosed as plethora, and so required phlebotomy, according to the wisdom of the day. Denman wrote that bleeding lessened the "general irritability of the habit" and was therefore invaluable, particularly in cases of incessant vomiting.[34]

Though doctors bled their patients regularly, they did not regard the procedure without some trepidation. They justified the painful and weakening remedy on the grounds that the battle of life and death necessitated such heroic measures. Their patients generally agreed with them. Lady Holland was bled toward the end of her seventh pregnancy in 1798. She recorded, in her clinically melodramatic and unpunctuated style: "I had an alarming complaint in my stomack the cause a total debility the effect a death like icy coldness from which torpor nothing but the strongest cordials could revive me—the Physician ventured upon a bold remedy and bled me success warranted the undertaking."[35]

Doctors did not hesitate to bleed their patients toward the end of their pregnancies, even though they and their patients recognized that it would leave them weakened. Lady Banbury had had many difficult pregnancies and confinements. In 1810 she was about to give birth to her tenth child. On April 7 her husband wrote that she was suffering from pain, fever, a cough, sleeplessness, and "several inconveniences of apprehension." She consulted Charles Mansfield Clarke who relieved her of twelve ounces of blood. Only three days later the Earl was again writing, this time to announce the birth of a son. "Her illness and Bleedings," he reported, "did not make her better prepared for the Event."[36] Lady Verulam was bled repeatedly during her 1810 and 1822 pregnancies—the latter time under the direction of Sir William Knighton.[37]

The practice of phlebotomy was nevertheless declining during this period, and it seems to have gone out of favor among England's fashionable accoucheurs and patients by 1840. Very few women were bled routinely after 1820 simply because they were pregnant. The latest reference to the practice among our fifty women occurred in 1838, when Lady Augusta Fox, pregnant, was bled for backache.[38] In 1842 Dr. Thomas Bull wrote that there was a prevailing notion among the lower classes that pregnancy in itself demanded a loss of blood. He made it quite clear, however, that doctors and enlightened patients no longer believed this to be the case, as they had fifty years earlier.[39]

The lowering plan, which provided the theoretical basis for much of the prenatal care experienced by the aristocracy, included several major elements: a low diet, exercise, and bathing. Taking spa waters and being phlebotomized were also somewhat common, though in the later case decreasingly so. Most of the women in our group were treated according to the lowering plan during some or all of their pregnancies.

The accoucheur had to devote disproportionate amounts of his attention to those women who had specific reproductive complaints or disorders. Among the most important and most common of these were the problems of infertility, difficult or symptomatic pregnancies, and miscarriages. Most reproductive wastage and ill health were experienced by a minority of women—something under a quarter of the group—many of whom also raised large, healthy families. These problems, trying as they were for women and their families, might also be exasperating for the accoucheur. It was in these areas that his patients were most likely to rely on his expertise, although these were areas where he had the least confidence in his methods. Restoration of the entire female constitution to a state of natural harmony remained the goal of medical treatment.

Although most women gave birth within a year or so after marriage, a substantial minority gave birth only after two or more years of marriage. Ten women in the group of fifty did not give birth within two years of their marriage. Of these, two—Lady Sarah Bunbury and Lady Anne Abdy—gave birth rapidly after their second marriages, indicating that the problem probably was with their first husbands. Indeed, since both women left those husbands and were divorced, it may well be that Bunbury and Abdy were not merely sterile, but impotent.

Indeed, Lord Wellesley believed that of Abdy, his son-in-law.[40] An extended period of adolescent infertility seems to be the most likely cause of the delayed fertility of most of the other eight women. Their mean age at marriage was only 18 ¾, compared to 20 ¾ for the fifty women as a whole—a large difference for so small a group. Indeed, the astonishing Duchess of Leinster was the only woman in the entire group of fifty who gave birth prior to the age of eighteen, though several women were married in their midteens. For most of these, time alone effected a cure.[41] Yet this is easier to see in retrospect than it was at the time. Most of these women, like the Duchess of Devonshire, considered themselves barren during the early years of wedded life. In 1781, after seven years of marriage, she wrote of how "obliged" she would be to "dear demure Dr. Denman" were he to enable her to have a child.[42] Thus, helping a woman to become pregnant was a major function of the aristocratic accoucheur. It was also one of his more difficult tasks, since the processes of conception remained poorly understood. Accoucheurs disagreed on the function of the menstrual cycle, for instance, though they agreed that its cessation was generally the first sign of pregnancy.[43]

In keeping with the general medical theories of the day, accoucheurs treated infertility by trying to restore the constitution to its natural harmony, rather than curing a specific problem. The change of air concomitant upon traveling and other external circumstances was thought to have beneficial effect on the constitution and could, therefore, restore the female reproductive system to its healthy, productive state. Mineral waters, such as those found at the fashionable spas, were not believed to be useful solely when a woman was pregnant. Because the waters were thought to regulate the menstrual cycle, they could foster fertility as well.

In 1782, after eight childless years of marriage, the Duchess of Devonshire took the waters at Bath to improve her prospects of pregnancy. She finally gave birth to her first child, a daughter, a year later. In 1788, after a second daughter's birth but still without the necessary son, the Duchess wrote pathetically to her mother: "The sea voyage, as it once before did, might occasion my breeding, and indeed if I am not with child before, we have nearly determined to go to Spa this summer." In April of 1789 she wrote to her friend and financier Calonne, "Les médicins croyent tous que le changement d'air et la salubrité des eaux me donneront un fils."[44] And indeed, the Duchess did conceive a son while taking the waters at Spa. Perhaps she and the Duke just needed to relax.

Lady Augusta Fox's sad, desperate letters to her in-laws, Lord and Lady Holland, give an excellent description of medical opinion and practice on infertility during the 1830s. Little had been learned in the half-century since the Duchess of Devonshire trusted in sea voyages and spas to make her fertile. Lady Augusta, the daughter of the Earl of Coventry, married Henry Fox, the future fourth Lord Holland, in May 1833, reportedly miscarried of twins in 1834, did not conceive again until 1838 (when she also miscarried), and finally gave birth in 1842 to a son who died within a few minutes. In 1844 she gave birth to stillborn twins—a sad reproductive history that resulted in the extinction of the family title. Though difficulties in conceiving were not Lady Augusta's only problem, she certainly did not conceive easily. At the time of her last reported pregnancy, she was still only thirty-two years old.

Lady Augusta's experience parallels that of many patients before and since. "Who can decide when Doctors disagree?" she asked after only a few months of marriage. The "famous" Dr. Hamilton, who had come to see her in Paris, diagnosed her complaint as "irritation" and prescribed some pills. He confidently assured Lady Augusta that she would have a "house full of children," and told her that her "great disposition to become *grosse* is the cause of the delay."[45] At another time that year, Lady Augusta saw a different accoucheur at the suggestion of Lady Keith, a friend of her mother-in-law's. This one who also inspired her confidence, advised her to keep "quite quiet."[46]

Consultation by mail and by mother-in-law was also in order. "I have seen Thompson who is persuaded all will come right with care and strict attention as to leeches and separation,"[47] Lady Holland advised her daughter-in-law. Leeches had been ordered to relieve inflammation, but evidently sexual intercourse was considered its cause. The Foxes therefore had to abstain from intercourse in order to relieve Lady Augusta from the irritation that was thought to be preventing conception. So a vicious cycle began. In October of 1834 Lady Augusta Fox wrote from Italy, "I feel better owing to the calming system & especially to the separation from Henry which my Doctor enforces."[48] Her letter indicates that Henry was very much with her (in fact, he added a postscript), so evidently the separation was only a sexual one.

It was little wonder that the Foxes failed to conceive when they embarked on a rigid program of sexual abstinence. Apparently they found this difficult and frequently lapsed, for in October of 1835 Lady Augusta wrote, "We have come to a *revolution* to be perfectly *good* until all symptoms of the complaint have disappeared—if it be but irritation as all have decided, quietude, my cooling system, and no cause given for aggravation, must at least get the better of it—being together only hurts me, frets me, I am determined to try to go on in this *good* state till I reach you & the doctors [in London]." In November she estimated that they would keep to this system for at least six months.[49]

Family friends contributed to the stream of advice offered Lady Augusta during these trying years. The Earl of Lauderdale recommended that Lady Augusta leave Florence, where the Foxes were then living, because he believed that "the relaxing heats of Tuscany are more injurious and debilitating than any medical aid can benefit." Lady Holland also passed on the advice of her friend, Lady Breadalbane, who recommended that Lady Augusta consult Dr. Locock. According to Lady Breadalbane, Locock had "a method of relieving internal inflammation that obviates all the torment of leeches & cupping."[50] Ignoring this well-meant advice, Lady Augusta assured everyone that she had confidence in her own doctor and that she was to take the sea baths, "which are to do me great good."[51]

About six months later Lady Holland decided that everyone had hitherto misdiagnosed Lady Augusta's problem, and she again urged her daughter-in-law to consult Locock. "In case however there should be a slight displacement of the uterus," Lady Holland advised the younger woman, "even that may be relieved, Dr. Locock has a method *entirely* of *his own* & a very ingenious mode of replacing that organ with scarcely any inconvenience and no pain & once replaced it will *enable the parts to perform their duty and probably give me a grandchild*," she added (italics mine). "From what I know of Dr. Locock's method of applying relief," Lady Holland assured Lady Augusta, "3 weeks or a month would do it effectively. It is nothing you may have heard of with horror of a wooden instrument & so forth, nothing of the kind."[52]

Lady Augusta Fox never did give birth successfully, despite the fact that she endured all the "cures" for infertility then currently available: phlebotomy, change of air, sexual abstinence, sea bathing, shower bathing, and "quiet." Nor was her condition ever diagnosed as anything beyond "irritation." Constitutional remedies to offset that irritation had a very limited success. Ironically, the problem may well have been Henry's. He was never examined, treated, or considered. The Foxes' series of reproductive catastrophes conforms to a pattern of veneral disease which he may have given her at marriage. This is not unlikely. He was thirty-one at marriage and had previously had several mistresses, including Theresa Guiccioli, Byron's last love. Indeed, the possibility had occurred to the sophisticated Lady Holland. Nevertheless, it was Augusta who suffered the blame. Her misery, Lady Augusta said in 1836, "was more distressing as it deprives Henry & his family of what they wish & ought with justice to obtain from a little lady of 23!"[53]

Once conception had taken place, the accoucheur's responsibilities became a continued part of aristocratic life. Many pregnant women suffered specific symptoms and discomforts from which they wanted relief. Their accoucheurs were generally ineffective in treating these problems, often because they did not really consider them to be problems. Morning sickness was then, as now, one of the most frequent complaints of pregnant women. Accoucheurs were not, however, as concerned by it as patients were, although there was a general belief among patients as well as doctors that morning sickness was desirable, since it was thought that those susceptible to the complaint would not miscarry.[54] Denman even suggested inducing vomiting with small doses of ipecacuanha.[55] Lady Morley echoed this prejudice in letters to her sister-in-law, who received daily accounts of her Ladyship's nausea. Having had two miscarriages following easy pregnancies, Lady Morley was, in a way, happy to develop morning sickness in her next pregnancy, though it made her very uncomfortable. At about nine weeks into her pregnancy, she wrote to her sister-in-law, "many thanks for your receipt—but in a *moral* point of view I think I ought to encourage the sickness to the utmost—I wished so much to be sick at first that it w^d be quite wicked & ungrateful in me, now that I have the power, not to *puke* all day long."[56] The belief in the wonders of vomiting persisted even as late as 1852. In that year, the new Lady Airlie's grandmother was delighted to hear that Blanche, the reluctant bride, was throwing up six months after her marriage. "Very good news of Blanche," she wrote, "the best, that is safest sign is being very sick, so she will get no pity nor ask for it."[57]

Natural or not, beneficial or not, most women wanted relief from morning sickness—whether palliative or cure. In cases where vomiting actually weakened the patient, both Denman and Thynne prescribed a variety of effervescent concoctions.[58] But, because of the generally sanguine attitude of medical men toward morning sickness, women were often forced to rely on their own home remedies to offset the complaint. Mrs. Villiers advised Lady Morley to use a mixture of cayenne pepper and laudanum for this purpose. Lady Frances Cole had a recipe for "panada for weak stomach" and a potion for "weak digestion," the latter containing oyster shell powder and pounded chamomile flowers. Presumably these recipes were well tested during Lady Frances's seven pregnancies.[59]

A variety of other aches and pains conspired to torment the expectant mother. Pain in the face and teeth were so common that Denman believed these to be "certain indications" of pregnancy. Since these pains were thought to be caused by uterine irritation consequent on pregnancy, Denman believed that only temporary relief could be afforded. Among remedies he suggested were "aether," solutions of opium, or blisters applied behind the ears.[60] Elizabeth, Countess of Sutherland, was relieved of a sore, blistered mouth during her first pregnancy in 1786 by use of "Asses milk and the Bark." Lady Morley used a homemade opium plaster to relieve her face ache in 1813, during the early weeks of her fourth pregnancy. It may well have been the same recipe that Lady Frances Cole used for the complaint. The recipe contained "Equal Quantities of Camphor and Opium with Gum Water," formed into a "plaister or leather."[61]

Toward the end of pregnancy, sleeplessness was often a major complaint, as women found it difficult to find comfortable positions for their unwieldy bodies. Again, Denman felt that discomfort should be welcomed as a healthy sign; he thought the sleeplessness was brought about by the fetus's increased demands for nourishment. Those women who suffered most from insomnia, Denman believed, though often reduced in appearance themselves, usually gave birth to the most healthy, vigorous babies. For those wishing aid, however, he advocated bleeding in small quantities and the use of laxatives. One simple remedy he proposed was to dip a towel in cold water and wrap it around the hand, with one corner hanging over the edge of the bed. This was consistent with the notion that pregnant women were usually overheated, or plethoric, and needed to be cooled. Although opium might be useful in large quantities, Denman recognized that it might be dangerous to both infant and mother, and therefore did not recommend it.[62] Nevertheless, patients had access to opiates without the aid of their physicians. Opium and its derivatives, especially laudanum, were common ingredients in the homemade plasters used by women like Lady Morley and Lady Frances Cole. Lord Verulam administered twelve drops of laudanum to his wife when she suffered from sleeplessness a month before her 1822 confinement. The laudanum "completely quieted her."[63] Queen Victoria suffered from sleeplessness during pregnancy. So did her eldest daughter, the Princess Royal, who had become the Crown Princess of Prussia upon her marriage. The Princess wrote home in 1858 asking her mother's advice while pregnant with the future Kaiser. Queen Victoria responded:

> I sent you today a bottle of camphor lozenges which I always have standing on my night table near my bed, wherever I go—since they were first recommended to me by Sir C. Locock, when I was so very restless before you were born, and I found them very soothing. They are perfectly simple and innocent; he said he found them the answer with ladies—and so have I.[64]

At best, such symptoms as sleeplessness, morning sickness, and various aches and pains may only have discomforted the prospective mother, without actually endangering either herself or her unborn infant. At other times, however, these and other symptoms could be associated with the impending disaster of a miscarriage.

Nineteen of the fifty women (38 percent) in the group suffered at least one miscarriage; eleven women suffered two or more. These eleven women, who composed 22 percent of the entire group, endured two-thirds of all the miscarriages experienced by the women. The proportion of women who suffered at least one miscarriage seems to have declined somewhat over the course of the century. The generations born after 1800 were the first in which fewer than a quarter of the women suffered any miscarriage at all. It may well be, therefore, that contemporary prenatal care was increasingly effective in preventing these accidents, or that women were simply becoming healthier altogether.

Accoucheurs attributed miscarriages to innumerable causes. Consistent with their notion of health as the midpoint of a continuum, doctors believed that women whose constitutions were either weak or plethoric were most subject to them. Denman, in an 1803 work, explained that women of weak habits were more subject to miscarrying because they were more susceptible to violent impressions; the plethoric were likely to miscarry because the vessels of the plethoric uterus had a "disposition" to "discharge its contents."[65] Most other discussions of miscarriage did not even account for a physiology as rudimentary as Denman's. In *Domestic Medicine* William Buchan listed the causes of miscarriage: the death of the child, relaxation or weakness of the mother, "great evacuations," violent exercise, lifting weights, reaching, jumping, vomiting, coughing, convulsions, blows to the belly, falls, fever, bad odors, excess of blood (plethora), indolence, "high living, or the contrary," and violent passions of the mind, including joy as well as fear and grief.[66] Later accoucheurs and physicians continued to attribute miscarriages to these causes, plus the additional ones of immoderate sexual activity and sudden changes in temperature.[67] Miscarriages were therefore often traced to things the mother had done, or thoughts she had had, rather than to independent and unavoidable acts of the constitution.

As a result, women generally blamed themselves for their "mishaps." In 1784 Lady Sarah Napier announced hers. "*J'eus la betise* to be frightened at the bad Cheshire roads and to miscarry on the first night of my arrival there. Was there ever such a stupid thing?" she asked her correspondent.[68] No doubt it seemed especially stupid to the fecund Lady Sarah, who had married for the second time at the age of thirty-six and went on to produce eight children, the first three born in less than three years of marriage. This miscarriage occurred only three months after the birth of her previous child. It seems more likely that her miscarriage was caused not by her foolish fright, but by the inability of her body to support another pregnancy at so short an interval, especially after such a succession of short-interval pregnancies. Or perhaps the bad Cheshire roads had really been responsible.

Frances, Countess of Morley, blamed her 1811 miscarriage on her own imprudence. During her pregnancy the following year she was "determined if I sh^d be as unlucky now as I was before it shall not be my own fault." But this was not to be. She miscarried again on December 28, 1812, and attributed the mishap to a walk she had taken on December 12 for the purpose of exercise. "I always thought I might walk with impunity," she wrote, "but the experience will teach me to take care of committing excesses even of that innocent kind in the future."[69]

Accoucheurs did their best to help women prevent such mishaps, even when a patient's carelessness was thought to be responsible. Again, the patient's constitution remained the primary criterion for determining the nature of the prophylactic regimen. In patients of weak habits, Denman and Clarke recommended strengthening diets supplemented by claret and other stimulants. On the other hand, patients of plethoric habits had to be phlebotomized and put on a lowering diet. A vegetarian diet might even be recommended.[70] Spells of dizziness were considered to be symptomatic of plethora. Thus in 1821, when Lady Londonderry became hot, dizzy, and nauseous, she was immediately relieved of fourteen ounces of blood to forestall a possible miscarriage. She was then given laudanum and put to bed.[71] The pregnancy proceeded successfully.

During the year 1812 Lady Morley wrote daily to her sister-in-law, describing in minute detail all the discomforts of her pregnancy. Her letters tell of the unsuccessful efforts of her medical attendants to prevent her miscarrying. Because she had miscarried the year before, her doctors wanted her to exercise a great deal of caution in her new pregnancy. At first Lady Morley thought the efforts made to reduce her level of physical activity were ridiculous. But she was willing to take any precaution rather than risk a recurrence of a miscarriage. On November 15, 1812, she wrote that her sedan chair had been "well-aired and new-cushioned" on the occasion of her pregnancy, which had only just begun, her companion, Miss Smith, "administered my food by the means of a spoon, as I don't think it is right to lift my hands to my mouth," she wrote, feeling the whole thing was very silly.

The first mention of real trouble was on December 17, a few days after the fateful walk in the wind. Lady Morley apparently began bleeding slightly. She told her sister-in-law:

> I yesterday took it in my head to have in a *very slight* degree the same freak that you used to have sometimes when you first began to be in a way—as it never happened to me before I began to think as you did that I was going to make an *Erroneous Sofa* but I believe it will go on very well, & Dr. Tomkins says nothing is so common. I think it is rather less today, but I have taken to the horizontal according to orders . . . I shall take great care of my valuable person.

Lady Morley's letters became less jocular and punning as "the freak" continued. On December 20 she reported bathing her back with "gallons of cold water." Tomkins, the local Plymouth practitioner, ordered her off the aperient rhubarb and chamomile she had been taking. A drive in her carriage on December 22, however, seemed to have increased the troublesome symptom. Her patience began wearing thin, both with herself and with her doctors. The day after Christmas she was completely confined to her sofa. "It would really wear out the patience of St. Anthony to keep all day long in this position I am condemned to," she complained, "& I am quite sure if he had had the expectation of a *fausse couche* amongst his trials his constancy would have worn thin." She had also begun using the "ice system," noting that she "only put it on the mons" but nevertheless she had been shivering all day—it was no doubt drafty in December in the largest house in Devonshire. Not having "profound faith" in Tomkins, Lady Morley decided to send for Dr. Hammick (later Sir Stephen), another Plymouth practitioner, "who is said to know a great deal abt. the matter." Hammick arrived, phlebotomized, and on the 28th Lord Morley had to tell his sister the bad news. "The bleeding of Saturday you will have learnt produced no sensible good effect," he wrote. "You will therefore not be surprised to hear this morning early the mishap occurred."[72]

In 1838 the occasion of Lady Augusta Fox's much-wished-for pregnancy raised family tensions to new heights, as everyone became concerned with ensuring a successful delivery. Here, too, efforts ended in miscarriage. Lady Augusta wished to remain in Florence for the duration of her pregnancy, although her husband had had to leave Italy on a diplomatic venture. Soon after, Lady Augusta received a succession of critical letters from her mother-in-law, Lady Holland, who believed from her own experiences and those of her friends that Florence was an unhealthy place for childbearing. She warned Lady Augusta that there were "*duties* as well as pleasures in life," and that one of these was to accompany one's husband. Lady Holland reminded her daughter-in-law that many women traveled during pregnancy without mishap. She demanded that the young woman "give up the *agrémens* of *théatres, compagni,* and *casini,*" which she argued were keeping Lady Augusta in Florence.[73] This time Lady Augusta responded angrily. "It is a hard and cruel thing to receive such letters from you as your last," she wrote her mother-in-law. "Very hard it is in the midst of bodily fear and pain, mental anxiety about Henry and my own relations, & after *2 months and ½* of *solitude* & lying up to be told to give up *'théatres, compagni, casini'* & etc. for *the duty* of pleasing you.!"[74] Nevertheless, alone and wishing to please, Lady Augusta hastily set off from Florence to join her husband and the Hollands in Paris, accompanied by Dr. Playfair. She had only reached Leghorn when she miscarried. In the wake of this cruel disappointment, a stream of epistolary invective ensued in which Lady Augusta blamed her in-laws and they blamed her for the miscarriage. No one blamed Dr. Playfair.

On the whole, complete bed rest, bathing, the application of ice, dietary regulation, and phlebotomy were the main methods accoucheurs had for combatting miscarriage. These recommendations are not very different from those prescribed for infertility. Quiet relaxation, perhaps with the aid of sea air or mineral water, had been advised in those cases. Whether miscarriage or infertility was the problem, accoucheurs turned to constitutional remedies to restore their patients to a healthy condition. It is appropriate, therefore, to evaluate these remedies in the context of all the prenatal care women received.

The lowering system was the regimen most often employed in the prenatal care of aristocratic women. A major component of that system was a spare diet. On the whole, that diet was probably a good one. These women had been eating well all their lives and clearly had the nutritional stores to support multiple pregnancies. The bland qualities of the prescribed diet were valuable in preventing the bladder infections to which pregnant women were particularly susceptible. A lack of salt would limit the retention of fluids and help keep blood pressure down, both of which were (and are) common problems during the latter months of pregnancy. (And, in the absence of any other antihypertensive agents, bloodletting may have been beneficial in some cases.) Prohibition of animal protein, though not necessarily desirable in itself, also eliminated undesirable animal fats. Abstinence from alcohol was wise, as was the emphasis on roughage in the diet. Bathing, another important element of the lowering plan, was likewise salutary. It is important in reducing vaginal infections and hemorrhoids, both of which commonly threatened pregnant women. Cleanliness continues to be an imperative of prenatal care today. Likewise, the emphasis on exercise was similarly conducive to good health and the maintenance of maternal well-being.

We can conclude that the lowering system, on the whole, made a positive contribution to the health and well-being of pregnant women. The debilitating effects of occasional bloodletting, the most negative element in the program (and even that was good for some people), moderated as time went on and did not hamper the progress of a healthy pregnancy. Certainly there was no superior alternative system of prenatal care available at that time.

Though healthy women flourished under this regimen, one suspects that weaker women—those with specific reproductive problems, as well as those debilitated by repeated short-interval pregnancies—did not fare so well. The low diet was particularly unfortunate for these women, probably aggravating the problems. Bloodletting probably weakened many too. The weakening system may therefore be in part responsible for the relationship between multiple forms of reproductive disorder. For instance, of the eleven women who suffered multiple miscarriages, seven were in the group who also suffered delays in initial fertility. These seven women clearly had significant health problems that may have been worsened by the lowering system. Elizabeth Bland Burges, for instance, was married in 1777 at the age of twenty-two, suffered two miscarriages, and died at the age of twenty-four. Her sister, Judith Milbanke, lived to a ripe old age, but had two miscarriages and gave birth to her only child fifteen years after marriage. Charlotte, Countess of Banbury, was perhaps more typical of the unhealthy group because she managed to produce a large family despite her difficulties. Married in 1795 at the age of eighteen, she had her first child somewhat more than two years later. She had two miscarriages and gave birth to eleven children, three of whom died in infancy. She was extremely ill after the births of several babies and died at the age of forty-one, two years after the birth of her last child. Poor

Princess Charlotte did not even live long enough to be classified as having suffered delayed fertility. Married only eighteen months, she had already had two miscarriages before she gave birth to a stillborn son and died a few hours later. Still, these seven women, who lived to an average age of fifty-one years, represent only 14 percent of the group studied. Most of the remaining 86 percent were able to sustain repeated short-interval pregnancies, give birth to healthy children, and live out a long life. The average age of death of these forty-three women was nearly sixty-nine years old. Sixteen women lived past eighty. For this large majority of healthy women, few of the accoucheur's efforts in these areas were truly harmful, and most of his suggestions were probably ineffectual. The psychological benefits of travel, rest, and relaxation, as well as the attention and reassurance of the accoucheur, may even have helped some women.

Although nature was promoted by doctors and hallowed by patients as a beneficial force, naturalness often implied pain and discomfort for women. Morning sickness and vomiting, like sleeplessness and other aches and pains, were viewed as good signs for the expectant mother. (Since there was not much an accoucheur could do to relieve these symptoms anyway, it was a splendid rationalization.) The emphasis on nature was therefore not entirely a happy one. Women were forced into a series of dilemmas. Encouraged to live normally during their pregnancies —and eager to do so—women were then criticized for living in an unhealthy fashion. Encouraged to be active and take exercise, women were blamed for their miscarriages, which were attributed to almost any activity they might have undertaken. Women were likewise blamed, and blamed themselves, for infertility. The husband's role in this situation was not even considered.

For many women, then, especially the younger and less confident ones, the emphasis on naturalness was not necessarily reassuring, wholesome, or consistent. The anxiety level of the pregnant (or would-be pregnant) woman, who was supposed to be responsible (if unwittingly) for so much, was bound to be high. What the accoucheur took with one hand, however, he gave with another. If many of his ideas might have created anxiety or discomfort, he also offered the means to relieve those very anxieties.

Much of the care he offered was socially and psychologically attractive to the aristocracy. The lowering system, designed to offset plethora, involved some minor sacrifices, but these were probably welcomed by the majority of aristocratic women. The elimination from a woman's diet of the most valued food, meat, enabled her to feel that she was contributing significantly to the welfare of her unborn child. Similarly, other aspects of the lowering plan were far more time-consuming than simply swallowing a pill. Bathing and visiting a spa, for instance, were both expensive and highly visible. Such practices, therefore, were not only reassuring to the prospective mother, but more importantly, they also loudly announced to the aristocratic family that substantial efforts were being made on behalf of future progeny. As long as a woman continued healthy, as did the majority, demanding relatives would be satisfied that everything possible was being done to ensure successful reproduction.

Aristocratic prenatal care gave careful consideration to the patient's rank. The leisurely travel recommended by accoucheurs, and gladly adopted by the aristocracy, could only be undertaken by the wealthiest of women, who could afford not only the expenses of the journey itself, but who were also able to spend months away from home, often in the company of their husbands, leaving household duties and children in the care of servants. Lady Holland, as we have seen, traveled in the most aristocratic of fashions, the sedan chair, endangering the lives of eight lower-class men in the process. When Lady Londonderry crossed the Channel during the eighth month of her 1823 pregnancy, she was able to rest in relative comfort inside a carriage that had been fitted up with a bed; she was accompanied by six nurses to tend to her every need.[75] When Lady Morley, who lived less than two miles from the ocean, wished to bathe in seawater, it was brought to her by servants in a hip bath. Thus prenatal care at the hands of a fashionable accoucheur could easily become an instrument of conspicuous consumption.

Prenatal care was a boon to all concerned. Anxious husbands and family members were assured that a prospective mother was doing all she could to ensure reproductive success. Any minor sacrifices or adjustments made under the rubric of the lowering plan would impress relatives with a woman's dedication to the ideals of motherhood. Furthermore, for the individual woman, extensive prenatal care must necessarily have been personally reassuring. Accoucheurs were uniformly soothing and optimistic. Their doctrine of natural care made it all sound quite simple, and patients might easily become more relaxed—and more successful—thanks to their comforting words. Too, the accoucheur was a valuable ally for the pregnant woman, surrounded as she was by conflicting opinions and demanding relatives. As long as childbearing was normal and successful (as it was for an overwhelming majority), the accoucheur, with his notions of naturalness and harmony, could be a useful ally of his patient's desire to lead as normal a life as possible during pregnancy. As long as a patient continued healthy, the accoucheur could justify any of her activities on these grounds. For him, of course, prenatal care was a financial windfall and a potential source of repute. It was also a function that seemed to elevate the accoucheur far above the midwife, whose services had traditionally been limited to the time of delivery.

This happy arrangement, however, could continue only so long as the aristocratic woman fulfilled her function of providing her husband's family with heirs. For most women, this was no problem. But when a woman's success was thwarted, her independence could not so easily be supported. The minor sacrifices of the lowering system, combined with a normal way of life, could no longer satisfy the demands of relatives, who wanted to see greater maternal efforts being made. Although reproductive success was often attributed to the skills of accoucheurs, failure was more often blamed on the hapless patient. The aristocratic woman, who had internalized her family's goals and was full of guilt and anxiety over her failures as a wife, had to turn to her accoucheur in a more serious way. Depending on him to bring her through this crisis, she became increasingly subjected to the accoucheur's interpretation of medical knowledge.

Although great strides had been made in the understanding of childbirth, there was still much to be learned about pregnancy and the mechanics of fertility. Lacking more specific knowledge of these conditions, the accoucheur often had little to offer. Given this situation, he tended to be cautious. Whether his goal was the prevention of miscarriages or the induction of fertility, the accoucheur prescribed rest, inactivity, travel, bathing, and taking mineral waters. These cures were designed to restore the patient's constitution to that state of natural harmony that would make healthy reproduction possible. And by removing aristocratic women from their normal urban social life, these cures helped eliminate part of the artificial environment that accoucheurs believed was responsible for much aristocratic ill health. Accoucheurs would have to wait for birth itself before they could intervene more actively.

The mutual trust and loyalty that developed between accoucheur and patient over the many years of their relationship and the sympathy and patience with which accoucheurs treated their patients were, if self-serving, nonetheless real. If in the twentieth century physicians are criticized for treating the disease and not the patient, one might say with equal truth that in the period 1760 to 1860, accoucheurs treated the patient and not the disease. The results for most women were relatively happy.

CHAPTER V

The Confinement: Childbirth

HYACINTHE, Lady Hatherton, had been married barely ten months when, on October 13, 1813, she began a letter to her brother, Gerald Wellesley, who was in India. "I shall expect your congratulations on the birth of a son and heir which I am daily expecting to make its appearance, & waiting for with the greatest impatience," she began her letter, "tho' there is little probability that my impatience will be satisfied before the end of the month." "However," she continued, "I am come up to Town for the express purpose of making all the necessary preparations & of being in full time ready for the Great Event." She had not long to wait. Two-and-one-half pages later, after detailing how she spent the summer, she wrote:

> Since writing the above I have been seized with every symptom of approaching confinement & every moment I am in terrible pain—I hope I shall be able to finish my letter before I am too bad to continue. This is quite unexpected as you see, for when I began I depended on being well for a fortnight longer—if I could but lye in, just in time to tell you before this is closed what I have produced it will come just apropos but I fear this must be off tomorrow, and as I suppose it will not be over with me *so soon* you will have to wait for future letters to tell you the event—Oh dear—I am in terrible pain.

Lady Hatherton filled several more pages with family news, interrupted only occasionally by expressions of pain. Her handwriting remained virtually undisturbed.

On November 5 she again wrote to her brother:

> Just three weeks ago I was sitting down to write to you under very different circumstances from the present, being already in the pains of labour & full of curiosity at the event . . . I cannot help writing a few words while laying at full length on my sofa, just to tell you that My Baby was born within a very few hours after the writing of my letter. They tell me I had a famous time, tho' in all conscience I thought it bad enough.[1]

Although few women went into labor while writing letters that were saved for posterity, we owe the detailed descriptions of scores of labors to aristocratic letter writers like Lady Hatherton. The quality and sensibility of such letters vary, of course, depending upon who was writing them. Most, however, describe the circumstances under which the mother went into labor, the length of the labor, the names of those present, and the condition of mother and child. More often than not, though, everyone's condition was said simply to be "as well as can be expected." The "perilous effort of maternal exertion," as Lord Castlereagh pompously phrased it,[2] was an event of unique importance to a woman and her family.

The fatal confinement of Princess Charlotte in 1817 is probably the most well-documented childbed scene of the nineteenth century. But although we know so much about that accouchement, it is still a topic that arouses controversy among medical historians. As in the management of pregnancy, accoucheurs of the day based their management of delivery on what they believed to be natural. As a result, Princess Charlotte was allowed to continue in labor for fifty hours because it was thought best to allow nature to take its course. "The tragedy of 1817," according to medical historians Ida Macalpine and Richard Hunter, "became the classic example of the danger to mother and child if instrumental interference were delayed.[3]

But accoucheurs of Charlotte's time believed it was natural for women to endure prolonged suffering.[4] If a woman suffered unduly, most accoucheurs were ready to blame the patient and the effete society in which she lived, rather than the inscrutable wisdom of Providence. Denman cited a familiar theme. "A consideration of their unimpaired constitutions and less exquisite feelings will likewise discover to us the reasons why the lower orders of women have more easy and favorable births, than those who live in affluence," he wrote, "the frame of whose bodies, and the sensibility of whose minds are altered, and often depraved by the indulgence and mistaken opinions of parents, when they are infants and by their own luxury and improper conduct when they are adult."[5] Whether or not Denman was correct, women did suffer in childbirth, poor and rich alike. Some, as in the case of Princess Charlotte, even died. The social niceties of which the aristocracy was so fond might make that reality easier to bear, but they could not disguise it.

Lady Hatherton's story illustrates much that was typical of an aristocratic confinement. The trip to London or "Town," the elaborate preparations, the difficulties in reckoning, Lady Hatherton's perception of childbirth as a "Great Event," her stoic good humor and prolonged recuperation, were all major elements in most aristocratic childbed scenes of her time. But during the century 1760 to 1860 many changes occurred in the aristocratic confinements—childbirth was in the process of deritualization and rationalization. On the one hand, these changes were consonant with the dominant view, among both aristocrats and their accoucheurs, of childbearing as a natural, healthy, and even beneficial process. In its deritualization, childbirth became less rigidly separated from the normal course of a woman's life. This transformation seems to have been related to changing notions about marriage and motherhood. While this may have resulted in less formal confinement for parturient women, it also meant that childbirth was becoming less special. This aspect of change is reflected, during the first half of the century, in the emphasis on nature in medical treatment. The process of rationalization would, however, ultimately push change in a different direction. By the 1820s doctors and patients alike were beginning to seek "improvements" on nature in the form of greater medical intervention. During the entire period 1760 to 1860 the predominant aristocratic perception of childbirth changed, becoming less a public event and more a private one. This is the meaning of much of the deritualization. As with other aspects of the rise of domesticity, changes in aristocratic childbirth customs proceeded hesitantly and unevenly. The model of swift change, completed before the end of the eighteenth century (as posited by Stone and Trumbach, for instance), does not conform to the realities experienced by these fifty women and their families.

Childbirth, anthropoligists have told us, is often carried out as a rite of passage. According to Arnold van Gennep, who first developed this classic theory, rites of passage are social devices designed to incorporate individuals into a new status group. According to later elaborations of van Gennep's early work, such ritual behavior can restore social equilibrium in the face of change.[6] Childbirth normally involves at least one such incorporation: that of the new infant into its social group. But childbirth also involves the change in a woman's social status. Particularly in a first birth, childbirth is the event that turns a woman into a mother. Subsequent births involve some social disequilibrium, too, for inevitably they change her relationship with existing children or make her the mother of an heir if earlier births had not.

Rites of passage generally involve three major phases: separation, transition, and incorporation, These phases normally proceed in gradual, though well-marked stages. The confinement of the English aristocrat conforms to this pattern. The initial phase of separation was exemplified by the process of "going to Town" for the birth. Throughout the century 1760 to 1860 most aristocrats were likely to go to London. This was especially true in the event of a first child, when the birth of an heir was anticipated. By the turn of the century women bearing second or later children would begin to consider staying in the country for their births, though a majority still went to London.

That "going to Town" functioned as a ritual of separation can be seen in three major ways: it was done with much public fuss; it involved a considerable amount of disruption of domestic space; and it was done quite at the last minute, thus emphasizing the relationship between the spatial movement and the changes in status wrought by childbirth,[7] however inconvenient this may have been for the family most nearly concerned. Indeed, as shall be seen at the recovery or incorporation stage of the confinement, households that were set up hastily for a long-awaited confinement were just as hastily dismantled once the recovery was ritually completed. The standard English aristocratic confinement of this century is in fact quite similar—in a rather sophisticated and ostentatious form—to the "hut-building" typical of birth rituals in many primitive societies.[8]

"Going to Town" for a confinement was indeed consistent with the notion of childbirth as a distinctive public event. The newspapers of the time so regarded aristocratic births, and an entry into London—complete with liveried servants and a coat of arms emblazoned on the coach—was something akin to a royal progress. "Lord and Lady Donegall passed by in their Chaise," Lady Mary Coke reported in 1769, "the newspapers say she is to come to Town to lie inn."[9] The publicity of a London lying-in was reinforced by the custom of placing straw on the street outside the home of a parturient woman. Though the rationale for this custom might well be in making the streets quieter, the whole scene is rather awkwardly reminiscent of the manger. But in making the street quieter, this strange custom would nevertheless increase a woman's degree of seclusion and separation from the "normal" world. The laying of straw, of course, most notably provided visible public testimony that a "Great Event" had taken place. In addition, door knockers were tied up with colored ribbons indicating the sex of the newborn, a measure that would also have muffled noise. These customs were referred to repeatedly in aristocratic correspondence of the 1760s, 1770s, and 1780s, though not after 1789, which is perhaps symptomatic of the decline in ritual beginning to occur after that date.[10]

Also typical of the public ritual that attended the London confinement was the large number of aristocratic visitors who paid courtesy calls during a lying-in. We may note, for instance, the rather ritualistic visit the Duchess of Grafton made to her daughter's lying-in room in 1805. Lady Mary Coke devoted much time to "making inquiries" at the homes of elegant parturients, many of whom she scarcely knew. Gradually, however, these formal visits came to be regarded as something of a nuisance and an imposition in a personal family matter. The Earl of Banbury, for instance, was quite hostile to the publicity of his wife's London confinement in 1804:

> It is a material difference laying in, in Town or in the country, as to what Regards being more at one's Pace in seeing People. Our numerous connections find much work for Civility, Bowing-Bowing, Sister by affinity, Law and Connection, Brother-by-Age, Hospitality and Marriage. Lord Help us as where will it all end our mighty etceteras of Blood and Affinity.[11]

Similarly, in 1831 Lady Dover believed the formal visits required at a London lying-in were an imposition on her sister Blanche, Lady Burlington. But the child born was someday to be Duke of Devonshire: his birth, therefore, attracted considerable public attention. "Blanche has made great progress during the last day or two," Lady Dover wrote. "They still wish, however, to keep her very quiet and I am a little afraid of her seeing too many people, as there are a good many of his relations and all the boys [her younger brothers or his?] who think they have a right to see her."[12]

Country confinements, as Lord Banbury suggested, did not

eliminate the presence of the "mighty etceteras," but they drastically changed the nature of their visits. These would no longer be dictated by etiquette, but by personal preference. By lying-in in the country, women and their husbands could choose who would come to stay with them. A decision to be confined in the country was often one that engendered considerable conflict with the "mighty-etceteras" themselves, who often resented being left out.[13] They perhaps understood that women who opted for country confinements were choosing private emotional satisfaction over the performance of their public duty. And indeed, even by 1860 going to town remained the normative aristocratic experience, though one that was increasingly resented or challenged.

The last few weeks of pregnancy were usually occupied in effecting the change in residence involved in going to town. Many peers' families, of course, maintained homes in London which would be opened for the confinement. Other families rented dwellings specifically for the occasion. These housing arrangements might be made at the last moment. This is consistent with the notion of going to town as an act of ritual separation—separating the period of birth, as it were, from what had gone before. Lord Worcester wrote from London lodgings that he and his wife were unable to find a house on reasonable terms for the confinement that was expected in three weeks.[14] Their own house was unsuitable because it was being painted. Lady Elizabeth Drummond also had problems in being housed for the birth of her first child in 1823. Her problems may have been compounded by her desire to remain in Hampshire as long as possible and to leave the arrangements to others. On January 5 her mother-in-law wrote that they could have "Miss Tate's House in Grosvenor Place" for the period of the birth, expected in March, to the end of the London social season. This plan must have fallen through, because a month later Lady Elizabeth's husband was still trying to secure a house, believing that they might have "Mrs. J.D.'s house if they liked it."[15] She would avoid these problems in her six subsequent births, which would take place at Cadland Manor, Hampshire. In 1822 Lady Londonderry and her husband rented the Duke of St. Albans' house on St. James Square at £500 a month, which even she admitted was "an immense rent."[16]

Perhaps the record for last-minute arrangements was set by Harriet, Duchess of Sutherland, in 1827. "She was taken ill early on Tuesday at Roehampton," her surburban home on London's South Bank; "they got to London soon after ten and in less than half an hour the child was born, a little before the time."[17] Such apparently ill-timed and unnecessary haste is particularly indicative of the ritualistic nature of the move to London.

Other women made very long and occasionally risky journeys at the end of their pregnancies in order to give birth in town. Lady Londonderry left her home in County Durham during the first week in March for the long trek to London, where she gave birth on April 15. Another pregnancy commenced in Vienna, but she crossed the Channel in her eighth month so that her child child could be born in London.[18]

The political need for a birth to take place publicly in London can be seen in the extreme case of the birth of Queen Victoria. Her parents, the Duke and Duchess of Kent, had been residing in Germany for thrift's sake when the Duchess became pregnant. The Duchess decided to make the journey of over four hundred miles so that her child, the potential heir to the British throne, might be born in London. She and her party, including an obstetrician named Madame Siebold, left Amorbach on March 28, 1819, and reached England on April 14. The future Queen Victoria was born exactly one month later.[19]

Even women already housed in London well before the confinement rearranged the rooms and furniture immediately prior to the birth. This was done so that the mother would have two rooms for her accouchement. Ideally these would be interconnected. One room, the inner, would be the actual location of the lying-in bed. The outer room would provide a gathering place for friends and relatives, who could selectively enter the inner sanctum. Often sleeping accommodations within the house also had to be found for the doctor and other medical attendants, who stayed over in anticipation of the birth. Lady Morley wrote the day before she gave birth to her first child that "the house is in great commotion with moving beds and changing apartments."[20] The entire household might well be upset in order to rearrange the rooms. Lord Verulam wrote in 1822 that his sons liked the "distribution of their Rooms which has been altered in consequence of Lady V.'s confinement." Two years later he noted that his sisters had come to help his wife in "setting her house in order" for the confinement that occurred about a week later.[21] Lady Dover's husband had only recently bought Melbourne House when she was confined but she turned everyone out of the rooms into which they had only recently moved, taking over the study and the tutor's bedroom for her confinement.[22]

English aristocrats did not, as is commonly thought, give birth in the ancestral bed where marriages were consummated and great lives came to quiet ends. The four-poster, where these events were supposed to have taken place, remained in the bedroom where it belonged. Into the newly arranged lying-in chamber was brought a fairly light weight portable folding bed, especially designed for the occasion. It was constructed to make linen changes easier and to keep the patient easily accessible to the doctor. Such beds were often passed along to women of the same family, since even in this group no one woman could keep her bed in constant use. Yet this sharing of beds was financially unnecessary and was often inconvenient. The practice may well have been part of the female bonding experience of childbirth. Lady Morley and her sister-in-law, Mrs. Villiers, shared a bed. Lady Morley wrote that her "Cot" had mistakenly been sent to Saltram, but as she planned to bring it to London for her expected confinement in 1813, she suggested sending it early so that Mrs. Villiers might make use of it first.[23] The Duke of

Sutherland described the sudden labor of his daughter Constance, Lady Grosvenor, which inconvenienced her sister, the Duchess of Argyll.

> Grosvenor and Constance had been to a play last night and went to bed all well and not the bed in which she intended to have the ceremony conducted. The Argylls were still in possession of this and were meaning to move away today to make things secure. Early this morning however they (the Argylls) were driven out of it and took refuge in their children's rooms—at least *he* did in one of the cribs, while the ladies were all in attendance on Constance who had been moved from her temporary place of rest into Elizabeth's room to act the same part Elizabeth did six weeks ago.[24]

The disruption caused by the rearrangement of furniture and rooms immediately prior to the birth seems to have represented a continuation of that process of separation from normal life that the move to London began. The domestic commotion reinforced the notion that childbirth was a "ceremony," as the Duke of Sutherland obligingly phrased it. The introduction of the portable bed ruptured the symbolic connection between sexual intercourse and birth which would have been more evident had the marriage bed been used for both purposes. Birth was thus cleansed of its sexual connotations and could therefore serve more effectively as a source of spiritual transformation. From both an anthropological and a historical perspective the most interesting aspect of the separation ritual is the involvement of the entire family. The confinement was not a solitary one, but one that involved the children and husband. The mother was only somewhat more separated, though not isolated, in her inner chamber.

Normally, the necessary preparations for the confinement would have been made far enough in advance so that the lying-in chambers were ready for the woman and her attendants. The entourage included not only the accoucheur, but also the monthly nurse and, when desired, a wet nurse. In the *Book of Household Management,* Isabella Beeton distinguished carefully between the last two. The wet nurse had only the function of breast-feeding the baby, while the monthly nurse, who was expected to attend for a month, attended the mother and assisted the accoucheur. According to Mrs. Beeton, the monthly nurse was to follow the orders of the doctor, administering medicine when he so prescribed and helping in household preparations for the birth. The monthly nurse was also supposed to be capable of delivering the baby in case the doctor failed to arrive in time.[25] She was therefore someone on whom both the doctor and the mother depended heavily. In keeping with the professionalization of obstetrics—at every level—which began at this time, the British Lying-in Hospital began a training program for monthly nurses in 1826. A similar one was established in Queen Charlotte's Lying-in Hospital in 1851.[26]

The monthly nurse tried to arrive at least several days before the mother's due date. She was usually in the house before the accoucheur arrived. Many accoucheurs and monthly nurses seemed to form a team, which saved a mother from the necessity of seeking out a nurse on her own. This could sometimes prove difficult for, as Mrs. Beeton observed, the best nurses had to be engaged months in advance, or a woman might find herself caught short. A month before her seventh confinement Lady Elizabeth Drummond had still not secured a monthly nurse. While she awaited the birth at their Hampshire seat, her husband, who was in London, attempted to find an appropriate nurse. His letter provides some insight into the selection process. "It is unlucky Mrs. Peyton being engaged," he wrote his wife,

> but Hedges mother-in-law had recommended a very respectable and nice woman who has been educated in a hospital and quite understands her business and has a fortnight at liberty. I am going to see her this evening and if I like her appearance and manners I shall send her down at once as at any rate you must have an attendant of this sort.[27]

Fashion as well as expertise entered into the aristocratic choice of a nurse, just as it did in the choice of an accoucheur. Lady Mary Bagot insisted on having the same monthly nurse as her "idol," Lady Cowper. According to the young Lady Harriet Cavendish, Lady Mary Bagot "raves about Lady Cowper and will have patterns of everything she wears and the young coxcomb is to wear," as well as the same attendants. Lady Mary sent for the lying-in nurse seven months before she expected to be confined of her first child to ensure the engagement of the woman's services.[28]

The majority of these nurses are veiled in the obscurity that history generally accords the humble. A Mrs. Griffiths evidently was the leading monthly nurse for many years. She worked with Croft, but her career lasted longer than his did. Although she was present at Princess Charlotte's fatal confinement, Mrs. Griffiths was apparently not considered responsible enough to be in the line of criticism. Her career seems to have suffered in no way from that event. The first mention of Mrs. Griffiths is in 1810, when she attended Harriet, Lady Granville, in her first confinement. She was also in attendance at Woburn Abbey before going to Claremont in 1817 to attend Princess Charlotte. In 1830 Mrs. Griffiths attended Harriet, Duchess of Sutherland, who was Lady Granville's niece. The following year she served the Duchess's sister, Blanche, Lady Burlington.[29] Mrs. Griffiths was regarded very affectionately by her aristocratic charges who called her "the Griff." After her fifth confinement in 1830, the Duchess of Sutherland wrote that she felt "quite low and helpless at parting with Griff yesterday." She added, "one does not feel the care and responsibility of another child till she is gone."[30] Gradually the aging Griff retired. During the Duchess of Sutherland's sixth confinement in 1832, the Griff was still nominally in attendance, but a new nurse, Mrs. Cooper, had been brought in to assist her. Lady Morpeth, the Duchess's mother, had reservations about the new nurse who was apparently of a less humble demeanor than Mrs. Griffiths. Mrs.

Cooper "looks too smart, with long gold earrings," reported the Duchess's sister, Lady Dover, who was in town for her sister's confinement.[31]

The acquisition of a monthly nurse, like the other arrangements made in preparation for the confinement, was dependent on the "reckoning," as the ladies termed it, of the day of delivery. Serious miscalculations in either direction produced a great deal of anxiety and disrupted the plans of the entire family. If Lady Hatherton was prepared for her early labor, many women were not.

Even the most carefully reckoned labors often took women by surprise. In fact, a fairly large number of women went into labor while away from home, or shortly upon returning home from a social engagement. As we have seen, Lady Constance Grosvenor (later Duchess of Westminster) went to a play a short time before going into labor. In 1810 Lady Verulam dined at Lady Aboyne's, stayed the evening, went home, and went into labor at 4:00 A.M. In 1822 Lady Verulam began labor while entertaining a large party at her home, all of whom stayed until well after the child's birth. Harriet, Duchess of Sutherland, was expecting her third child in 1827 and, recorded her sister, she had felt unwell the whole day, but so slightly that they did "not even put off the Mount Charles' for dinner." She was "brought to bed" at half past ten.[32]

Of course, when the reckoning was even further off, matters became much more inconvenient, because the necessary preparations might not have been made. Catherine Wellesley-Pole, whose husband became the fourth Earl of Mornington, was surprised by a premature labor in 1813 at her country seat. She had planned to go to town for the birth and was completely unprepared. Her husband wrote his mother: "Mrs. Wellesley's confinement at Wanstead was quite unexpected and frightened me to death. Her son was brought into the world without there having been any cloathes been prepared for him, so that I understand he was wrapped upon the housekeeper's flannel Petticoat."³³ Georgiana, Lady Morpeth, planned to be with her sister during Lady Granville's 1812 accouchement in Staffordshire. When she got there, however, she found it was all over. Lady Cecilia Ridley wrote on July 24, 1844, that she did not expect to be delivered until the end of September, "but really I do feel so enormous now that I don't know what I shall do if I go on increasing all that time." She gave birth to twins only three days later. Lady Frances Cole was philosophical about the unexpected birth of her daughter Fanny. "As she appears quite *compleat* I supose she knew better than me & I am heartily glad to have got rid of her!" she wrote.³⁴

Postmature babies also presented problems, giving everyone involved a long time to become anxious. Lady Sarah Napier, for instance, was supposed to give birth during the beginning of July 1782. By August 8, still undelivered, she wrote, "I have been three weeks in hourly expectation of being confined," she told her sister, "having been very uneasy and very cross as you may guess at not being over this tiresome business." Her sister, too, was growing impatient and wished that Lady Sarah "would not be so tedious on a job of so little amusement."³⁵ Lady Caroline Capel, who had already given birth to twelve children, was more sanguine about her delayed delivery at the age of forty-two. Still, it was June 1815 and she and her large family were living outside Brussels. On the very day of the Battle of Waterloo, she wrote, "In spite of all I am perfectly well, my spirits are good, you know I never come a moment before my time. In some constitutions nothing will affect this; two or three days, at the utmost must decide whether it is safe to remain here, and I shall have ample time, if necessary, to reach a place of security and settle myself there before my confinement."³⁶ The baby was not born until early July.

Sometimes a baby arrived so late that the time of conception must have been seriously miscalculated. This could be profoundly inconvenient and unnerving. Lady Londonderry expected her first child in January 1821 in Vienna, where her husband served as British ambassador. He asked and received the government's permission to leave an international conference at Laibach, Germany, soon after it had started, to be home with Fanny in January since the child was expected daily.[37] In fact, it did not arrive until April. Similarly, in 1835 Susan, Lady Rivers, expected her second child in February. She did not give birth until May 28. This upset the course of family life, since she had planned to visit her parents, the Granvilles, in May, well after the baby was supposed to have been born and herself recovered. All through February she was in daily expectation of going into labor. On March 4 she wrote that it seemed to be "so funny to be in March and not confined." Life became increasingly confusing. "My size, the motion of the child, etc., put that [delivery in June] out of the question, & therefore we have no sort of guide in our calculations, I cannot feel sure of a single day," she told her mother. In early April her doctor, Boutflower, was already sleeping in the house "as it may come on at any time."[38] It is not clear whether he stayed at Mistley Hall with the Riverses until the actual delivery.

Both Lady Londonderry and Lady Rivers gave birth four months after they had expected to. They obviously had not become pregnant as early as they believed; we can conclude that their children were actually conceived when they believed themselves to be four months pregnant. This is perhaps the strongest possible evidence of the continuation of sexual activity during pregnancy. Lady Rivers, who had had her first child in March 1834 and expected the second in February 1835, apparently never resumed menstruation after the first birth and so assumed she had become pregnant immediately. Both she and Lady Londonderry were relatively inexperienced mothers. Inexperience, however, cannot extenuate the errors of the doctors involved. Yet Lady Rivers recorded that on February 20 Boutflower "declared he cannot guess when I shall be confined as my long delay has defeated his calculations."[39]

Most of these highly privileged women seem to have been psychologically, as well as physically, hardy. They were prepared to endure pain and fatigue, and if they were not always cheerful about their situation, they were, like Lady Caroline Capel, stoical and even able to respond with humor. In 1843, for instance, a few minutes after giving birth to her second child, Lady Cecilia Ridley said, "it was really nothing," though she did not "care to have one every week."[40] There were women who, like Lady Holland, maximized the misery of childbearing. But she had endured three miscarriages, two of which occurred in Spain during the Peninsular Wars. She also tended to have very prolonged labors. In 1799 she was "safely delivered of a nice little boy" after "6 days of lingering labor."[41] She was furious on one occasion when a male guest at Holland House denied that childbirth was painful at all.[42] In so doing, Palmer implicitly denied that women were heroic creatures possessing fortitude and endurance. If childbirth pain did not exist, women were merely juvenile attention-getters who complained without cause.

Later generations of women, however, often seemed to minimize the discomfort of pregnancy and the agony of birth. Lady Bessborough was astonished at how both her daughters-in-law comported themselves during pregnancy. Lady Duncannon, she said, was "the only one disposed not to make a fuss if they would leave her to her own judgment and discretion about it."[43] Similarly Lady Charlotte Guest prided herself on expeditious deliveries that minimized their inconvenience to her. According to her diary she enjoyed surprising her husband with these quick births. In 1843, on the occasion of the birth of her eighth child, she sent her husband and son off to lunch without telling them she was in labor.

> However I went to bed as soon as they had left me, and in a very few minutes Merthyr came up again to see why I had not followed them down. I tranquillized him as well as I could and he again went out of the room, but only to be recalled almost immediately to see the eighth child to which, thank, I had given birth to with as little

pain as I suppose it is possible to suffer on such occasions.... She was born at a quarter past four p.m. being only three quarters of an hour from the moment of my having finished writing and dated my journal.[44]

But the general level of fortitude in this group of fifty women is perhaps even better exemplified by those who, though members of this privileged class, gave birth in unusually stressful circumstances. They, too, were able to carry through to a successful delivery. Lady Frances Cole and Lady Elizabeth Foster were two of these.

Lady Frances Cole lived on the island of Mauritius, off the coast of East Africa, for several years during her husband's term as governor. At the age of forty she gave birth to her sixth child during a fierce hurricane that began on April 9, 1824. Her husband wrote back to their family in England that

> The gale commenced on the morning Fanny was taken ill & lasted with increased violence until the 12th inclusive—I was obliged to remove the children downstairs . . . the rain . . . literally poured into Fanny's bed room & I was in considerable alarm that I should have had to remove her to another room, but fortunately it did not reach her bed. . . . She behaved as she always had done on every occasion with great self-possession & you may well suppose that if she had no anxiety for herself she felt a good deal for the safety of the brats.[45]

Lady Elizabeth Foster's situation was equally far removed from that of the normal fashionable English lying-in. Lady Elizabeth's pregnancy in 1785, by the Duke of Devonshire, was illegitimate. The Duchess of Devonshire was her best friend. Lady Elizabeth necessarily went to great efforts to conceal both the pregnancy and the birth. Her worldly-wise brother, Lord Hervey, brought her to a suitably obscure place for her confinement—in southern Italy—a far cry from the usual scene of the aristocratic birth. She disguised herself as the wife of her own servant and the paramour of her own brother, both of whom accompanied her to the home of the so-called Archi-prêtre des Amoureux, where Lady Elizabeth was destined to give birth:

> Imagine a little staircase, dark and dirty, leading to the apartments of these people. The family consisted of the Archi-prêtre des Amoureux; his woman-servant, a course, ugly, and filthy creature; the doctor (his brother) and his wife—the doctor an honest man, the wife everything that one can imagine of wicked, vulgar, and horrible; two young girls, pretty enough but weeping all day; a married elder sister—who was the best of the lot; the nurse who was to take care of my child; and some babies which cried from morning till night—there you have the family of the respectable *archi-prêtre,* who had a sort of seraglio about him.

After a week, Lord Hervey had to leave, although Lady Elizabeth was still undelivered. His departure increased her misery, she wrote in her diary, and "I prayed to God with bitter tears to end my sufferings." Finally, after fifteen more days of anxious waiting, "just as I was thinking of looking for another refuge," she wrote, "on August 16 at 9 o'clock in the morning, after strong but short pains, I gave birth to a daughter . . . weak as I was, I took her into the bed and tended her myself, seeing the ignorance of those about me."[46]

During the more typical at-home labor, where the stresses were not usually as great as those faced by Lady Frances and Lady Elizabeth, the psychological atmosphere was likely to have been more reassuring and presumably more conducive to a favorable birth. The presence of family members created an emotionally sympathetic atmosphere. The birth of the Duchess of Devonshire's long-awaited first child in 1783 was such an occasion. She was attended by her husband (nicknamed Canis) and his sister, the Duchess of Portland, her own mother Lady Spencer, and her maid Dennis. "I was laid on a couch in the middle of the room," the Duchess of Devonshire recalled in a letter, curiously enough, to her husband's mistress Lady Elizabeth Foster:

My mother and Dennis supported me—Canis was at the door and the Duchess of Portland sometimes bending on me and screaming with me and sometimes running to the end of the room and to him. I thought the pain I suffered was so great from being new to me—but I find since I had a very bad time. Towards the end some symptoms made me think the child was dead—I s^d so and Dr. Denman only s^d there is no reason to think so but we must submit to Providence. I had then no doubt and by watching my mother's eyes . . . I saw she thought it dead, which they all did except Denman who dared not to say too much—when it came into the world I s^d only let it be alive—the little child seemed to move as it lay by me but I was not sure when all at once it cry'd. Oh God! I cry'd and was quite Hysterical. The Duchess and my Mother was overcome and they cry'd & all kissed me.[47]

Later generations of men would become more physically and emotionally involved with the births of their children than had been the phlegmatic Duke of Devonshire. Moreover, by 1830 it seems to have become perfectly acceptable for male relatives other than the husband to be present—at least in the outer room of the lying-in chamber. We do not mean the austere presence of a forbidding father-in-law, but rather the loving presence of someone who cared deeply for the welfare of the woman and her child. Lord Gower, who was then a bachelor, came to stay at Tixall for the Staffordshire birth of his uncle's second child (though probably Gower was not present in the lying-in chamber itself) and had become an experienced witness at these events when his wife's sister was confined in 1831. "Lord Gower arrived towards the end," a third sister wrote a fourth "and was very near being quite overcome, as he always is with Harriet, and I believe thought us rather unfeeling because we were not so." Husbands actually stayed at their wife's bedside. The twenty-three-year-old new father on that occasion, William, the Earl of Burlington, was "very *rayonnant* tho' rather nervous, which showed itself by laughing in the most hearty manner when he first came out of her room." He had been with his young wife "all the time." Also present, though like Lady Burlington's sisters, in the outer chamber, was her teenaged bachelor brother. "Morpeth was very much in the room (next to it) with us, which was perhaps not quite right. He received I imagine many new lights," Lady Dover wrote. Although the family thought Morpeth's presence, "not quite right," they seem to have been more amused than outraged.[48]

The change to a more domesticated childbirth scene, in which male and female relatives alike might be present, is particularly clear in the cases of royal births. When Caroline, Princess of Wales, gave birth to Princess Charlotte in 1796, her sense of personal isolation must have been tremendous. She had been married less than a year to a man who notoriously despised her; she spoke little English and was under the care of Dr. Underwood, the accoucheur of her husband's mistress, Lady Melbourne. Even her wet nurse had been chosen for her by her mother-in-law. The birth took place at Carlton House, the Prince's grand residence in town. Present at the birth were the officers of state, including the Archbishop of Canterbury and three noblemen who attended "at the special invitation of the Prince." No one seems to have been there on Caroline's behalf. When her daughter Charlotte gave birth in 1817, the scene was quite different. She had chosen Richard Croft to be her accoucheur. This was considered a triumph for the Whigs. The Tories, including her father the Prince Regent, had hoped she would be under Knighton's care.[49] The confinement took place at Claremont, the country home where she and Prince Leopold had lived their short married life. Leopold himself was present for the entire duration of her prolonged and ultimately fatal ordeal. The royal family—particularly Charlotte's father the Prince Regent and her grandmother Queen Charlotte, an experienced mother—were severely criticized, both publicly and privately, for their failure to be with Charlotte during her confinement.[50] By 1817 apparently aristocrats expected women to be attended by members of their families when they gave birth. Yet it is well known that when Queen Victoria gave birth in 1840 to her first child, she wanted no one there but Locock, Prince Albert, and a maid. This is usually considered symptomatic of the queen's prudery, but Locock did not so interpret her wishes. "As to delicacy," he said, "she would not care one single straw if the whole world was present."[51] In fact, Queen Victoria simply wanted only the company of those she cared for—and she had no one but Albert. Lacking a father or siblings, she had only a mother toward whom she was extremely hostile. Albert behaved at the birth as any impeccably domesticated aristocratic father of his time would have. "The Prince was present at Queen Victoria's side almost all the time," according to one account, "there remaining to lift and carry and comfort and help, to read and sing and summarize dispatches."[52] The officers of state were there too—in the outer chamber, from whence they could both see and hear the Queen—but their presence clearly did not have a chilling effect on this cozy scene. Present too, of course, were Locock and the monthly nurse, Mrs. Lilley, both of whom would be with Victoria at all nine confinements.

The accoucheur and monthly nurse were also likely to be supportive emotional presences. As we have seen, the accoucheur was more likely to be a figure of reassurance than of intimidation. His authority emanated from the trust his patients had in him. In fact, during the first stage of labor the responsibilities of an accoucheur were largely psychological: there was little he could—or would—do. During the second and third stages, accoucheurs had the expertise to intervene more effectively, but until about 1820 they were normally reluctant to do so. Medical orthodoxy until that time relied on the principle of trusting in nature to see a woman through her delivery. When doctors began at about that time to intervene more effectively, they did so as much at the behest of their suffering patients as in their own self-interest. Furthermore, Princess Charlotte's death in childbirth after a heroic fifty-hour labor made it evident to even the archest conservative that there were occasions when nature was inadequate. Death, after all, had been perfectly natural in her case. It is appropriate, therefore at this point to look at the medical management of childbirth which, according to some historians, was the field on which the battle of the sexes was played in the nineteenth century.

Sometimes after a woman went into labor, the accoucheur was called, either from an adjoining room where he was staying or from his own home, to attend her. Just as women were relatively free of restraint during pregnancy, so too during labor. They were not expected to take to their beds the moment labor came on. In fact, doctors generally recommended the opposite approach. Denman wrote that putting women to bed raised the expectation of a speedy delivery, which might easily prove disappointing. "It will always be found more comfortable and useful" he advised, "to leave the patient to her own choice in these matters and her inclination will be her best guide. . . . The patient will often find relief, either by walking or standing, pursuing some amusement, or choosing that position which she herself prefers, because she will instinctively seek that which is proper."[53] Other doctors of the time were in agreement.[54] It seems likely that patients preferred accoucheurs who allowed them to go their own way, in this as in so much.

Through internal examinations, in which the extent of cervical dilatation was ascertained, accoucheurs could estimate the progress of the labor, but they could not accurately predict the duration of the labor. The patient nevertheless was very eager to know how long her pain might continue. Charles Mansfield Clarke considered this an important problem in dealing with his patients. He told his medical students how to conduct the management of the patient in labor:

> When you introduce yourself to your patient, just go in to her in the same manner as if, she was not in labor, & do not, all at once, begin talking of labour, such as enquiring into present symptoms

of labour, but make any common remark in the day & etc. until a pain or two comes on when you wish to make an examination. . . . Never on any account seem tired: As you cannot in any case tell the length of the labour so never give a prognostic: but if after making as many evasions as you can without success, tell you cannot possibly say the time.[55]

Accoucheurs necessarily devoted many of their efforts to increasing the psychological comfort of the patient. "It behoves every Practitioner," Thynne told his students, "to soothe his Patient, with the hopes of her ultimately doing well." Patience and perserverance," he added, "are very necessary qualifications in an accoucheur."[56] Although the accoucheur might leave the patient's bedside from time to time, she was never left completely alone. The nurse was always there: so, too, were her husband and possibly some of her friends and relatives, particularly her mother and mother-in-law.

The accoucheurs all emphasized that a healthy attitude on the part of the patient, which they did their utmost to promote, was essential in procuring a satisfactory labor and delivery. Of course, the accoucheur often saw himself as the fount from which courage flowed; nevertheless, the prospective mother was expected to contribute through her own efforts to a successful delivery. It had been observed, Denman wrote, that

> a cheerful flow of the spirits, which arises from the hope of a happy event, inspires women with an activity and resolution which are extremely useful and favorable in that situation. In the time of a labour proceeding very slowly or irregularly, doubts and fears in the mind of the patient have an evident and great influence upon the pains. When these are removed, and her resolution confirmed, she will go on with courage and effects will be produced, which would have been impossible if she had remained in a state of depression.[57]

The progress of a labor, according to Denman, was "often retarded by such passions as depress the spirits; as on the contrary, it is accelerated by cheerfulness, by resolution, and a certain preparation of the mind for enduring pain and fatigue."[58]

A skilled accoucheur might be of some technical value, even during an uncomplicated delivery. There were many important tasks in the supervision and management of birth. Accoucheurs of this century were particularly concerned with preventing laceration of the perineum by providing sufficient lubrication and manual support to the area. Accoucheurs also emphasized the need to evacuate the patient's bowels and bladder during labor to prevent them from posing obstacles to the passage of the child and discomfort to the mother. During prolonged labors it was usually necessary to catheterize the patient.[59] Charles Mansfield Clarke told his students that it was best to keep the patient on a very light diet during labor. Bread and barley water were good sources of nutrition, he told them, while wisely recommending that laboring women avoid rich foods like oysters.[60]

Buchan asserted in *Domestic Medicine* that bloodletting was an excellent means of reducing the pain of labor by weakening the patient as a whole. Bloodletting during labor, up to fifty ounces, he believed would decrease the rigidity of the soft parts and facilitate dilitation.[61] Denman, however, believed that it was improper to phlebotomize during labor. As a preferable method for treating fevers that developed during parturition, Denman recommended the administration of cool drinks, keeping the lying-in chamber cool and airy, and giving the patient an emollient enema.[62] These suggestions were far safer than bloodletting, and the aristocratic accoucheurs of whom we have spoken were likely to have followed Denman's plan, since he was usually their authority in the management of birth. This may well be another facet of obstetric care in which the aristocracy received better treatment than did much of the rest of the population.

Once the baby's head began pressing upon the perineum—

the end of the first stage of labor—the patient took to her bed in preparation for delivery. According to Clarke, the woman was placed on the side of the bed, so that after delivery she could be moved to the bed's dry center. "The dress of the woman," Clarke recommended, "should be a shift tucked up under the arms with a short petticoat placed about the hips which is to be removed after labour and the dry shift drawn down."[63] Thus both comfort and modesty were protected.

The position assumed for delivery—as for the vaginal examination—was the Sims position (as it is now termed), in which the patient lay on her left side, with her back toward the edge of the bed, and her knees bent and drawn up to the abdomen.[64] Denman regarded the position as one that was "by far the most convenient as well as decent."[65] The accoucheurs apparently rigidly enforced this posture, although they were aware that others were possible. In 1857 Dr. Edward Rigby of St. Thomas' Hospital and the General Lying-in Hospital reported on a bizarre set of experiments designed to determine what was the most "natural" position for delivery, and concluded happily that the Sims position was.[66] The inflexibility of accoucheurs in their preference for this position can also be seen in some correspondence that appeared in the London Medical Gazette in 1838. One Henry Coles wanted to know, innocently enough, why the right side was not as advantageous as the left. The reply, by a Dr. McIvor of Harley Street, emphasized that the left side was preferable for making examinations and using instruments "without the patient seeing either the practitioner or what he is about, which is of the greatest consequence." He continued, "it is the position of all others in which a woman can be delivered in accordance with that high and sensitive feeling of delicacy which at all times, and more particularly at this, pervades the female breast." So although accoucheurs believed the Sims position to be a technically superior one, they also preferred it because the accoucheur and patient did not have to look at each other, enabling the mother to "save face" in what was assumed to be an embarrassing situation. "Certainly no one is justified in exposing the patient," McIvor continued, "and *Still less in looking,* and then apologising by saying she was not conscious, just as if it was possible, which I maintain it is not, for the accoucheur to tell whether the patient was or was not conscious of being exposed. Women do not make known all the wounds they receive on those occasions from imprudence."[67]

The accoucheurs who in the early years of the eighteenth century had superseded the midwives, had done so in large measure through their ability to intervene with instruments during difficult labors. By 1760, however, successful accoucheurs were one or more generations removed from the pioneering efforts of men like Manningham and the Chamberlens, and were now in a position to evaluate the work of their predecessors.[68] The major point on which they criticized their professional forefathers was that they had been, in their eagerness to prove themselves indispensable, overly zealous in their use of the forceps. Caution about the use of forceps was in keeping with the later generation's philosophic predilection for nature. As Andrew Thynne told his medical students in 1807, it was best during labor to "give Nature a fair trial." He believed that "the practice of Midwifery 50 or 60 years ago was too instrumental," and that this had "brought the profession into disrepute."[69] Denman was one of the leaders in the conservative movement in midwifery and had, through his teaching and writing, a great deal of influence on the younger generation of accoucheurs. "It may be doubted whether any part of medicine has been more improved within the last sixty or seventy years than the practice of midwifery," Denman wrote in 1815, the last year of his life, "by returning, as it were from too much artifice to the simplicity of nature" and "by relying on the general efficacy of the powers of the constitution in overcoming the difficulties which occur in childbirth."[70]

In prolonged labors, Denman insisted that the accoucheur wait for contractions to cease entirely for six hours, with the fetus low in the pelvis, before using forceps to deliver. This came to be known as Denman's law. According to one medical historian, the opposition of Denman and such colleagues as William Osborne and William Hunter practically obliterated the use of forceps in England during the last half of the eighteenth century and the early decades of the nineteenth century.[71] Later generations of accoucheurs—beginning perhaps as early as 1817 with the death of Princess Charlotte—would reevaluate the conservatism of the accoucheurs who had practiced at the turn of the century.

Accoucheurs like Denman were able to maintain a strict conservatism in the use of instruments because they did not believe that a prolonged labor was in itself dangerous. "After the completion of a slow or lingering labour," Denman wrote, "patients usually recover better than after those which are quick."[72] Thynne echoed this belief when he told his medical students that "it does not follow" that a lingering labor "is proportionately painful. On the contrary," he continued, "a woman who is delivered in 6 hours may suffer as much, or more than another, when the child is not born till after 24 or 36 hours. Women generally recover as soon after a labourious, as after an easy labour," he concluded.[73] As with many of the discomforts of pregnancy, Denman went so far as to assert that pain was positively wholesome. "No woman has ever had a pain," he wrote in his influential textbook, "which was in vain." "Every pain," he concluded, "must have its use." He found contrary notions to be dispiriting.[74]

This reluctance to use instruments might well have approached neglect. Croft, for instance, did not even bother to bring his obstetric instruments with him when he attended the Duchess of Devonshire in Paris in 1790. About a week before the Duchess gave birth, Croft wrote to his mother-in-law in England:

> As the instruments did not come by Lady Spencer in my opinion they need not be sent at all at least beg the Doctor will not give himself the smallest trouble about 'em as I have no reason to think I can want to use them, but if he thinks I ought to be prepared with 'em he may easily send them by the Coach which comes three times a week from the White Bear Picadilly, directed to me of the Duke's party, L'Hotel de l'Université Paris, when I shall get them in about 5 days.[75]

The forceps was not the only instrument in the obstetric black bag. The vectis, an instrument like the forceps designed to extract a living infant when uterine contractions proved insufficient, was used even less frequently. It was constructed of a single obstetric pincer—something like an elongated shoehorn. Other instruments had a more gruesome purpose. In cases where a prolonged labor was due not to insufficient contractions or a malpresentation but to the disproportion between the infant and the birth canal, the baby's head would become impacted. In such a case the instruments were designed to kill the infant rather than extract it alive. The operation usually performed was called a craniotomy. A blunt hook was used to open the infant's head, and the brain was brought out piecemeal, the rest of the body following in similar fashion. Dreadful as the operation was, it was the only way to save the life of the mother, who would otherwise die undelivered. In these cases, it was quite clear that the life of the mother was always preferred to that of the infant.[76] Caesareans were not then performed on living women.

On those rare occasions when a forceps intervention was necessary, the patient's comfort was attended to as far as was reasonably possible. While Clarke evidently believed that covering forceps with leather would make them more comfortable for the patient, Thynne quite rightly believed that they were more difficult to clean that way and could become a means of transmitting disease. He believed forceps should be made of steel, kept clean and bright, and warmed with water before use.[77]

Accoucheurs, sensitive to the potential dangers of instrumental intervention, believed it was essential to be honest with each patient, keeping her and her family informed of all the procedures they were about to perform. Charles Mansfield Clarke warned his students never to apply instruments without first consulting the patient. Thynne, too, emphasized that using instruments "clandestinely, wantonly, and unnecessarily without the patient's knowledge and approval would endanger the reputation of the practitioner."[78]

It would have been unlikely for any patients to have objected to the use of instruments by the time their conservative accoucheurs suggested using them. Patients were rarely as complacent about the pain they were suffering as their accoucheurs could afford to be. Accoucheurs even feared that their patients would force them to intervene before they themselves thought it appropriate. A Norfolk doctor complained in 1819 that "in private practice the impatience of ye patient or the interference of her friends may so teaze the practitioner as to bias his judgment and urge him to have recourse to instruments sooner than he deems absolutely necessary."[79] Family letters announcing a birth always expressed a more favorable attitude toward a short labor than toward a long one. A twelve-hour labor could be considered distressingly prolonged. The Earl of Banbury told his sisters of his wife's confinement in 1800: "At two this morning she was taken ill, continued at intervals so, and at half an hour after two this afternoon all was well. . . . Conceive my happiness, the whole Period my darling children were at times comforters. I own I began to be extremely uneasy, and thought it long before the accouchement took place."[80]

Accoucheurs might also be called upon to intervene in the third stage of labor—that is, after the child was born and during the delivery of the afterbirth. Accoucheurs recognized that the patient was not out of danger until the placenta had been completely expelled. Denman believed that whether the placenta came down naturally or had to be brought down manually (after some time had elapsed), it should be left in the vagina to be expelled naturally by the pains. This was one area in which Thynne took exception to Denman's teachings. "We are not to imagine," he told his medical students, "that the expulsion of the Placenta can be safely left to the efforts of nature, on the contrary, we should never think our patient safely delivered or *leave her chamber till it comes away,* as many women have died from a neglect of this circumstance."[81] As late as 1841, however, Denman was still the authority with whom doctors had to reckon. In an article appearing in the *London Medical Gazette* in that year, Dr. Robert Robertson, a lecturer in midwifery at the University of Aberdeen, disagreed with Denman. "Every woman, after the birth of her infant," he wrote, "feels more or less anxiety of mind until the afterbirth is expelled, and not without good reason." Leaving the placenta in the vagina, Dr. Robertson reasoned, could conceal the presence of a dangerous hemorrhage.[82] When Croft attended Princess Charlotte in 1817, a difficult third stage of labor was one of the many problems he faced: his conduct of that stage, according to Denman's principles, became an issue in the controversy that ensued. That case—one of the most notorious cases of obstetric failure in history—provides us with the perfect opportunity for judging the strengths and weaknesses of medical orthodoxy of the time.

Princess Charlotte first went into labor at seven in the evening of Monday, November 3, 1817. A statement prepared by the attending physicians after Charlotte's death claimed that "instruments were in readiness in case they might have been required, but the Employment of them never became a question, because the labour, though proceeding slowly, advanced naturally."[83] This is an important point, since in later years the main charge against Croft was his failure to intervene instrumentally. Had he done so, however, he would have been acting contrary to the established procedures. Dr. Sims, who had been named consulting accoucheur, was called in by Croft and arrived at two on Wednesday morning. He concurred with Croft's management of the case, as did Matthew Baillie, Croft's friend and brother-in-law, who, as the Physician-in-Ordinary, was also in attendance. At the time he arrived at Charlotte's lying-in chamber, Sims wrote later, "the state of the labour at that time precluded all thoughts of having artificial assistance therefore D^r. Baillie & I thought such introduction was then, both unnecessary and unadviseable. As the labour continued from that time, to the end, progressive, there was no period of it, at which a question about the use of instruments could have been entertained."[84] Prolonged labors, as we have seen, were not in themselves considered dangerous. It was Croft, in fact, who had attended Lady Holland during her labor in 1799 which, she claimed, lasted six days. Croft had spent four days and nights in the house prior to the delivery, and Lady Holland recovered well.[85] Therefore it is not surprising that Croft remained relatively undisturbed during Princess Charlotte's less-prolonged labor.

Although the doctors realized that Princess Charlotte's contractions were slow and inefficient, the labor was gradually progressing, and the parts dilated properly, though slowly. The Princess gave birth to a stillborn male on Wednesday evening at nine o'clock, some fifty hours after the labor had begun. Throughout the two days, there had been little cause for alarm among the doctors. The Princess, it was reported, showed "no marks of deficient strength during her labor." Though she slept a little on Monday and Tuesday evenings, during the day she was "generally up & frequently walking about the room" and she remained up until a short time before the delivery.[86]

The irregular action of the uterus during the labor led Croft to suspect that it might contract irregularly and that the third stage of labor would be difficult. He was not surprised, therefore, to discover, after the child's birth, that there was an hourglass contraction of the uterus, with the placenta retained in the upper portion. Croft removed the adhering placenta manually, about thirty minutes after the birth: but in accordance with Denman's teachings, he left it in the vagina to be expelled naturally. About thirty-five minutes afterward, the Princess complained of the discomfort the afterbirth was causing her, so Croft took it away, noting that very little blood came with it.[87] For the next two hours Princess Charlotte appeared "as well as Ladies usually are, after equally protracted labors she talked cheerfully and took frequently of mild nourishment."[88] A little before midnight, however, the Princess complained of a "singing noise in her head" and of feeling sick. Croft gave her some camphor mixture which she quickly vomited. She then took some tea, appeared more composed, and slept for about a half hour.[89] A little before one o'clock, however, she became very irritable and restless and may well have suffered convulsions. These were described by Croft as "spasmodic affections of the Chest." Her breathing became difficult, and her pulse irregular.[90] Cordials, nourishment, antispasmodic medicine, and opiates (including twenty drops of laudanum in wine and water) were given in an attempt to soothe and calm the patient. Their efforts were to no avail, and the Princess died about five-and-a-half hours after giving birth.[91]

Although Croft enjoyed the support of Sims and Baillie, other attendants, and the royal family, the public outrage at the Princess's death could not be stemmed. Many of the reproductive casualties suffered by the aristocracy in the year following Charlotte's death were blamed on the shock caused by that event.[92] In February, attending a patient who died after a similarly protracted labor, Croft killed himself.

One of the many reasons why the public was so upset was that the doctors never released the results of their autopsy on the Princess, and the cause of death was never sufficiently explained.⁹³ The public could only surmise that Croft had poorly managed the case and was covering up. The truth was that the doctors themselves did not know why she had died.

Even modern doctors, looking at the same evidence, disagree as to the cause of her death. Dr. Harvey Evers in 1950 cited a possible pulmonary thrombosis. The doctors would not have recognized the various signs of coronary disease, but Evers cites as the most crucial finding of the autopsy the presence of at least two ounces of fluid in the pericardium. He described the labor as "a sinister combination of premature rupture of the membranes, incoordinate uterine action, disproportion, . . . delayed third stage with constriction ring and haemorrhage." He also believed the Princess showed signs of preeclampsia—a condition characterized by high blood pressure, edema, and albumin in the urine, which could well have combined to cause the thrombosis.[94]

In a well-known 1951 article Sir Eardley Holland reached a different conclusion. On the basis of the autopsy, Holland believed that Charlotte died of postpartum hemorrhage, although other commentators have believed that the blood loss was not sufficient.[95] Given the presence of the hourglass contraction and constriction ring, both Evers and Holland agree that the Princess would have died even sooner if forceps had been attempted.

Macalpine and Hunter reopened the controversy in 1969 by attributing the Princess's death to a fulminating attack of porphyria, the disease that they believe she inherited from her grandfather, George III. They cite the Princess's cheerfulness during her prolonged labor as a sign of mental imbalance. "The medical controversy over this distressing and enigmatic event may now be closed," Macalpine and Hunter confidently concluded.[96]

Their thesis is attractive but not convincing. While it is possible that the Princess had porphyria, the very difficult circumstances of her labor indicate that her death could have resulted from less arcane factors. Married only eighteen months, she had endured two miscarriages before this last, fatal pregnancy. The Princess had endured a very difficult pregnancy even before labor began. She had suffered constantly from pains in the groin and lower abdomen, bladder problems, and even kidney stones—sure signs of kidney disease. These symptoms, combined with the aggravating circumstances of postmaturity, an exhausting labor, and the signs of preeclampsia, which Evers believes were present, would seem to indicate that Charlotte may have suffered fatal postpartum eclamptic convulsions. Only an early induction of labor might have saved the Princess and her child.[97] But not even Croft's critics suggested such an action, since the induction of labor was not then performed for reasons other than cephalic-pelvic disproportion.

In a pamphlet that appeared shortly after Croft's suicide, one Thomas H. Green went against the stream of opinion that had condemned Croft. Green declared that "had it not been for the groundless insinuations and atrocious calumnies with which that unhappy gentleman was so cruelly assailed," Croft might still have been "a *living* honour to his profession."[98] The public, however, was inconsolable, especially in view of the fact that Charlotte's death opened the succession to her dissolute uncles. Even Lady Morley, who had been one of Croft's patients, could not view his role compassionately. "Poor Princess Charlotte is indeed a most grievous loss—on every possible account," she wrote after hearing the news. "I think there ought to be some proper statement from the Doctors of the circumstances that immediately caused her death for they certainly do not satisfactorily appear."[99] Lady Caroline Stuart Wortley perhaps best understood Croft's role in this tragedy. "I never read anything more touching and shocking than the account of the whole melancholy business" she wrote from Paris on November 11, after the news of Charlotte's death had reached her. "And it worries me," she continued, "that if she had been any insignificant person, she or the child, or even both would have been saved, but that the medical men were timid! Poor Croft, I wish he had acted upon his own judgment."[100]

As details of the case became known, accoucheurs realized that Princess Charlotte had died, not as a result of mismanagement, but as a result of what was then believed to be the best care possible. Long afterward medical men still referred to the case of Princess Charlotte to discredit the naturalistic theories of Denman and his followers. In an 1827 article in which the surgeon Sir Anthony Carlisle deplored the use of men as childbirth attendants, he drew an invidious comparison between the medical treatment of Princess Charlotte and that received years before by her grandmother, George III's consort Queen Charlotte, who gave birth to fifteen children. "That exemplary Queen was personally attended by good Mrs. Draper without difficulties or misadventures," Carlisle pointed out, "whereas the contrary result, under male management, in the fatal affair of the Princess Charlotte will be long remembered."[101] At a meeting of the Obstetric Society of London in 1879, the chairman referred to Croft's management of the Princess and condemned the leading accoucheurs of that time. "These illustrious men," he told the assembled obstetricians, "thought it right to exert all their authority in discouraging the use of instruments, in inculcating blind faith in nature as the better way. So earnest was their zeal, so commanding their authority that men were driven into the opposite extreme of supine inaction. Rules were laid down and widely obeyed which too often allowed women to drift into danger, injury, and death."[102]

After 1817 the medical profession seems to have been increasingly likely to intervene in childbirth to hasten delivery. Of course, Princess Charlotte's death was not the only factor in this trend, but her case did much to legitimize it. Anthropologist Margaret Mead and psychologist Niles Newton believe that cultures that "emphasize the value of time, and personalities that enjoy rapid action, may be particularly drawn to the philosophy of labor speeding" during childbirth.[103] Such a description indeed fits English society after 1817, and certainly the momentous social and cultural changes of the day would have been reflected in the medical practices. A nation that had developed the steam engine, the railroad, and had otherwise harnessed natural energy for productive purposes, might well apply technology and "labor-saving devices" to women's distinctive form of labor. Finally there may have been a perfectly mundane consideration, but one relating to the rise of the medical profession: shorter labors made more efficient use of the doctor's time.

The new presence of men in the lying-in chamber must also have been a factor in increasing medical intervention. In the eighteenth century husbands had been notoriously uninvolved in the births of their children. They were interested in begetting heirs and were not terribly concerned with what their wives endured to procure them; later generations of male relatives were more emotionally involved. From the vantage point of the lying-in chamber, it was difficult to deny or ignore the existence of maternal suffering. Prince Albert's presence at the Queen's confinements gave rise to a discussion in the pages of *Lancet* in 1841 on the proper conduct of husbands. Only one letter suggested it was neither "delicate nor decent" for the husband to be there. The other six letters encouraged the spousal presence. "If husbands were present," one physician wrote rather confidently, "they would be less likely to question the propriety of the physicians' conduct."[104] But it also seems apparent that husbands and other relatives present at a lying-in were in a better position to influence the physician's conduct than were absent husbands. As noted earlier, family members were far less tolerant of maternal suffering than were doctors, who were conservative by training and timorous of reputation. And since the husband was likely to be accompanied by his wife's relatives rather than his own, the combined group seems to have presented a united front on behalf of the alleviation of maternal misery.

Whatever the precise combination of causes, doctors gradually gave signs of trying to improve upon, and even to control, nature. An 1827 issue of *Lancet,* for instance, urged the use of ergot of rye to speed up action of the uterus in protracted labor.[105] Then in 1847 came the most drastic innovation of all with the introduction of anesthesia by Sir James Simpson. Brilliant propaganda by Simpson and the demands of patients—notably Queen Victoria—quickly made anesthesia acceptable to the obstetric profession as a whole, in spite of much initial resistance. By 1850 a critic felt it necessary to object that the expeditious "chloroform and forceps" treatment "had suddenly become fashionable."[106]

Anesthesia challenged the earlier attitudes of doctors and patients toward parturient pain. Opposition to anesthesia was not based on the potential harm the drug might cause, but on the idea that pain was a good thing for women.

> Pain during operations is, in the majority of cases, even desirable, its prevention or annihilation is for the most part, hazardous to the patient. In the lying-in chamber, nothing is more true than this; pain is the mother's safety, its absence her destruction. Yet there are those bold enough to administer the vapour of ether, even at this critical juncture, forgetting it had been *ordered* that "in sorrow" she shall bring forth.[107]

Others referred to the wisdom and justice of Providence in ordaining that women should bring forth their children in sorrow.[108] One clergyman wrote a medical friend condemning chloroform as a "decoy of Satan." "In the end," he warned, chloroform, while posing as a blessing to women, would "harden society and rob God of the deep earnest cries which arise in time of trouble for help."[109] The clergymen probably feared the decline of childbirth as a religious experience. Women who became more dependent on obstetric skill would be less dependent upon God.

Simpson, the seventh son of a poor Scots baker, was able to use his own familiarity with the Bible to good effect, showing how Scripture could be used to sanction the use of anesthesia. In history's first surgical procedure, he pointed out, God himself "caused a deep sleep to fall upon Adam" before removing his rib.[110] Simpson then went on to reveal the religious critique for the sexist cant that it was. Man, after all, was cursed to earn his bread by the sweat of his brow, though Simpson pointed out wryly, "instead of his own sweat and personal exertions he employs the horse and the ox-water and steam power—sowing, reaping, thrashing and grinding machines, etc. to do his work for him." Furthermore, God had ordained that men and women alike were to die, and yet every day of a physician's life was spent trying to contravene that fate.[111]

In a different version of the "pain is good for women" theory, W. Tyler Smith argued in an 1848 issue of *Lancet* that ether was immoral because it incited sexual passion. Although he admitted the wonder of pain "being metamorphosed into its antithesis," he nevertheless thought pain was better for women than lust.

> May it not be that in women, the physical pain neutralizes the sexual emotion, which would tend very much to alter our estimation of the modesty and retiredness proper to the sex, and which are never more prominent than on these occasions? If this be so, women would scarcely part with pain, hard as their sufferings may be to bear, chastity of feeling and above all, emotional self-control, at a time when women are receiving such help as an accoucheur can render, are far more important than insensibility to pain.[112]

Simpson's response to this bunkum was succinct. "Pain," he concluded with Galenic authority, "is useless to the pained."[113]

The response among English aristocrats to Simpson's anesthetic method was immediate. Within a few months of his first etherized delivery in November 1847, Lady Stanley of Alderley and her friends were already discussing its use. "I went to see Emma Mainwaring yesterday who was full of her intention to be delivered without knowing it," she wrote on February 3, 1848. Emma told Lady Stanley that "Dr. Locock either had made use of chloroform or had expressed approbation of it as a boon not to be rejected." Ultimately Emma was "dissuaded" from its use "and had the best and shortest labour she ever knew."[114] But another friend went ahead and tried the new technique in 1849. "Mrs. Leycester has produced a son under chloroform," Lady Stanley reported. "The last hour was an anxious one and would have been a very bad time in a common way—but there was no suffering."[115] When Lady Stanley's own daughter gave birth in 1865, she herself administered the chloroform even before the doctor arrived.[116] Queen Victoria, of course, put the ultimate imprimatur of respectability on chloroform by using it during the birth of her eighth child in 1853. She pronounced the new drug "the greatest blessing to suffering humanity," or so the Duke of Rutland told his daughter.[117]

By mid-nineteenth century, anesthesia was not the only example of the sort of intervention Denman and his colleagues would have deplored. The speeding of labor likewise came to be a routine aspect of medical practice. By the twentieth century premature induction of labor, once a rare procedure designed to save the life of baby and mother, had also become a routine procedure, especially in Great Britain, where it is used in even the healthiest of mothers to enable the doctor to fit all his deliveries into his busy schedule. Such techniques as episiotomies have also become routine. Caesarean section, the most artificial form of delivery, has become increasingly common as it has become safer, involving less risk, at times, than a forceps intervention. In fact, by the middle of the twentieth century, delivery has come to be perceived as a surgical procedure. The parturient women often finds herself strapped onto the operating table as would a sick person awaiting an operation. And an operation is, in fact, what she may well undergo.

Anesthesia and the full technologicalization of childbirth have been blamed for robbing women of an experience that was a source of spiritual redemption and a passage into adulthood. In an increasingly capitalist world, reproduction became reduced to production—as efficient and rationalized a procedure as possible. This process has reached its fullest culmination in the practice of in vitro fertilization—the production of the so-called test-tube babies. Yet it would be wrong to blame doctors for this theft, if theft it be. They and their patients were only responding to much larger changes in society. As shown earlier, anesthesia would not have been adopted by numberless patients had not English aristocrats already reduced the religious and psychological significance of childbirth. At the time anesthesia was introduced, the joy at being released from age-old suffering was so great that few women questioned whether or not they might be losing as well as gaining something. The idea that women had no choice in life but to suffer had been discredited—and that was probably the greatest gain of all.

CHAPTER VI

The Confinement: Recovery

Had Princess Charlotte survived, she would have become the central figure in the confinement—a term that applied both to the birth itself and to the succeeding period of recuperation. The confinement or lying-in, as it was usually called in the eighteenth century, lasted four to six weeks and followed a flexible, but fairly predictable pattern. It was at this point that the accoucheur, who was so much in evidence during pregnancy and birth, usually left the scene. During the confinement, the mother was likely to receive visits from friends and relatives, many of whom would have shared in the drinking of caudle, the hot spiced wine mixture she had imbibed to ease her labor pains. Mothers who chose to nurse their infants themselves would begin breast-feeding during the period of confinement. The confinement ended when the mother had been "churched" and her child christened. This represented the end of the rite of passage with the mother's reincorporation into society—her return from childbirth, as it were. Nevertheless, the process of deritualization was as apparent during the recovery as it had been in earlier stages of the confinement. Women became significantly less isolated during the century 1760 to 1860, their condition less a matter of taboo.

The traditional aristocratic confinement was highly ritualized, emphasizing the degree to which parturient women were separated from society and from their own usual mode of living. Besides being limited to a low diet of broth and gruel during the first postpartum month, the new mother was traditionally confined "to a room whose every crevice was kept shut, with the windows battened down with shutters, curtains and blankets. The hinges of the doors were greased, and the very keyholes blocked up." Communal caudle-drinking, something of a social occasion for the women of the aristocracy, was another aspect of this ritual.[1] Dr. Buchan complained in *Domestic Medicine* (1762) of the hazards of the formal aristocratic confinement. "The better sort of women run the greatest hazard from too much heat" during their confinements. "They are generally kept in a sort of bagnio for the first 8 or 10 days," he wrote, "and then dress out to see company."[2] Lady Judith Milbanke's vivid and unhappy memoir of her younger sister's birth in 1755 recalled just such an occasion.

> The first *Event* of which I retain a perfect recollection was the birth of my sister Elizabeth when I was 3½ years old, wondering *how* she came and *whence* she came. It was the fashion to tell children in those days that infants were found in the *Parsley Beds*. This was told me of my sister when I was first shown her in her cradle and did not satisfy me. I had seen my mother very large, I had seen my Cradle again introduced into the Nursery, and had observed bustle, preparation, and expectation, that the *Doctor* was sent for, and when I again saw my mother, she was in bed in a darkened room and appeared ill. . . . I was not so much completely deceived as was imagined, but I well remember drawing this inference—that it was a wrong thing to have a child.[3]

Perhaps this memory was a factor in Lady Judith's decision in 1792 to have her own child born in Durham, away from what she regarded as the artificial and unwholesome atmosphere of London.

By the 1770s, Randolph Trumbach has assured us, much of this formal etiquette had changed. "The doctors outlawed caudle," windows were opened, women arose from their beds more quickly, and light was allowed to enter the lying-in chamber for the first time—as were gentlemen of the lady's acquaintance.[4] Perhaps one of the most significant changes cited by Trumbach was the widespread adoption of maternal nursing by the aristocracy, which, he believes, occurred between the years 1765 and 1780. By 1780, according to Trumbach, most aristocratic women were breast-feeding, and the figure of the wet nurse, he says, had virtually disappeared from the aristocratic home.[5] Lawrence Stone agrees with Trumbach's assessment of nursing behavior in the aristocracy.[6] These changes, Trumbach has concluded, are indicative of the healthier attitude of British aristocratic society toward the subjects of reproduction and infant care, the domesticity that encouraged the growth of that new attitude, and the closer infant-mother relationship that developed as a result.[7] These changes could also be described as exemplifying a decline in ritualized behavior.

The evidence, however, does not fully support Trumbach's thesis. Various elements of the aristocratic confinement that he believes were eliminated by the end of the eighteenth century continued to appear well into the middle of the following century. Rather than a period of sudden change, the 1770s merely inaugurated an era in which postpartum behavior was evolving gradually and becoming less structured, more natural, and less ritualized. The portrait of a slower rate of change drawn in this chapter is consistent with the notion that a new system of domestic values did not fully triumph until the second or even third decade of the nineteenth century.

One of the earliest recorded examples of the "new confinement" was that of the Duchess of Buccleuch in 1772. "In the evening I went to Town to see the Duchess Buccleuch," wrote Lady Mary Coke, "who is perfectly well in her great room with all the windows open, and no one thing that conveys the idea of a lying-in Lady, but a great Boy."[8] But Lady Mary evidently was surprised by the conduct of the Duchess's lying-in. The new confinement had by no means yet become the normative aristocratic experience.

In 1794 Dr. William Moss of the Liverpool Lying-in Charity echoed the complaints William Buchan had made concerning aristocratic accouchements a generation earlier. Ladies who had "lain-in" in London told him they had been kept "in a perpetual stupor and state of intoxication there." In *Essay on the Management, Nursing, and Diseases of Children from Birth; and on the Treatment of and Diseases of Pregnant and Lying-in Women* he continued to criticize the etiquette surrounding the traditional confinement. "The mother's life, during her lying-in is often in danger, and sometimes actually lost, by her being compelled to submit to and go through the many rules and ceremonies that are thought indispensable upon such an occasion," he wrote, "many of which are not less disagreeable than injurious and by which the *constitution* is always weakened."[9]

Nineteenth-century confinements continued to reflect many of these older rules and ceremonies. The emphasis on the darkness of the lying-in chamber seems to have remained particularly consistent. The confinement of Maria, Lady Duncannon, in 1812 seems very like those that Trumbach has said were out of fashion before the end of the eighteenth century. "Certainly, poor Maria's room is a damper; she is well but weak," her mother-in-law, Lady Bessborough, wrote.

> Maria must not talk much or yet be read to, nor let remain to her own thoughts, as her Spirits are low. She must not be too much interested or too much entertained, but constantly talked to, in a calming, soporifick way, which has a wonderful effect on me, for added to the darkness of the room, I could slumber away the day very quietly, and should probably, were it not for the dissipation of Mr. Croft's and Mrs. Griffith's conversation to enliven us now and then. Oh, what stories I could tell you of cross births and hard labours.[10]

Lady Bessborough seemed to take the darkness of the lying-in chamber quite as a matter of course: she did not find it curiously old fashioned, or yet, the modern revival of an old custom.

Indirect evidence also suggests that lying-in chambers were usually kept darkened, at least during the early part of confinement. Many letters of the period indicate that women's eyes were unusually sensitive to light, probably as a result of continued darkness. All activities requiring their use were postponed, even until after the woman began moving about. The first letter written was therefore an important point in the recovery process. In 1782 Lady Sarah Napier wrote a long letter to her sister on the eleventh day of her confinement, and her correspondent replied that she was concerned that "dearest Sally" had "hurt her poor eyes" as a result of writing so soon. Three weeks after giving birth to her first child in 1786, Elizabeth, Countess of Sutherland, wrote to her mother-in-law, saying that this was the first time she had been allowed to do so.[11] Similarly, in 1825 the Duchess of Rutland wrote a letter to her daughter, Lady Elizabeth Drummond, four days after the latter had given birth, saying that Andrew Drummond should read the letter aloud to Lady Elizabeth, "as it is *not proper* to *read* too soon." And even so late as 1850 Emmeline Way shocked her mother, Lady Stanley of Alderley, by attempting to use her eyes too soon: "I only hope Emmy will not be too venturesome Lou Way tells me she tried to *read* and *write* on the 9th day, but found her eyes would not stand *that* effort, & Albert quickly removed the book & pen—but the mere wish shows how well she felt."[12]

The advent of men into the lying-in chamber may have proceeded more slowly than Trumbach suggested, in the passage quoted earlier. According to the old ways, no man entered the lying-in chamber during the first two weeks after birth; ceremonial visits of close male relatives were allowed during the third week; and all males could visit during the fourth week. This schedule was certainly not out of fashion by 1780. During her first confinement in 1786, for instance, the Countess of Sutherland wrote precisely on the twenty-first day that she had just seen Lord Uxbridge, "the first gentleman who has visited me." The following day, "Mr. Selwyn is to dine with me."[13] This suggests strongly that males had not been allowed to visit her during the first three weeks of her confinement, although her husband seems to have been with her most of the time. Of course, this may simply have been a matter of chance, but other evidence indicates that rules concerning male visitation privileges continued to be invoked, even a generation after the Countess of Sutherland's confinement.

Georgiana, Lady Morpeth, gave birth to her seventh child on December 23, 1809. The following day her sister, Lady Harriet Cavendish, had married Lord Granville Leveson-Gower, and Lady Morpeth had missed the wedding. Lady Morpeth was sorry that Lord Granville had not been allowed to visit her in her lying-in chambers. On Christmas Day—two days after giving birth—she wrote her newly wed sister that "I have pined a little at not seeing Ld Granville last night—I think on such an occasion [his marriage to her sister] the usual etiquette might have been laid aside, & for my Brother too."[14] If Lady Morpeth was unhappy with the etiquette of her day, it is not surprising that she did not protest when that etiquette finally changed, as it did for her daughters' generation, when men and women appear to have been allowed in on the same basis. Her daughter Blanche, Lady Burlington, for instance, was attended by Lady Morpeth, two sisters, husband, bachelor brother, and two brothers-in-law, during her 1831 confinement. The following day, Lady Burlington's uncle, the Duke of Devonshire, was one of the first visitors to the chamber.[15]

An important part of the visit to a lying-in chamber was drinking the new mother's caudle. While it is, again, difficult to tell how common caudle-drinking was, the practice did survive the turn of the nineteenth century. Curiously, both examples we have of caudle-drinking include men. At Lady Burlington's 1831 confinement, her brother George, Lord Morpeth, was invited to drink caudle prior to his departure from London. In 1840 Lord Leveson was at Buckingham Palace when Queen Victoria gave birth to her first child. He was invited to drink caudle with the lady-in-waiting and maids of honor.[16] In neither of these cases was caudle-drinking viewed as a strange or old-fashioned custom. Our guess is that caudle-drinking remained a custom of confinements, but that its use had become diffused to include the male visitors to the lying-in chamber. Caudle-drinking may therefore have lost something of the ritual about it when it became less exclusively the prerogative of women—less an opportunity for, and symbol of, bonding between women.

The confinement itself was composed of a set of clearly defined stages in the recovery process. While these provided something of a guideline for the recovery of all women, they were flexible enough to allow for individual differences. Generally, the stages consisted of increasingly long forays from bed to sofa; thence to the outer or dressing room of the lying-in chambers; downstairs, possibly to dine with the family; and finally to take her first leave of the premises. The entire process lasted from four to six weeks. While the stages remained the same in all families, the timetable for reaching them varied from woman to woman and from pregnancy to pregnancy. These stages, or levels of recovery, were regarded as an index of the woman's state of health and were often considered of enough moment to be noticed in correspondence and diaries. Thus we find letters like the one of Lady Hatherton, quoted in the last chapter, wherein she tells her brother that she writes "while laying at full length on my Sofa." That was a clue to her condition.

"Going downstairs" was a particularly important stage in the recovery process, because—as visitors to any country house can recall—the downstairs is the public part of the house. Elizabeth, Marchioness of Westminster, gave birth to thirteen children in the twenty years between 1820 and 1840. She was usually "put on the sopha in the bedroom within a few days of giving birth and within a week or ten days of the event she would be downstairs."[17] The Duchess of Devonshire came out of her lying-in chamber exactly one week after the birth of her third child in 1790. Frances, Marchioness of Salisbury, left her room for the first time eleven days after giving birth to her seventh child in 1834. Blanche, Countess of Burlington, left her dressing room for the first time four weeks after the birth of her first child in 1831, which might indicate that she was then well enough to go downstairs. Charlotte, Countess of Verulam, was downstairs for the first time three-and-one-half weeks after the birth of her fourth child in 1813. Ten years later she dined downstairs for the first time exactly one month after the birth of her ninth child. She expressed gratitude for what she considered a "speedy recovery."[18]

Family members often had very strong ideas about when the new mother should reach a given stage of recovery. Harriet, Duchess of Sutherland, had to tailor her recovery to suit the firmly held expectations of her parents-in-law. After the birth of her fifth child in 1830, she received the Duchess of Gordon while reclining on her sofa. She then got word that her husband's parents were coming up the stairs to see her, "upon which I instantly found my legs and my strength," she wrote, thus surprising her in-laws. "Lord S. turned sharply around," she recorded, "and said 'It is the day month.' They wish me to be quite about which I do not feel equal to yet."[19] More commonly, families warned new mothers of the dangers of recovering too quickly. "The better she is now, the more careful she should be," the Dowager Lady Stanley wrote concerning the fate of her granddaughter, Lady Airlie, in 1854. "Ellin sent a melancholy account of a young friend of hers who recovered so well, she was downstairs in a fortnight—caught cold and died."[20]

Most women felt well enough to end their confinement after a month. Anything slower was considered somewhat backward. Just four weeks after the birth of her first child in 1787, Lady Bessborough was reported as being "not yet out of her confinement . . . she recovers but slowly."[21] By contrast, four weeks after Lady Charlotte Guest gave birth to her first child in 1833, she went out with her young brother for a "ramble in her carriage" to visit London gin shops and other haunts of the lower classes.[22]

The end of the confinement was ritually signaled by a religious ceremony called "churching." Traditionally, a woman was to pay her first visit upon leaving home to her church. The custom was an ancient one,[23] no doubt related to Levitical injunctions that have resulted in similar practices elsewhere, such as the Jewish ritual of postpartum bathing. According to the *Book of Common Prayer*, the woman was, at the usual time after delivery, "to come into the church decently apparelled, and there shall kneel down in some convenient place." Such ceremonies have been interpreted to mean that women needed to be religiously "cleansed" before mingling once again in society. Edward Shorter has expressed surprise that women concurred so readily in a ceremony that defined them as contaminated.[24] But in fact, if one looks at the actual liturgy of churching, it did not bespeak purification. It was formally named the "Thanksgiving of Women after Childbirth." Most of the service emphasizes a woman's gratitude toward God for her full recovery. "For as much as it hath pleased Almighty God of his goodness to give you safe deliverance, and hath preserved you in the great danger of childbirth: you shall therefore give hearty thanks unto God," intoned the priest in the opening words of the service. "I am well pleased that the Lord hath heard the voice of my prayer," responded the woman, "the snares of death compassed me round: and the pains of hell got hold upon me." This is a service that emphasizes the danger of the experience the woman had endured. She has returned from childbirth and has been redeemed by the experience. Aristocratic women indeed seem to have regarded churching as a means for expressing their gratitude. In her diary for 1810 Charlotte, Lady Verulam, recorded, "I was churched on this day by Mr. Robert Hodgson, and returned thanks to Almighty God for the recovery of my dear children and my own." A week later Lady Verulam attended the opera and Lady Shaftesbury's ball. Two years later she was churched on April 29 and went out for the first time on May 1.[25] The Duchess of Grafton was churched on January 21, 1786, and went out for the first time on the same day. The ceremony of churching also reinforced the notion that bearing children was a religious act performed primarily in the service of God and secondarily in the service of men. "Children," according to the liturgy, "are an heritage and gift that cometh of the Lord." Then it continued, "Happy is the man that hath his quiver full of them."

The aristocracy, with its increasingly domesticated and deritualized view of childbirth, became somewhat lax about churching. Despite exhortations to the contrary, aristocratic women were increasingly likely to be churched at home. They believed it was unhealthy for women to visit a cold damp church after being closely confined at home for upward of a month. At home—usually in the lying-in chamber itself—a woman could be decently appareled and give thanks in much greater comfort. A month after she gave birth to her son in 1807, Lady Caroline Lamb was warned by her grandmother that she should be churched "before she stirs out of the house."[26] How clearly the act had been transformed from one of religious, to one of domestic significance. No wonder the aristocracy in adopting anesthesia did not worry that they were robbing God of their "deep earnest cries." They had already begun the process of secularizing the event.

A ceremony conducted with much greater fanfare was the christening of the infant. The christening symbolized the introduction of the new individual to the religious and social community into which it had been born. It usually served as the mother's first public appearance after the birth. It thus continued her phased re-entry into society. The christening was therefore delayed until she was well enough to attend. Although often coming within a few days of the churching, the christening inevitably followed that ceremony. The Duchess of Devonshire planned the Parisian christening of the heir, the Marquess of Hartington, for a date six-and-one-half weeks after his birth—and it was postponed even further because of the illness of his elder sister. She, Lady Georgiana Cavendish, had been christened not quite four weeks after her birth in 1783. Lady Verulam had her fourth child christened only three weeks after its birth in 1813, and her ninth child, born in 1822, at four weeks. Lady Frances Cole celebrated the christening of her seventh child six weeks to the day of its birth in 1826.

The christening ceremonies were usually elaborate affairs, emphasizing the high social rank into which the infant was born. The selection of the godparents, who were highly visible, played an important part in reaffirming the family's high status and exalted connections. Lady Cowper's first child was christened in 1807 as part of a double ceremony with its cousin Augustus, the first child of William and Lady Caroline Lamb. The Prince of Wales stood as "sponsor" to the two infants in the ceremony conducted at the fashionable St. George's Hanover Square.[27]

After the religious service, usually held at a fashionable church, the christening was capped by a large dinner given at home to celebrate the event. The Londonderrys did not spare themselves on the occasion of their eldest daughter's christening on May 18, 1822, four weeks after the infant's birth. They had thirty-four guests including "Esterhazys, Becketts, Lievens, Munster, Duke of Wellington, Camdens" in fact, the Tory elite.[28] Similarly, Lord and Lady Salisbury also entertained the Tory elite (including, again, the Duke of Wellington) at the christening of their seventh child in 1834.[29] Festivities seem to have been no less grand for younger children than for older, and for daughters no less than sons. All were welcomed into the society of the British aristocracy.

Extravagant display was an essential element in the christening. Childbed linen, christening robes, layettes, and other small, lacy items could well cost upward of several hundred pounds. For her first child, born in 1783, the Duchess of Devonshire spared no expense. "Her cradle, robes, baskets, & etc. are, I am afraid, foolishly magnificient," she told Lady Elizabeth Foster. "They are cover'd with the finest lace, the baskets Laycock and Brussels lace. I had been so extravagant about myself I c'd not bear indulging this occasion." The Duchess had even made part of her daughter's layette herself, indulging in the sort of domestic whim her husband's family disliked.[30] More typically, these items were ordered from childbed warehouses weeks, or even months, before the expected accouchement.[31]

An astute clergyman's wife wryly noted the contradictions between the religious and social functions of a christening. Her husband was the chaplain to the British embassy in Vienna, where Lord Londonderry was ambassador in 1821. "She had a profusion of diamonds in her hair," Mrs. Bradford wrote of Lady Londonderry, whose infant was being christened on this occasion. The ambassador himself was

> in full hussar uniform, yellow boots and all, not to mention a gold chain clasped with a ruby and an emerald set in diamonds, and a diamond serpent which he always wears. . . . The proxies renounced in the babe's name all the pomp and vanities of this wicked world, while the unconscious little innocent was dressed and surrounded with every vanity and pomp which money could purchase.[32]

The mother's presence at the baby's christening was of utmost significance. In many traditional cultures, women are denied access to the religious ceremonies in which their infants are named and otherwise ritually incorporated into society. Anthropologist Ashley Montagu has remarked that, generally, sex roles are clearly defined and segregated during birth. While only women are allowed to assist with the delivery of the child, "the mother is too busy having the baby to be herself engaged in any ceremonial procedures."[33] By contrast, English men played important roles during delivery, and women played important parts in the religious ceremonies that welcomed the newborn infant. When Lady Horatia Seymour (1762–1801) gave birth in 1793, her husband, who was in the navy, was out to sea. "I feel most impatient to know a great deal about our fourth little boy," he wrote her, "and to learn in what ways you had arranged the ceremony of his Christening, which I had pleasure in leaving to yourself."[34] Participation of English women in these ceremonies indicate that the mother's ancestors were also considered part of the child's lineage and that the mother was as important a parent as the father. The mother's contribution was not limited to the physical, profane one of giving birth: she also had access to the sacred elements of her culture, though she did not control them.

Once the christening was over, the mother was free to resume her normal social life. Elizabeth, Countess of Sutherland, was not atypical in this regard. She gave birth to her first child on August 8, 1786, and was confined until September 6, when the christening of the heir took place. The following day she attended a drawing room, held a whist party at her home, and gave a large dinner. A week and a half later, she and her husband left for Europe.[35]

Soon after the christening, the aristocratic household set up specifically for the confinement was closed, and the family moved on. Most went back directly to their country seat. Others traveled to a seaside resort or spa to complete a prolonged recovery under very pleasant circumstances. In fact, leaving one's home directly after the confinement was the expected pattern of behavior. Only three weeks after his sister Susan, Lady Harrowby, had given premature birth to her sixth child in 1805, Lord Granville had to be assured that she had not yet left town. His own wife, Harriet, went to Brighton six weeks after giving birth in 1810. In 1820 Emily, Lady Cowper, also went to Brighton six weeks after the birth of her child. The Londonderrys left London six weeks after her ladyship gave birth to their child in 1823, while the Duchess of Sutherland left London about seven weeks after she gave birth in 1830 to visit some country houses. Even Queen Victoria found it desirable to go from Buckingham Palace, where she had given birth to the Princess Royal in 1840, to Windsor Castle a month later, which, she assured her uncle, "will quite set me up."[36] Established quickly in time for the birth, the household was just as quickly dispersed after the confinement was completed. The entire family continued to move in accord with the state of the wife and mother. The termination of the confinement was the most rigorously followed part of the experience and completed the cycle of events.

Within this general pattern, other aspects of postpartum behavior showed more variety, probably because they were more dependent on the condition of the mother. Among these were medical attention, diet, breast-feeding, and the exhibition of nervous complaints.

Chapters 4 and 5 noted that prenatal care and the attendance of an accoucheur were features of all aristocratic pregnancies and births. After the birth, however, the accoucheur's work was, for the most part, completed. Unless the patient recovered poorly, she was not likely to receive much medical attention—for there was little for a doctor to do. Since most of the hormonal and anatomical changes of the postpartum period were not recognized by medical men of the time, not a great deal of interest was shown in normal postpartum care. Most of an accoucheur's attention was focused on the diseases of lying-in women, most prominently, puerperal fever. The women in our study who did receive extensive postpartum care usually suffered either from pain, fever, or both.

Painkillers were often used to ameliorate afterpains (a problem particularly severe among women who have borne many children) or other discomforts of the lying-in state. Ten days after the Duchess of Devonshire gave birth in 1790, Croft thought it wise to administer laudanum for a "nervous toothache" that had developed.[37] This was the first medication the Duchess had been given since the birth. From that point on, however, the use of opiates increased. Two days later Croft noted that the Duchess "is at this instant better both in health and spirits than she had ever been before," but that he was going to give her "one grain of opium as a preventative." On the sixteenth day of her confinement, though she was doing well, the duchess was taking "Saline Draughts, Bark, Wine, and Bitters, with Opium in the

Evenings."[38] She was perhaps in that state of intoxicated stupor that Moss was to condemn.

Nearly twenty years later, the Duchess's elder daughter, Lady Morpeth, was attended by Croft at her seventh confinement. She was given laudanum the day after the birth.[39] Lady Morpeth's daughter, the Duchess of Sutherland, was also given opiates during some of her confinements. In 1832, after the birth of her sixth child, she was reported to be "light-headed," "talking a great deal in an unconnected way," and "fancying she saw things such as a white swan." Locock was consulted and it was finally decided that the "narcotics may not have agreed."[40] In this case, it is impossible to tell whether her hallucinations were induced by high fever or by drugs.

When fever was a problem during the postpartum period, it was treated as it would have been at any time of life—by the lowering plan. Charlotte, Lady Banbury, was extremely ill after her sixth child was born in January 1804. Her husband wrote to his sisters that

> Charlotte is now I think after the most acute pains in her stomach, & weakened by never once this fortnight having anything but gruel or Slop, mended, and I hope she will not be thrown back—She had as fine a time at lying-in as could be expected, but these Hot Pains coming so soon after, accompanied with the most profuse Perspiration, was almost too much for any Constitution to stand. Indeed I fear'd for your favorite Wally at his early age knowing the loss of a Parent—opening Draughts upon each other & no food with little abatement of pain has been hard work.[41]

The lowering system did little to alleviate Lady Banbury's misery, and she continued to suffer throughout the month of February. Her mouth and throat were covered with a thick white crust, owing, it was thought, "to the violence of the Byle." On February 16 Lord Banbury again wrote at length, much troubled by his wife's condition. Dr. Clarke had by this time been called in.

> Poor Charlotte continues so ill, her disorder returning with double Violence and an agonizing Rheumatic Gout, now ascertained, in her Hands & Arms & Feet.... I thought she was better & Dr. Clarke cheers me up by saying *there is no reason to be afraid, tho much to be discouraged*.... Early yesterday morning I was so ill, I did not know what to do, anxiety has almost worn me out.[42]

Lady Banbury survived this illness, only to endure the births of six more children and suffer a miscarriage. She finally died in 1818 at the age of forty-one, two years after the birth of her last child.[43] Fortunately, few women suffered to this extent and so they knew less of the accoucheur's methods or his reassurance.

Diets, however, were prescribed for most postpartum women. General medical opinion of the time recommended gruel and tea for at least three or four days after delivery, possibly keeping to a "low diet" for some time after.[44] It was left for the patient and her family, however, to see that the diet was enforced, so many women simply ate as they wished. Lady Morley gave birth to her first child on June 10, 1810, at half past three in the afternoon. An hour later her husband was writing news of the event and remarked that her ladyship was "quite stout and well, & going to eat some chicken." By contrast, for the first few days after giving birth in 1840, Queen Victoria only drank coffee and some gruel.[45] Mary Howard, the Carlisles' daughter-in-law, gave birth on August 12, 1843. A week later she ate "chicken and mutton chop and a simple jelly made with calves foot leaves, sugar and sherry and a few caraway seeds in it, merely a small pinch. She is to have her first glass of porter today." At about the same date, another woman thought it quite extraordinary that a friend of hers should have eaten a veal cutlet one week after giving birth.[46] Harriet, Duchess of Sutherland, ate little solid food during her difficult confinement in 1832. Finally, three-and-a-half weeks after the birth, her sister wrote joyfully that Harriet was on the road to recovery, noting that "she had taken her breakfast and 2 basins of vermicelli with more appetite than usual and is to have fish or chicken for dinner.[47] Nineteenth-century definitions of indigestible or overly stimulating foods are not necessarily consonant with twentieth-century ones. Six weeks after giving birth in 1810, on the road back to the Morley estate in Devonshire, Lady Morley wrote that she had been enjoying "a quantity of tea, and as much hot toast!!! as I chose to eat." "For being an extraordinary case," she told her sister-in-law, "the usual restrictions were taken off."[48]

Perhaps the most significant element of postpartum behavior showing a striking diversity among the group of fifty women is that of infant feeding. While there may well have been more women breast-feeding by the 1780s than in earlier generations, it had become by no means a uniform practice, contrary to the suggestions of Stone and Trumbach.[49] Many women continued to make use of wet nurses throughout the first half of the nineteenth century. Stone also asserts that women who did breast-feed did it out of a sense of duty and found it a "tedious chore."[50] Contrary to these findings, the women in our group who breast-fed enjoyed the experience, and those who were against the idea usually did not feel compelled by custom to take up the practice against their own preferences. This is an area in which women exercised a high degree of autonomy.

The Duchess of Devonshire was one of those women who had been a follower of Rousseau and for whom the fashion for "naturalness" suited her temperament and instincts.[51] When the Duchess gave birth to her first child in 1783, it was reported that she was "taken up with nothing so much as the prospect of nursing her child herself." According to Lady Sarah Napier, the Duchess spoke of nursing "with so much eagerness as if her whole happiness depended upon succeeding."[52] The Duchess became intensely attached to her daughter during the nursing period. She postponed weaning little Georgiana until she was well past her first birthday.

I do miss my Dear little girl so I do not know what to do—I have been twenty times going to take [her] up in my arms & run away and suckle her—I would give the world for her dear little eager mouth at my breast. This is the first night of my sleeping away from her for months and my room looks so dreary—oh dear, dear, but it is for her good.[53]

Two generations later the Duchess's granddaughter Harriet, Duchess of Sutherland, was equally devoted to nursing her child. She also dreaded weaning her infant "as a sort of separation from the darling thing."[54] Lady Banbury was devoted enough to her nursing to continue to do so even in the throes of her serious illness during her confinement in 1804.[55] Lady Frances Cole, who had earlier experienced difficulties in nursing, was happy to succeed when she gave birth to her sixth child in 1824. Then living on the East African island of Mauritius, she told her parents, "I should much dislike taking a black woman in that capacity."[56]

Many women received the support of their families in their decision to nurse. Mary Noel told her niece, Lady Judith Milbanke, that it made her "excessively happy" to hear that Lady Judith intended to nurse after the expected birth of her baby in 1792. Lady Elizabeth Drummond was warmly encouraged to nurse by her mother-in-law, Lady Mary. In 1827, shortly after the birth of Lady Elizabeth's fourth child, her mother-in-law wrote, "The next time I hear from you or Andrew mention how your nursing is going on—it makes me happy to hear in general that both you and the baby are quite well, but it will be a great additional pleasure to me, if I find you are able to persevere in *enjoying* the *greatest of all pleasures*, that of nourishing your own dear little Frederica."[57] Had Lady Elizabeth found herself unable to nurse, however, her mother-in-law's strong opinions might well have made her feel inadequate and unhappy. Lady Duncannon had to give up nursing her first child only a few days after its birth, "as they were alarmed at the great weakness of the child."[58]

Maternal nursing was, as noted earlier, far from universal among the aristocracy. The very short birth intervals that characterized our group indicate that the majority of women probably did not nurse their own children.[59] Women who used wet nurses were members of every generation (e.g., the Countess of Sutherland, born in 1765, the Marchioness of Westminster, born in 1797, and Queen Victoria, born in 1819). Lady Judith Milbanke, who nursed, had a sister, Sophia Curzon, who did not. The Duchess of Devonshire's elder daughter, Lady Morpeth, whom she nursed with such pleasure, used wet nurses when her time came. Wet nurses, too, had their disadvantages, but women who wanted them persevered in making use of their services. After the birth of her fourth child in 1805, Lady Morpeth had "20 troubles about wet nurses," her sister wrote, "as she is obliged to change the one she has at present and cannot find one that seems likely to suit her."[60]

Not all families were in favor of maternal nursing. Sophia Curzon's mother in-law, Lady Scarsdale, warned Sophia to have a "whet-nurse" from the country when she gave birth to her first child in January 1779. Nearly a century later, Lord Clarendon, the British foreign secretary, reported that Queen Victoria was hostile to maternal breast-feeding. "Our Gracious Mistress," Lord Clarendon wrote, "is still frantic with her two daughters making cows of themselves."[61] Other family members who opposed maternal nursing did so because they disliked what they perceived as its contraceptive effects, preferring that the young women produce the maximum-possible number of children. This was especially true if no heir had yet been born. The Duchess of Devonshire, for instance, nursed her daughter despite the opposition of her husband's family. Rather forlornly, the Duchess wrote her mother that her in-laws "abuse suckling" because of "their impatience for my having a son and their fancying I shan't so soon if I suckle." Their hostility was upsetting to the Duchess. "How can one help being anxious," she asked her mother, adding, "as usual I am the most nervous of beings."[62]

To the Cavendishes, the Duchess's penchant for nursing probably appeared foolish, self-indulgent, and capricious. And yet the Duchess prevailed.

Other families, however, welcomed the contraceptive effects of lactation, however unreliable they might be. Thus, some women chose to use wet nurses during the early years of marriage and later adopted maternal nursing as a form of birth control.[63] Lady Verulam, for instance, used wet nurses for at least her first four children. But she began nursing when the arrival of more children became increasingly undesirable. She nursed her younger children for exceptionally long periods of time in hope, probably, of avoiding impregnation. She was still nursing her fifteen-month-old son, Charles, her seventh child, in 1819, when she again became pregnant. In 1824 she finally weaned her ninth child after eighteen months of nursing. Three months later she was pregnant again.[64]

We can conclude that, with respect to infant feeding, a variety of options opened to the aristocratic mother. No single custom prevailed. Women might nurse or wet-nurse, or behave differently during different pregnancies. Reasons varied for the choices made. Certainly some women nursed their infants out of a sense of sentimental devotion to their babies. But they might also nurse for one or more other reasons: out of a rational belief that this was the healthiest way to bring up baby; because of family pressure; out of distaste for the lower classes, from whose ranks wet nurses were recruited; or out of a desire to avoid pregnancy. Similarly, those who chose wet-nursing were also motivated in a variety of ways: to avoid the inconvenience or indelicacy of nursing; to save their figures; because of an inability to nurse successfully; family pressure; and a desire to become pregnant again as soon as possible. Some mothers, perhaps, even believed that wet-nursing would be healthier for their babies. They might certainly feel that way if, like the Duchess of Devonshire, they became acquainted with the argument of some medical men that delicate or nervous women were bad nurses.[65] (This did not make the Duchess cease nursing, however. It only made her worry more about it.) The medical profession was wont to believe that "women of fashion" were especially likely to be delicate or nervous during their confinements.[66]

The exhibition of nervous complaints during the postpartum period was not recognized by the medical profession as a specific disease peculiar to that point in the reproductive cycle. Doctors were necessarily ignorant of the hormonal changes that play a large role in creating postpartum depression. Yet they were aware—as were mothers—that the confinement was, for some women, a nervous unhappy time. Lady Emmeline Stuart-Wortley (1806–1844) suffered a clear case of postpartum depression. The second daughter of the Duke of Rutland (and sister of Lady Elizabeth Drummond and Katherine, Lady Jermyn), Lady Emmeline married Charles, the second son of Lord Wharncliffe, in 1831. "Charles has just been declaring," Lord Jermyn told his sister-in-law, Lady Elizabeth Drummond, that

> he would not have another child for £1,000 for that her Ladyship takes no part of the management on her own shoulders, and that he has to make its bed, and to cook its victuals with his own hand—& that Emmeline w^d let it starve and sleep on the floor if he were to be accidentally out of the way.[67]

The Stuart-Wortleys had two more children. Queen Victoria suffered from a severe bout of postpartum depression after the birth of the Prince of Wales in November 1841. He was her second child; she had been married less than two years. "Christmas has brought its usual round of festivity and its agreeable accompaniment of presents," her husband's secretary recorded on December 26. "The Queen was not at all well again yesterday, being again troubled with lowness. . . . I should say that Her Majesty interests herself less and less about politics."[68]

There were many potential sources of anxiety and nervous irritation during the postpartum period for these aristocratic mothers. The feeling that one had too many children, that they were coming too quickly, or that one had too many of one sex, might well be depressing after suffering the pain and exhaustion of childbirth. In a matter of so much importance to them, women must often have felt helpless. It would indeed by discouraging to receive a congratulatory letter like that addressed to the Staffords, after Lady Stafford gave birth in 1772 to her third girl in as many years. (Her husband also had three daughters from an earlier marriage, but only one son between the two wives.) "Tho I can't possibly wish you joy of your hundredth girl," wrote a family friend, "I do very sincerely of Lady Gower's [as she was then styled] recovery and hope she will bring better luck nine months hence." Lady Londonderry was depressed after giving birth to her second girl in 1823, especially after enduring a difficult twenty-six-hour labor. When Lady Westminster gave birth to her eighth girl in 1834, she wrote in her diary, "The catastrophe of a daughter was a bore, but what can't be cured must be endured, for even adjured, and never mentioned."[69] Other mothers were unhappy when they had a surplus of sons.

In these highly domestic families in which affective relations between spouses predominated, the behavior of husbands might be another source of discontent. Lady Verulam often felt that her husband was not as attentive to her as she thought he should be. The day after she gave birth to her ninth child in 1822, her husband went out shooting with his friends "and had good sport," as he wrote in his diary. The men came back to Gorhambury for dinner, dining downstairs, and then went to nearby Hatfield House to spend the evening with Lady Salisbury. Lord Verulam was annoyed to find his wife nervous and irritable when he returned home, and she continued so for several days.[70] The extent of Lady Verulam's resentment toward her husband—and by extension toward men in general—can perhaps be gauged by a story about her that was circulated in 1835. Her married eldest daughter, Lady Catherine Barham, "had a stillborn child the day before her sister was married," a young nobleman recorded in his diary. "The story goes," he continued, "that Lady Verulam wanted to keep it to show Mr. Barham, & so pickled it and salted it and hung it up by the hindheels in the Ice House with the Venison, where it was exhibited to all the visitors at Gorhambury."[71] Lady Verulam might well have agreed with Queen Victoria that childbearing "is indeed too hard and dreadful," and that "men ought to have an adoration for one, and indeed to make up, for what after all, they alone, are the cause of!!"[72]

Most women, however, learned through experience and adjustments how best to cope with their confinements. Elizabeth, Lady Westminster, who gave birth to most of her children privately at Eaton Hall in Cheshire, resumed her normal domestic routines as quickly as possible. Lady Charlotte Guest, though devoted to her children, allowed their births to disrupt her busy schedule as little as possible. In 1838 she gave birth to her fourth child. On the fifth day she resumed work on the Welsh epic she was translating. For a brief respite, she told her mother, she amused herself by "Making a calculation of prices for Great Western Rails." When she had her fifth child the next year, she followed a similar pattern during her recovery. Research and writing kept her occupied, and "every moment that I am not suckling my infant," she wrote about two weeks after its birth, "is fully taken up."[73] As with her pregnancies and labors, Lady Charlotte minimized the separation of childbearing from the normal course of her life. All her later children were born in Dowlais, where she had the expeditious labors described earlier. Lady Charlotte, having scarcely separated from society—whether from the society of London or of her normal routine—hardly needed to be reincorporated.

For other women, the practice of traveling immediately after the confinement helped ward off depression or other emotional problems. Indeed, some were even aware that this was the case. "Change of air for me after a confinement is indispensable to keep off a whole train of nervous disorders," Lady Holland wrote in 1809, five weeks after the birth of her ninth child.[74] By then she had the experience to know her own reactions to childbirth and to respond accordingly. Traveling, which so occupied the mother that it forestalled or banished symptoms of depression, was the usual sequel to an aristocratic confinement. This perhaps, at least in part, explains its popularity. Travel or work were probably both better calculated to eliminate the depression of the puerperium than the opiates and low diet that doctors were likely to have prescribed.

Perhaps the question of the relation of language to reality is best left to linguists, but it does seem curious that the term *lying-in* gave way to *confinement* during the century under study. An analysis of the literary evidence of the fifty women studied indicates very clearly that this change had occurred by the first decade of the nineteenth century, when the terms *lying-in* and *brought to bed* faded away.[75] The term *confinement*, with its connotation of restrictions, might seem to run counter to the notion that postpartum behavior became less ritualized and more open, healthy, and well integrated into the normal course of family life. And, as noted earlier, the pattern of postpartum behavior changed quite slowly. But it may be that the new use of the word *confinement* expressed the resentment that women felt toward this experience: not that they *were* more confined, but that they were more likely to perceive accouchements as confining. Indeed, the double meaning of the word was not lost on these women. Lady Sutherland described her confinement in 1792 as being "at least equal to being in the King's Bench."[76] This confirms the notion that women, and their families, were less willing to consider parturient suffering as either normal or tolerable. When they could diminish suffering, they did; when they could not, they were resentful. It is clear that women, as a whole, tried increasingly to minimize the disruptions of childbearing.

However, no clear dichotomy existed between highly ritualized "old-fashioned" confinements, characterized by darkness, caudle-drinking, wet-nursing, low diet, and an absence of men, and "modern" confinements, which included daylight, an absence of caudle, the presence of men, and maternal nursing. Each confinement was likely to have elements of both. The model of swift, well-defined change, as described by Trumbach, does not, therefore, seem appropriate. Aristocratic custom, medical opinion, and biology provided the parameters within which aristocratic women lived out their childbearing lives. As long as they were willing to "be fruitful and multiply," they were likely to do so through the exercise of a high degree of autonomy. Accoucheurs, far from being imposed upon unwilling or overly docile women by authoritarian husbands, were usually useful allies in womens' struggles to minimize the disabilities imposed upon them by childbearing. Women were anxious to integrate childbearing into the normal course of their lives. The direction was clear, if the speed was uneven: women sought less isolation, less disruption, less taboo.

With the end of confinement, women prepared to go out into the world again, perhaps only to have more children and more confinements. Confinement, like childbearing itself, was an episode in the lives of aristocratic women. It was, nonetheless, an important episode—part of a process that brought together love, money, tradition, and the perpetuation of family lines. Childbirth represented women's most important function in aristocratic society. To accomplish it successfully, women and their husbands spared little expense and experienced some discomfort we might regard as needless. Their achievement—and that of the accoucheurs who attended them in the earlier stages of childbearing—can be measured both in high fertility rates and in the continued strength of the aristocracy in a century of rapid change.

In Conclusion

THE social construction of childbearing is largely dependent upon three variables: a society's need and ability to support an increasing population; its understanding of reproductive physiology; and the role of women in directing their own reproductive lives. Analytically separate, these three factors are, in reality, inextricably entwined. The dialectic of change during the period in question came from the different weight and interpretation of these features. With the help of the nascent obstetric profession, the British peerage during the century 1760 to 1860 attempted to satisfy the perceived reproductive needs of their class. They increasingly tried to do so without unduly sacrificing the well-being of individual women within that class.

The demands of aristocratic society can hardly be doubted. The peerage was an enormously privileged and powerful group in late eighteenth- and early nineteenth-century England. Most of the economic, political, religious, and legal institutions of the nation were under its control. Yet the survival of the peerage, based as it was on the principle of inheritance, was as dependent as that of lesser families on the vagaries of an element beyond their control—reproductive biology. Each landed family required a male heir and other male children to ensure the preservation of the family estate from which they derived their wealth and power. Such families also required a pool of healthy female offspring, worthy and capable of bearing these heirs. "Founding a family" was an essential task in joining the upper class, as essential as was the acquisition of a large landed estate: the two went hand in hand. Quivers full of children were a part of the ostentatious display that characterized aristocratic life. Large families were also useful for the maintenance and extension of those vast networks of patronage that underlay so much of English society. Elaborate family connections simply helped the politics of the day work in one's favor. An abundant progeny, quite simply, helped support one's rank.

The opposition to birth control which so markedly typified the English aristocracy during this, its most fertile century (in stark contrast to the practice of their French contemporaries), could not be overcome until private needs would supercede these public demands, or until public demands changed. Ultimately, by the latter part of the nineteenth century, the rise in meritocracy would make family factions less essential in the business of politics, while the decline in land values after 1873 would make large families more difficult to support. But for the century 1760 to 1860, political reality made large families desirable, while economic reality made them easy to accommodate. For this century, the control of reproductive biology was normally exercised to augment, rather than to limit births.

Aristocratic society of the years 1760 to 1860 was characterized by two major trends: expansionism, which provided the direction, and romanticism, which provided the style. Expansionism is perhaps the more apparent of the two forces. The British aristocracy was at the zenith of its worldwide wealth and power during this century. Its surplus wealth had reached unprecedented proportions, and new outlets for investment and consumption were constantly sought. The aristocracy had the confidence to greet the twin challenges of the French and Industrial revolutions by an increased determination to assure the continued supremacy of their class. Landed families became intent on the rational development of their resources, even when that meant expanding into nonlanded sources of wealth, such as urban real estate, mining, and canal and railroad enterprises. Many of the families whose domestic lives we have studied so closely were doing just that.

Frances Anne, Marchioness of Londonderry, personifies the unlikely marriage of expansionism with romanticism in aristocratic society. In addition to the homes she had inherited and acquired through marriage, she had built a cottage *ornée* called Rosebank near Richmond. Her friend Benjamin Disraeli described Rosebank as "a thatched cottage on the banks of the Thames, surrounded by groves of the flowers which gave it a name," and, he continued, "where, to render the romantic simplicity complete, Lady Londonderry, in a colossal conservatory, condescended to make tea from a suite of golden pots and kettles."[1] But most of the Londonderry wealth that supported this romantic simplicity came from the coal mines Frances Anne had inherited from her father, Sir Harry Vane Tempest. In order to exploit more fully the profitability of these mines, her High Tory husband (brother and heir to Lord Castlereagh) had bought the coastal estate of Seaham from the Milbankes in 1821, built a deep-sea harbor at Seaham, and later constructed a railroad from his coalpits to his harbor. By 1836 the Londonderrys were exporting 373,000 tons of coal annually from Seaham.[2] Of the six residences the Londonderrys called home, Lady Londonderry preferred Seaham, nearest the source of her wealth. Disraeli described her in 1861 as "surrounded by her blast furnaces and her railroads and the unceasing telegraphs, with a port hewn out of solid rock, screw steamers, and 4,000 pitmen under her control." When asked once if she did not mind the smoke that hovered about Seaham Hall, she replied that she did not, as she knew "the furnaces were making money for her."[3] This was a most untraditional attitude for a woman whose family honors went back to the Battle of Poitiers in 1356!

In matters of childbearing, romanticism and expansionism also coincided nicely. Husbands were expected to care for the emotional well-being of their families, just as they needed to develop their resources pragmatically. A woman's childbearing capacity was one of those resources. English aristocratic men were willing to take an increasingly active role in the childbearing lives of their wives. They were even willing to allow other men to do so. The great concern for healthy childbearing in the aristocracy was mirrored by that of the medical community, which was, in the eighteenth century, beginning to take a scientific interest in the study of obstetrics. The support of the aristocracy for the new scientific midwifery was part of their policy of controlled growth which dominated the aristocratic world view of the time. This support was normally expressed through the patronage of individual accoucheurs and lying-in institutions. A few ambitious, well-educated, consummately polished accoucheurs won the confidence of the aristocracy during the century 1760 to 1860 and so solidified lucrative and prestigious careers. The social and medical expertise of the accoucheur gave him a stature in the aristocratic household that the female midwife could not have hoped to attain. The accoucheur's authority could even be used as a counterpoise between his client and her family when their concern for her reproductive life became too intrusive.

But romanticism was more than a gloss covering the increasingly sooty foundations of aristocratic wealth. Much of the success the aristocracy achieved in enhancing maternal health and in augmenting fertility was accomplished through a romantically derived philosophy of medical care that emphasized nature rather than artifice, and health rather than illness. Accoucheurs resorted to schemes of constitutional restoration instead of specific remedies in treating their aristocratic patients. With their holistic perspective on health, doctors necessarily became more involved in the moral and physical environments of their patients than do modern physicians, who usually prefer to isolate the disease process. The accoucheurs' soothing doctrine of natural care, in welcome contrast to the anxious emotions of family members, provided the theoretical basis for the freedom from physical restriction during childbearing that most women wanted. The doctrine of reliance on nature was also advantageous to women because only they could interpret their own instincts. It thus gave them a rationale for a greater measure of control over their reproductive lives than they might otherwise have had. But the penchant for nature also served another important function: it enabled British aristocrats to throw off the restrictive bonds of patriarchal etiquette that had traditionally surrounded childbearing. Indeed, once this had been accomplished, the emphasis on nature appears to fade as a theoretical basis for obstetric practice. This trend seems particularly apparent after 1820.

Mark Girouard has reminded us that only a very sophisticated society "could react against their civilization and go back to nature." "The nature" an English aristocrat saw from his drawing room window, Girouard has said, "was 'nature' in quotes—devised by Humphrey Repton."[4] If the enthusiasm for nature was somewhat meretricious in landscape design, so too, we suspect with domestic life. The images of the Duchess of Devonshire crocheting her daughter's layette or of Lady Londonderry pouring tea at Rosebank are, at bottom, uncomfortably close to that of Marie Antoinette playing peasant at Le Hameau. However useful the emphasis on nature had been at one period, that usefulness could not have lasted. Civilization, after all, was thought to be a product of upper-class life: nature, as Dr. Rigby's experiments illustrated, was identified with the lower classes. One might wish to enthuse over the Noble Savage, but one seriously would not want to live like one. Perhaps the biggest long-term obstacle to the sway of nature was that the aristocracy was far more interested in creating distance between themselves and the lower classes than they were in closing that gap. Distance was necessary to maintain the privileges of rank. Similarly, nature, except in its most artificial interpretation, provided so little opportunity for display. Ultimately, the upper-class desire to consume conspicuously would outweigh any theoretical allegiance to the simplicities of nature. Furthermore, nature could not have survived as a dominant theme if only because accoucheurs could not profit too readily from it. Obstetricians desperately needed to prove their utility: they could realistically only do so by intervening in the natural process.

Yet it seems to have been the medical profession that clung longest to the notion of the beneficence of nature, which can only be understood by looking at the dark face that nature presented. Nature, after all, was held responsible for morning sickness, sleeplessness, fifty-hour labors, and maternal and infantile death. Doctors could disclaim responsibility for such misfortunes that, after all, were perfectly natural. Aristocratic patients and their families were far less tolerant of nature's darker side than their doctors. The aristocrats were accustomed, under other circumstances, to a large measure of control in their lives: why could not something be done to alleviate human suffering, however natural it was? And indeed, while doctors excused massive amounts of maternal suffering as "natural," patients were increasingly loath to do so. This growing resistance to the notion of the inevitability of maternal suffering is perhaps the key to understanding the changing meaning of childbearing in this period. And that can be best understood by a review of how domesticity transformed family life.

Social change, we have constantly emphasized, occurred slowly. Domesticity, whether measured in language, naming patterns, marriage, or childbirth customs, did not become fully normative until the second or even third decade of the nineteenth century. In many cases, domesticity simply provided emotional reinforcement to sustain the patterns of the past. Virtue became its own reward, guilt its own punishment. At other times domesticity might not so easily coexist with traditional patriarchy. A major aspect of domesticity, after all, was to accentuate the private, emotional meaning of an event. This emphasized the growing distinction between an individual's social status and his or her personality. Henry Fox, fourth Lord Holland, was a bachelor for some time before deciding to marry Lady Augusta Coventry in 1833. His social standing, he found, was a real impediment to the acquisition of a "true love." He told his mother in

1827 that he wanted a wife, though of "creditable connexions," who would love him for his own sake.[5] Such a condition implies, of course, that "his own sake" existed independent of his rank. How perplexed and amused might a traditional patriarch like the Earl of Carlisle or the Duke of Devonshire have been by this notion. Girls, too, were expected to develop autonomous personalities. Henry Fox's little sister Mary was thought by her contemporaries to have been hindered in the marriage market by her stunted personality growth. In May 1826 Lady Mary Fox was described as being "so tied by the leg, so watched by the eye, so regulated, so tamed, so told not to say this, not to do that, not to go here, not to stay there, to cut this man, to avoid that girl, that she has lost all effect in society but that of being *gêned* herself and a *gêne* to others."[6]

The romantic elevation of the individual human personality has been alternatively attributed to the intellectual content of Protestantism, romanticism, or both. It is not within the scope of this book to argue about its origins. But we can see that its consequences were an asset to the aristocracy in their desire to hold onto power in the face of those changing economic and political circumstances that marked the century 1760 to 1860. To the degree that domesticity emphasized the individual personality over an ascribed role, the individual aristocrat was perhaps better able to cope with the forces of change. The rational augmentation of one's resources surely demanded some work, some attention, some internal motivation. The Duchess of Devonshire once asked her husband for an estimate of his income. He told her he had no idea; he paid no attention to his business affairs.[7] Later generations of aristocratic men—and even aristocratic women—could not afford to be so casual. Lady Londonderry, whom we have glimpsed amidst the roses and the soot, again provides a useful example of how the aristocracy coped with social and economic change by placing new demands on themselves. "This is a remarkable place," Benjamin Disraeli wrote from Seaham Hall in 1861, "our hostess a remarkable woman."

In the town a mile off, she has a regular office, a fine stone building with her name and arms in front, and her flag flying above, and here she transacts, with innumerable agents, immense business— and I remember her 5 & 20 years ago, a mere fine lady; nay the finest in London! But one must find excitement if one has brains![8]

In an earlier chapter motherhood was described as having been an ascribed status; it became an achieved one. In a sense this change was true of aristocrats in general. Like motherhood, aristocracy was an inexorable biological fact—one derived one's status from an inherited position. But that was no longer enough. One had to work to defend one's position. The Evangelical movement, the reform of manners, the expansion into new sources of wealth, the political reform movements on one side and political intransigence on the other—these were all attempts by the British aristocracy to avoid the plight of their French counterparts. New notions of motherhood were invaluable in these efforts. Mothers were the ones who, through affectionate bonding,[9] inculcated the sense of self that their children would need to succeed. They nurtured children at the breast and in the schoolroom, and perhaps most importantly, they conveyed aristocratic values directly to children in a way that servants were incapable of doing. Motherhood became a moral, intellectual, and emotional pursuit. It became a woman's greatest source of dignity and emotional satisfaction. This was certainly not true earlier, when motherhood only required that one produce children—an autonomous act of the constitution that necessitated breeding but no brains. The disinterest in birth control can be seen here, too, in the absence of other meaningful outlets for women's energies and talents.

Earlier we saw how the new notions of motherhood depleted the symbolic richness of childbirth. Birth was no longer the end of a process, the culmination of an effort: it was now the beginning. As aristocratic childbirth became less ritually separated, it also became less special. Once this had occurred, women were willing to be "delivered without knowing it." Childbirth was no longer the great rite of passage into adulthood, the great hour of trial. It had become merely a painful experience to be gotten over as quickly and easily as possible so that one could get on with the business of life. Elisabeth Badinter believes it was in the "interests of patriarchal society to blur the distinction between childbearing and childrearing."[10] Whether or not this is true, it is clear that this blurring did occur during the century 1760 to 1860. And once distinctions were blurred, the need for childbirth as a major rite of passage became inappropriate. The truth of this can be seen in subsequent developments: by 1984 American women, in the interest of a so-called natural childbirth, are once again ritualizing the experience and treating it as an occasion important in itself. They are, at the same time, refusing the sole responsibility for the upbringing of those children. What was blurred is once more brought into focus.

No society can live entirely without ritual, and the society of the British aristocracy was no exception. As childbirth diminished in its ritual significance, so marriage grew. Curiously, this is perfectly consistent with that growth of emotional richness and sense of personal autonomy that characterized domesticity, though it has rarely been seen that way. The central aspect of the traditional patriarchal wedding, such as that of the Duke and Duchess of Devonshire or of Lady Sarah to Sir Charles Bunbury, had been the disposition of property. The loss of the bride's virginity was important primarily in defense of male property rights. There was no need to celebrate—or mourn—the loss of virginity. Only the consequences of that loss, is the form of a child, was worthy of celebration. The birth of an heir represented the preservation and continuation of the male property line. "Happy is the man that hath a quiver full of them [children]," English women had recited at their churching since the sixteenth century.

The Victorians, of course, sentimentalized virginity and made its loss the central symbol of their more highly ritualized wedding. This was essentially a private rather than a public concern. The preservation of virginity in and of itself now transcended its significance for property arrangements. And in that change one senses the growing respect for the autonomy of the female person. The loss of virginity implied the loss of a woman's physical integrity: it was no longer to be dismissed lightly. If "love" was bruited about as a new essential in marriage, it was only because love, in some degree, mitigated the sense of personal violation. Marriage came to be the great rite of passage into adulthood for women, separating the asexual from the sexual stages of life. As such, marriage from the 1820s onward was frequently regarded as a rather melancholy—if inevitable—state for women. The married state itself, like childbirth, was probably no more offensive than it had always been. But married women like Queen Victoria perceived it that way, as their sense of personal autonomy grew. It is no accident that English women would ultimately rally behind the slogan "Votes for Women! Purity for Men!" in their long struggle for suffrage.

This sense of growing personal autonomy for women is also reflected in changing attitudes toward adultery. Peter Gay is wrong in declaring the 1857 Divorce Act a new sign of women's subordinate status.[11] Women had always been subordinate. The parliamentary divorce procedure that preceded the 1857 act had been instituted in 1692 solely for the protection of male property rights. The eighteenth century regarded adultery primarily as an economic problem. A woman's adultery was a means for the introduction of "spurious issue" into the male line of descent. A husband's adultery was virtually unworthy of notice because the descent of property was not blighted—at least not in *his* home. The suit for criminal conversation reified this economic notion of adultery. It was technically a suit for trespass, and financial damages were awarded in compensation. We have said that social change occurred slowly. It is true that divorce was not awarded to women on the same basis as it was to men until 1923. But the Matrimonial Causes Act (as it is properly termed) of 1857 did represent a small, but significant step in that direction. By granting women the legal right to divorce their husbands—even though adultery had to be compounded by other offenses, such as incest or sodomy—the act provided the first legal recognition that adultery had a damaging effect beyond the issue of male property rights. The Divorce Act also affirmed that there was indeed some legal limit to what married women might have to endure. This notion was quite new, and as conservatives of the time rightly feared, it represented only the narrow end of the wedge. The criminal conversation procedure was also eliminated by the 1857 act. It was replaced by a procedure in which wives, as well as husbands, could sue spouses and alleged paramours. The main argument used by M.P.'s against the old criminal conversation procedure was that it reduced a woman's chastity to a matter of property: but of course that was precisely what the procedure was supposed to do. By 1857, however, such an unsentimental, mercantile view of chastity was abhorred by the Victorian public. Finally, as with the Infant Custody Act of 1839, married women were gaining an independent legal existence. It is perhaps curious that this recognition of a woman's legal personality should have come first to protect her emotional life as wife and mother. But that, after all, is what domesticity was all about.

Finally, we witness the growth in personal autonomy in changing attitudes toward childbearing and birth control. It is apparent that, for the century in question, the social valuation placed on "quivers full of children" was so high that widespread use of birth control was both inappropriate, unnecessary and, unimaginable. Even though women like the Countess of Sutherland often resented childbearing, the motivation to practice birth control was simply not strong enough to overcome all the social norms that favored "natural" and prolific childbearing. After giving birth to her third child in Paris in 1792, she wrote her mother-in-law back in England, "The French ladies are all astonished at how anybody can be *si bête* as to have *trois enfans*."

"They are perfectly right," she continued, "and I shall mind what they say another time."¹² But she apparently did not care enough to persevere, or else was unable to get her husband's cooperation. Lady Sutherland went on to have four additional children.

Women were always aware, of course, that pregnancy and childbirth could be uncomfortable, painful, and even fatal. But it took the growth in personal autonomy before they could openly admit, even to themselves, that excessive childbearing interfered with their lives or, indeed, that they had lives beyong the bearing of large numbers of children. The undercurrent of resentment was always there, but, combined with the social pressures and authentic pleasures women found in their children, it created a mainstream of ambivalence. The Duchess of Leinster's failure to menstruate three months after she had been "brought to bed" of her eleventh child in 1762 made her fear that she was once again pregnant. But resignation to one's fate was the order of her day. "I have resolved not to grumble!" she wrote. "After all, are not my pretty babes a blessing? When I look round at them all, does not my heart rejoice at the sight, and overflow with tenderness? Why then, repine?"¹³ Evidently she was repining, or she would not have needed to convince herself to be happy at the prospect of her twelfth child.

As domesticity gained sway, a larger network of kin—increasingly including her husband—was there to care about the welfare of each individual woman. The ambivalence became more marked. In 1809 Lord Morley needed to be convinced that it was a good thing that his young wife had become pregnant immediately. Yet his inward sense told him that her headaches and illnesses were unfortunate. But this sensibility could not be easily affirmed. His skepticism did not fit into the traditional scheme of things, which insisted that it was both natural and divinely ordained for women to become pregnant and bring forth in sorrow. His wife's experience was simply part of women's lot. Lord Morley's contemporary, Lord Verulam, also regretted the miseries continued pregnancies caused his wife. He often took solitary walks whenever his wife's menstrual periods were delayed. His diaries gave him an outlet to express his anxieties: one wonders if he ever shared these with poor Charlotte. (Perhaps in Lord Verulam's ambivalence we witness the origins of that sexual guilt for which the Victorians are notorious.) Nevertheless, Lord Verulam continued to get his wife pregnant: she ultimately had ten children. For this couple, and probably for many of their contemporaries, breast-feeding was perhaps a passive way of limiting conception without acknowledging what one was about.

Lords Morley and Verulam were born in 1772 and 1775 respectively. For later generations, the balance in the ambivalence equation shifted. As the hold of nature began to decline, so too the belief that it was natural for women to suffer lost some credibility. Henrietta, Lady Stanley of Alderley, induced an abortion in 1847 during a tenth pregnancy. "A hot bath, a tremendous walk and a great dose have succeeded," she wrote her husband.[14] The threatened child would have interfered with her duties to her eldest daughters, who were coming out that year. The need to control one's life, even in the interests of one's children, was the major factor in Lady Stanley's decision. Her perception, in line with the new notions of motherhood, was that she could be a better mother if less frequently a mother. But the ambivalence was still there. Guilt, however, replaced the resignation of earlier generations. The following year Lady Stanley gave birth to a daughter who died in infancy. She blamed its death on her abortion the year earlier. Only in the generation of her daughter, Lady Airlie (born in 1829), did aristocratic women admit freely their resentment of childbearing. "She seems to like Lady Newport," Lady Stanley wrote of her newlywed daughter in 1851, "who says she hates having a child, & that all the women there speak as if they hate having any."[15]

The birth rate in the British aristocracy would plummet after 1865. Birth control was perhaps the last "private practice" to be fully accepted by them. It had had the most to overcome. Earlier in the century, enormous affluence had made large families easier to accommodate. By the second half of the century, the desire of English aristocrats to control reproduction could work to limit, as well as to augment, family size. Women's personal well-being had legitimately become a question for family consideration.

Modern feminists who romanticize the highly ritualized childbirth of traditional societies often forget that this was a ritual based on the inevitability of female suffering. The modern movement toward "natural" childbirth emphasizes the trained control of pain, not its passive endurance. The difference is an enormous one. The old identification of womanhood with the passive endurance of pain and the celebration of womanhood at the moment of greatest agony was essentially masochistic, suiting a society in which women occupied a subordinate place and in which endurance was hailed as the prime female virtue. As with labor pain, traditional society recognized no reasonable limit to what a woman might have to endure.

This notion gradually changed after 1760, gathering momentum in the nineteenth century. Later generations of women became increasingly eager to associate motherhood with dignity, more anxious to live lives free of artificial restraint, more likely to wish to minimize the pain of birth and the suffering in their lives. More importantly, they increasingly felt they had the right to do so. When anesthesia was introduced in 1847 to relieve the pains of childbirth, it was welcomed by the women of the aristocracy. The arguments of those who were against its use are telling. They attacked anesthesia not on the basis that chloroform might inflict harm, but on the basis that pain was good for women. Similarly, the cantankerous Victorian philosopher Thomas Carlyle was reported to have written as late as 1854 that, "No woman has any right to complain of any treatment whatsoever," but that she should instead, "patiently undergo all misery."[16]

Can we blame the aristocratic women of England for disagreeing with him?

Appendix

SUMMARY OF GROUP EXPERIENCE

Women are identified and alphabetized according to the title used throughout the text. Additional titles are also listed. Number of children includes those who died in infancy but is exclusive of stillbirths and miscarriages.

1. Blanche, Countess of AIRLIE (1829–1921). Daughter of second Lord Stanley of Alderley and Henrietta Maria, Lady Stanley of Alderley (see below). Known as Hon. Blanche Stanley until she married in 1851 the seventh Earl of Airlie. Six children, no reproductive casualties.

2. Charlotte, Countess of BANBURY (1777–1818). Daughter of Ebeneezer Blackwell, Lombard Street banker. Known as Miss Blackwell until she married in 1795 the titular eighth Earl of Banbury. Discontinued use of title after 1813, following a resolution of the House of Lords. Afterward known as Mrs. Knollys. Thirteen children; two miscarriages; two infant deaths.

3. Charlotte, Duchess of BEAUFORT (1771–1854). Daughter of first Marquess of Stafford and Susan, Marchioness of Stafford (see below). Known as Lady Charlotte Leveson-Gower until she married in 1791 Henry, Marquess of Worcester, heir of Duke of Beaufort. She was styled Marchioness of Worcester until 1803, when her husband succeeded to the dukedom. Well-known Evangelical. Thirteen children; one infant death.

4. Lady Anne BENTICK (1788–1875). Natural daughter of Marquess Wellesley and Hyacinthe Roland (parents married subsequent to her birth). Known as Miss Wellesley until she married in 1806 Sir William Abdy. Then styled Lady Abdy, as she was known until 1816, when Sir William divorced her. She then married in 1816 Lord Charles Ben-

tick, third son of the third Duke of Portland. She was thereafter known as Lady Anne Bentick. Husband died 1826, when she was thirty-eight years old. Grandmother of sixth Duke of Portland and of Lady Ottoline Morrell. Great-Grandmother of Queen Elizabeth, the Queen Mother. No issue of first marriage. Six children from second marriage; one miscarriage.

5. Harriet, Countess of BESSBOROUGH (1761–1821). Daughter of first Earl Spencer. Known as Lady Harriet Spencer until she married in 1780 Lord Duncannon, heir of Earl of Bessborough. Known as Lady Duncannon until 1793, when her husband succeeded to the earldom. Afterward known as Countess Bessborough. Whig political activist; confidante of Prince of Wales, Fox, and Sheridan. Mother of Lady Caroline Lamb (see below), Lord de Mauley, General Frederick Ponsonby, and Lord Duncannon. Four children, no reproductive casualties, from her marriage. Two children, no known reproductive casualties, by Lord Granville Leveson-Gower.

6. Elizabeth Bland BURGES (1755–1779). Daughter of Viscount Wentworth; known as Hon. Elizabeth Noel until she married in 1777 James Bland Burges (later Sir James), when she became Hon. Mrs. Burges. Two miscarriages, no live births.

7. Blanche, Countess of BURLINGTON (1812–1840). Daughter of George, sixth Earl of Carlisle, and Georgiana, Countess of Carlisle, also known as Lady Morpeth (see below). Known as Lady Blanche Howard until she married in 1829 William Cavendish, great-grandson of fourth Duke of Devonshire and grandson of first Earl of Burlington. Known as Lady Blanche Cavendish until 1834, when she became Countess of Burlington. Husband became seventh Duke of Devonshire after her death. Mother of liberal politician Lord Hartington (eighth Duke) and Lord Frederick Cavendish (Secretary of State for Ireland, assassinated in Phoenix Park, 1882). Five children; one infant death.

8. Lady Caroline CAPEL (1773–1847). Daughter of first Earl and Countess of Uxbridge. Known as Lady Caroline Paget until her marriage in 1792 to Hon. John Capel, second son of fourth Earl of Essex. Afterward known as Lady Caroline Capel. Thirteen children; one infant death.

9. Princess CHARLOTTE (1796–1817). Daughter and heir presumptive of King George IV and Queen Caroline. Known as Princess Charlotte of Wales until her marriage in 1816 to Prince Leopold of Saxe-

Coburg and Gotha. The Princess took on additional title of Princess of Saxe-Coburg and Gotha. Two miscarriages, died five hours after giving birth to stillborn son.

10. Frances, Lady CHURCHILL (1780–1866). Daughter of third Duke and Duchess of Grafton (see below). Known as Lady Frances Fitzroy until her marriage in 1801 to Lord Francis Spencer, second son of the Duke of Marlborough. Known as Lady Frances (Fanny) Spencer until 1815 when her husband was raised to the peerage as Baron Churchill in his own right. Thereafter styled Lady Churchill. Twelve children; no reproductive casualties.

11. Lady Frances COLE (1780–1847). Daughter of the first Earl and Countess of Malmesbury. Father was a well-known diplomat. Known as Lady Frances Harris until her marriage in 1815 to Lieutenant-General Sir Galbraith Lowry Cole, second son of the Earl of Enniskellen. Afterward styled as Lady Frances Cole. Husband stationed in Calais during early years of marriage. He was later Governor-General of Mauritius, where they lived for many years. Seven children, no reproductive casualties.

12. Emily, Countess COWPER (1787–1869). Daughter of the first Viscount Melbourne and Lady Melbourne, the great Whig hostess (see below). Known as Lady Emily Lamb until her marriage in 1805 to Earl Cowper. Thereafter known as Countess Cowper. After husband's death in 1837, she married in 1839 the statesman Lord Palmerston, with whom she had been involved for some thirty years and who probably fathered her two youngest children. Known as a Whig hostess, especially when Lady Palmerston. A Lady Patroness of Almack's as Lady Cowper. Five children; no reproductive casualties.

13. Hon. Sophia CURZON (1758–1782). Daughter of Viscount and Viscountess Wentworth and known as Hon. Sophia Noel until her marriage in 1777 to Nathaniel Curzon, heir of Lord Scarsdale. (Husband succeeded to title after her death.) Known as Hon. Mrs. Curzon after marriage. Two children.

14. Emma, Countess of DERBY (1805–1876). Daughter of first Lord and Lady Skelmersdale. Known as Hon. Emma Bootle-Wilbraham until her marriage in 1825 to Edward, Lord Stanley, heir of Earl of Derby. Known as Lady Stanley until her husband succeeded to the earldom in 1851. Husband was the Tory Prime Minister; eldest son served as foreign secretary. Six children; three died on day of birth.

15. Georgiana, Duchess of DEVONSHIRE (1757–1806). Daughter of first Earl and Countess Spencer. Known as Lady Georgiana Spencer until her marriage in 1774 to fifth Duke of Devonshire, when she became the Duchess. A great leader of society and the greatest of Whig hostesses; confidante, with her sister Lady Bessborough (as above), of the Prince of Wales, Fox, and Sheridan. Wrote novels and poetry. Three children of her marriage; two miscarriages. One additional child by Charles Grey (later Earl Grey).

16. Lady Elizabeth DRUMMOND (1800–1886). Daughter of the fifth Duke and Duchess of Rutland (a daughter of the fifth Earl of Carlisle); known as Lady Elizabeth Manners until her marriage in 1822 to Andrew Robert Drummond, son of Andrew Berkeley Drummond and Lady Mary Perceval, daughter of Earl of Egmont (sister of Spencer Perceval, the Prime Minister). After marriage styled as Lady Elizabeth Drummond. Mother of Frederica, Countess of Scarborough (see below). Seven children, no reproductive casualties.

17. Maria, Viscountess DUNCANNON (1787–1834). Daughter of the tenth Earl and Countess of Westmoreland. Known as Lady Maria Fane until her marriage in 1805 to John, Lord Duncannon, heir of the Earl of Bessborough. He succeeded to the earldom only after Lady Duncannon's death. Fifteen children; two infant deaths.

18. Lady Elizabeth FOSTER (1757–1824). Daughter of the fourth Earl (the Earl-Bishop) of Bristol and Lady Bristol. Known as Elizabeth Hervey until her marriage in 1776 to John Thomas Foster. Known as Lady Elizabeth Foster after her marriage and her father's elevation to the earldom in 1779. Well known as a great beauty and notorious as the apex of the Devonshire House triangle. Two children of her first marriage. Married (after the deaths of their respective spouses) in 1811 to the Duke of Devonshire, with whom she had lived for nearly thirty years. Two additional children by the Duke, born before their marriage. No known reproductive casualties.

19. Lady Augusta FOX (1812–1884). Daughter of the eighth Earl and Countess of Coventry, who were separated during her childhood. Known as Lady Augusta Coventry until her marriage in 1833 to Henry Fox, heir of third Lord Holland. Known as Lady Augusta Fox until 1840, when her husband succeeded to the barony and she became Lady Holland. Spent much of her life before 1840 living in Italy. Patron of the arts; established painter G.F. Watts at Little Holland House, where he

lived for many years. Converted to Catholicism, probably as early as 1851, and died in the Roman Catholic faith. One child, died on day of birth; stillborn twins; two miscarriages. No surviving children.

20. Elizabeth, Duchess of GRAFTON (1745–1822). Daughter of Sir Richard Wrottesley, Bart., Dean of Windsor, and Lady Wrottesley. Known as Miss Wrottlesley until her marriage in 1769 to the third Duke of Grafton. Afterward known as the Duchess of Grafton. Her husband had been a notoriously unpopular prime minister, the subject of the "Junius" attacks. He was known for gambling and consorting with prostitutes. He had divorced his first wife in 1769, who later became Lady Ossory. Thirteen children; no reproductive casualties.

21. Harriet, Countess GRANVILLE (1785–1862). Daughter of fifth Duke and Duchess of Devonshire (see above). Known as Lady Harriet Cavendish until her marriage in 1809 to Lord Granville Leveson-Gower, second son of the Marquess of Stafford. Styled Lady Harriet Leveson-Gower until 1815, when her husband was raised to the peerage as Viscount Granville. Styled Viscountess until 1833 when her husband was elevated to an earldom. Afterward styled Countess Granville. Well known as a letter writer, both before and after marriage, and as a hostess during the years 1824–1828 and 1830–1841, when her husband served as ambassador to France. Mother of Susan, Lady Rivers (see below). Mother of Lord Granville, the Liberal foreign secretary, and Lady Georgiana Fullerton, a popular Victorian Catholic novelist. Five children; two miscarriages.

22. Lady Charlotte GUEST (1812–1895). Daughter of the ninth Earl and Countess of Lindsay. Known as Lady Charlotte Bertie until her marriage in 1833 to Josiah John Guest, the great Welsh ironmaster. Known thereafter as Lady Charlotte Guest. Husband died in 1852, when she was forty. Married in 1855 to Charles Schreiber, her sons' tutor. Translated and published the *Mabinogian*, a medieval Welsh epic. Wrote technical articles on iron and steel. Most widely known as a collector of playing cards, fans, and porcelains—collections that she bequeathed (as Lady Charlotte Schreiber) to the British Museum. Ten children of her first marriage; no reproductive casualties.

23. Susan, Countess of HARROWBY (1772–1838). Daughter of first Marquess and Marchioness of Stafford (see below). Known as Lady Susan Leveson-Gower until her marriage in 1795 to Hon. Dudley Ryder, eldest son of first Baron Harrowby, after which styled Lady Susan

Ryder until 1803, when her husband succeeded to the barony. Afterward known as Lady Harrowby. Her husband was created Earl of Harrowby in 1809. She was thereafter styled as Countess of Harrowby. Her husband was Lord President of the Council, and it was at their home that the Cato Street Conspiracy was to have been carried out. Ten children; one infant death.

24. Hyacinthe, Lady HATHERTON (1789–1849). Daughter of Marquess and Marchioness Wellesley, but born before their marriage. Known as Miss Wellesley until her marriage in 1812 to Edward John Littleton. Known as Mrs. Littleton until 1835, when her husband was raised to the peerage as Baron Hatherton. Afterward known as Lady Hatherton. Four children; no reproductive casualties.

25. Elizabeth, Lady HOLLAND (1771–1845). Daughter and heiress of Richard Vassall, a West India planter, and his wife, later Lady Affleck. Known as Miss Vassall, until 1786, when she married Sir Godfrey Webster. Styled Lady Webster until 1796, when Sir Godfrey divorced her. Married a second time in 1796 to Henry, the third Lord Holland. Subsequently known as Lady Holland. The greatest hostess of her time; patron of literary men and Whig politicians. Four children, one infant death of first marriage. Six children, one infant death, three miscarriages of second marriage. One of the Holland children was born prior to the Holland marriage.

26. Katherine, Countess JERMYN (1809–1848). Daughter of fifth Duke and Duchess of Rutland. Known as Lady Katherine Manners until her marriage in 1830 to Frederick, Earl Jermyn, heir of the Marquess of Bristol. (He succeeded to that title only after his wife's death). Known thereafter as Countess Jermyn. Ten children; two infant deaths, one stillbirth. Died after giving birth to the stillborn child; said to have had smallpox at the time.

27. Sarah, Countess of JERSEY (1785–1867). Daughter of tenth Earl of Westmoreland and Countess of Westmoreland, the former Sarah Child. Through her mother, Sarah was heiress to the huge Child banking fortune, including the Osterley Park estate. Known as Lady Sarah Fane until her marriage in 1804 to Lord Villiers, when she became known as Lady Villiers. Husband succeeded to earldom of Jersey in 1805. Afterward known as Countess of Jersey. Lady Patroness of Almack's and well-known Whig hostess. Eight children; one infant death; one miscarriage.

28. Lady Caroline LAMB (1785–1828). Daughter of Earl and Countess of Bessborough (see above). Known as Lady Caroline Ponsonby (or "Caro") until her marriage in 1805 to Hon. William Lamb, heir of Viscount Melbourne. Known thereafter as Lady Caroline Lamb. (Husband succeeded to his father's title after her death, and, as Lord Melbourne, became Queen Victoria's first and muchly beloved Prime Minister). Known for her well-publicized love affair with Lord Byron, her unconventional behavior, and her society novels, including *Glenarvon*. Two children; one infant death; one miscarriage.

29. Lady Caroline LASCELLES (1803–1881). Daughter of sixth Earl and Countess of Carlisle (see below, as Lady Morpeth). Known as Lady Caroline Howard until her marriage in 1823 to William Lascelles, second son of second Earl of Harewood. Thereafter known as Lady Caroline Lascelles. Twelve children; one infant death; one miscarriage.

30. Emily, Duchess of LEINSTER (1731–1814). Daughter of second Duke and Duchess of Richmond (and therefore a great-granddaughter of King Charles II). Known as Lady Emily Lennox until her marriage in 1747 to twentieth Earl of Kildare. Known as Countess of Kildare until 1766 when her husband was created Duke of Leinster. Thereafter known as Duchess of Leinster. Husband died in 1773 when she was forty-two years old. In 1774 she married William Ogilvie, her sons' tutor, but continued to be known as Duchess of Leinster. One of her sons was the great Irish patriot, Lord Edward Fitzgerald. Eighteen children of first marriage; one infant death. Three children born of second marriage; one infant death. Last child born at age forty-seven, after thirty-one years of childbearing.

31. Frances Anne, Marchioness of LONDONDERRY (1800–1865). Daughter and heiress of Sir Henry Vane Tempest, Bart., and his wife Anne, Countess of Antrim, in her own right. Known as Lady Frances Vane Tempest until her marriage in 1819 to Lord Charles Stewart, second son of Marquess of Londonderry and brother of Lord Castlereagh. Known as Lady Stewart until her husband succeeded in 1822 to the marquessate after the deaths of his father and brother. A great Tory hostess and developer of vast coal mines she inherited from her father. Seven children; one infant death; two miscarriages.

32. Elizabeth, Viscountess MELBOURNE (1751–1821). Daughter of Sir Ralph Milbanke, fifth Bart., and Lady Milbanke. Known as Miss Milbanke until her marriage in 1769 to Peniston Lamb. Known as Mrs.

Lamb until her husband was elevated to the peerage in 1770 as Baron Melbourne and in 1781 as Viscount Melbourne. Thereafter known as Lady Melbourne. Whig hostess; favorite of the Prince of Wales; mother of Lord Melbourne, the Prime Minister; mother of Lady Cowper (see above). Eight children; including premature twin girls—one was stillborn, the other died in infancy.

33. Lady Judith MILBANKE (1751–1822). Daughter of second Viscount and Lady Wentworth. Known as Hon. Miss Noel until her marriage in 1777 to Hon. Ralph Milbanke, Bart. Afterward known as Lady Judith Milbanke. Daughter was to marry the poet Lord Byron. One child; two miscarriages.

34. Frances, Countess of MORLEY (1782–1857). Daughter of Thomas Talbot, Esq. Known as Miss Talbot until her marriage in 1809 to John Parker, Viscount Boringdon. Known as Lady Boringdon until 1815, when her husband was created Earl of Morley. Known thereafter as Countess of Morley. Two children; two miscarriages.

35. Georgiana, Lady MORPETH (1783–1858). Daughter of fifth Duke and Duchess of Devonshire (see above). Known as Lady Georgianna Cavendish until her marriage in 1801 to George Howard, Lord Morpeth, heir of fifth Earl of Carlisle. Known as Lady Morpeth until 1825, when her husband succeeded to his father's earldom. Thereafter known as Countess of Carlisle. Mother of Blanche, Lady Burlington, and Lady Caroline Lascelles (see above), and Harriet, Duchess of Sutherland (see below). Twelve children; no reproductive casualties.

36. Lady Sarah NAPIER (1745–1818). Daughter of second Duke and Duchess of Richmond. Last surviving great-grandchild of King Charles II. Known as Lady Sarah Lennox until her marriage in 1762 to Sir Charles Bunbury. Known as Lady Sarah Bunbury thereafter. Divorced by Sir Charles in 1776. Married in 1781 to Col. Hon. George Napier; afterward known as Lady Sarah Napier. (Mother of Sir Charles Napier, conqueror of the Scinde, and William Napier, historian of the Peninsular Wars.) One child of first marriage, (probably child of Lord William Gordon); eight children, one miscarriage of second marriage.

37. Lady Cecilia RIDLEY (1819–1845). Daughter of first Lord Wensleydale. Known as Miss Parke until her marriage in 1841 to Sir Matthew White Ridley, Bart. Afterward known as Lady Cecilia Ridley. Died at age twenty-six, probably of tuberculosis. Four children; one infant death.

Summary of Group Experience 241

38. Lady Susan RIVERS (1810–1866). Daughter of first Earl and Countess Granville (see above). Known as Lady Susan Leveson-Gower until her marriage in 1833 to George Pitt, fourth Baron Rivers. Known thereafter as Lady Rivers. Thirteen children; one infant death; one miscarriage.

39. Frances, Marchioness of SALISBURY (1802–1839). Daughter and heiress of Bamber Gascoyne II. Known as Miss Gascoyne until her marriage in 1821 to Viscount Cranborne, heir of the Marquess of Salisbury. Known as Lady Cranborne, until her husband succeeded in 1823 to the title. Mother of the future Prime Minister. Died at the age of thirty-seven, probably of diabetes. Seven children; two infant deaths.

40. Frederica, Countess of SCARBOROUGH (1826–1907). Daughter of Andrew and Lady Elizabeth Drummond (see above). Known as Miss Drummond until her marriage in 1846 to Viscount Lumley, heir of the Earl of Scarborough. Known as Lady Lumley until 1856, when her husband succeeded to the earldom. Afterward known as Countess of Scarborough. Seven children; one miscarriage.

41. Lady Horatia SEYMOUR-CONWAY (1762–1801). Daughter of second Earl Waldegrave and Lady Waldegrave, later HRH Duchess of Gloucester. Known as Lady Horatia Waldegrave until her marriage in 1786 to Lord Hugh Seymour-Conway, fifth son of the Marquess of Hertford. Eight children; one infant death; one miscarriage.

42. Susan, Marchioness of STAFFORD (1731–1805). Daughter of sixth Earl and Countess of Galloway. Known as Lady Susan Stewart until her marriage in 1768, as his third wife, to the second Earl Gower. Known as Lady Gower until her husband was created Marquess of Stafford in 1786. Afterward Marchioness of Stafford. Mother of Charlotte, Duchess of Beaufort, and Susan, Countess of Harrowby (see above). Four children; no reproductive casualties.

43. Henrietta Maria, Lady STANLEY OF ALDERLEY (1807–1895). Daughter of thirteenth Viscount and Lady Dillon; raised in Italy. Known as Hon. Miss Dillon until her marriage in 1826 to Edward John Stanley, heir of first Lord Stanley of Alderley. Known as Hon. Mrs. Stanley until 1848 when her husband was raised to the peerage in his own right as Lord Eddisbury. Called Lady Eddisbury until 1850, when her husband succeeded his father as Lord Stanley of Alderley. Actively promoted higher education for women and was a founder of Girton College, Cambridge. Mother of Blanche, Lady Airlie (see above).

Grandmother of Bertrand Russell. Twelve children; two infant deaths; one induced abortion.

44. Elizabeth, Countess of SUTHERLAND (1765–1839). Daughter and heiress of William, eighteenth Earl of Sutherland, and known as Countess of Sutherland from the age of two, when she succeeded to the title. Married in 1785 to George Leveson-Gower, Earl Gower, heir of the Marquess of Stafford. Known as Lady Sutherland until her husband succeeded to the marquessate. Often called Lady Stafford after that, although she continued to use Sutherland title as well. Husband created Duke of Sutherland in 1833, after which she was known as the Duchess-Countess of Sutherland. Probably the wealthiest women of her time, having inherited over one million acres in the Scottish Highlands. Mother of Elizabeth, Marchioness of Westminster (see below). Seven children; two died in infancy.

45. Harriet, Duchess of SUTHERLAND (1806–1869). Daughter of sixth Earl of Carlisle and Countess of Carlisle (see above, as Lady Morpeth). Known as Lady Harriet Howard until her marriage in 1823 to Earl Gower, heir of the Marquess of Stafford, later Duke of Sutherland (as above). Called Lady Gower until her husband succeeded to the dukedom in 1833. Afterward Duchess of Sutherland. Served for many years as Queen Victoria's Mistress of the Robes. Criticized for entertaining Garibaldi at her home, Stafford House. Mother of Constance, Duchess of Westminster (see below). Eleven children; one infant death.

46. Charlotte, Countess of VERULAM (1783–1863). Daughter of first Earl of Liverpool, sister of the Tory Prime Minister. Known as Lady Charlotte Jenkinson until she married in 1807 James Grimston, heir of third Viscount Grimston and first Baron Verulam. Known as Lady Charlotte Grimston until husband succeeded to the title of Verulam in 1809. Husband created Earl of Verulam in 1815; afterward titled Countess of Verulam. Ten children; one infant death; one miscarriage.

47. Queen VICTORIA (1819–1901). Daughter of Edward, Duke of Kent, and the Duchess of Kent, a Princess of Saxe-Coburg and Gotha. Known as Princess Victoria of Kent until she succeeded to the throne of England in 1837 as Queen Victoria. Married in 1840 her first cousin, Prince Albert of Saxe-Coburg and Gotha. Named Empress of India in 1877. Mother of King Edward VII of England and of the German Empress Frederick. Grandmother of George V of England, Kaiser Wilhelm

Summary of Group Experience

of Germany, and Empress Alexandra of Russia. Nine children; no reproductive casualties.

48. Constance, Duchess of WESTMINSTER (1834–1880). Daughter of second Duke and Duchess of Sutherland (see above). Known as Lady Constance Leveson-Gower until her marriage in 1852 to her first cousin, Earl Grosvenor, heir of Marquess of Westminster. Known as Lady Grosvenor until her husband succeeded to the marquessate in 1869 and was raised to the dukedom in 1874. Afterward known as Duchess of Westminster. Eleven children; two infant deaths.

49. Elizabeth, Marchioness of WESTMINSTER (1797–1891). Daughter of first Duke and Duchess of Sutherland (see above, as Countess of Sutherland). Known as Lady Elizabeth Leveson-Gower until her marriage in 1819 to Lord Belgrave, heir of Earl Grosvenor, later Marquess of Westminster. Known as Lady Elizabeth Belgrave until her husband succeeded to the marquessate in 1845. Afterward known as Marchioness of Westminster. Thirteen children; one infant death; one miscarriage.

50. Priscilla, Countess of WESTMORELAND (1793–1879). Daughter of third Earl of Mornington. Known as Lady Priscilla Wellesley until she married in 1811 Lord Burghersh, heir of tenth Earl of Westmoreland. Became Lady Westmorland in 1841, when her husband succeeded to the earldom. Eight children; two infant deaths; one stillborn.

Notes

INTRODUCTION

1. Queen Victoria to Crown Princess of Prussia, March 9, 1859, in Roger Fulford, *Dearest Child*, 165–166.
2. Some of the original works that first attacked the male medical establishment of the nineteenth century include G. J. Barker-Benfield, *The Horrors of the Half-Known Life: Male Attitudes toward Women's Sexuality in Nineteenth-Century America*; Charles Rosenberg and Carroll Smith-Rosenberg, "The Female Animal: Medical and Biological Views of Woman and Her Role in Nineteenth-Century America;" Ann Douglas Wood, "The Fashionable Diseases: Women's Complaints and Their Treatment in Nineteenth-Century America;" Patricia Branca, *Silent Sisterhood: Middle-Class Women in the Victorian Home*; Jane B. Donegan, *Women and Men Midwives: Medicine, Morality and Misogyny in Early America*; and John S. and Robin M. Haller, *The Physician and Sexuality in Victorian America*. However extreme and unsophisticated their arguments may now appear, these original treatments were a necessary antidote to what was then the accepted version of the history of obstetrics, one established by the medical profession and its own historians. According to that account, self-sacrificing men of courage and vision entered the field of obstetrics to save women from age-old pain and suffering; women should be duly grateful to their benefactors for all the miracles of modern medicine.
3. Lawrence Stone, *The Family, Sex, and Marriage in England, 1500–1800*, and Edward Shorter, *A History of Women's Bodies*.
4. See in particular Jill Suitor, "Husbands' Participation in Childbirth," 282. Suitor concurs with Catherine Scholten that it is practically impossible to get patients' accounts of childbirth from American

sources. See Scholten's article, "On the Importance of the Obstetrical Art."

5. Anne Oakley, "A Case of Maternity," 628.

6. F. M. L. Thompson, *English Landed Society in the Nineteenth Century*, 27.

7. To a certain extent only, because the landed aristocracy was a wider, more inclusive group than the peerage. Some great landowners remained commoners, while some peers possessed little land, especially the newer peers who were honored for political or military services. Because of the difficulties of defining the aristocracy without including innumerable exceptions, I have decided, for the purposes of this study, to include only peers and their immediate families.

8. Arthur S. Turberville, *The House of Lords in the Age of Reform, 1784–1837*, 478.

9. T.H. Hollingsworth, "Demography of the British Peerage."

10. Ibid., passim, especially 23, 30, 42, 45, 49–50, 67. I excluded childless women from the study since I was primarily interested in pregnancy and childbirth experiences. There were three women in the group who never gave birth to a surviving child, but all three (Hon. Elizabeth Bland Burges, 1755–1779; H. R. H. Princess Charlotte, 1796–1817; and Lady Augusta Fox, 1812–1889) were pregnant at least twice, and thus had some reproductive experience to record.

11. See Neil McKendrick, "Josiah Wedgwood and the Commercialization of the Potteries," 115. See also 28, 62, 82, and 112 for other references to the Duchess's impact on English merchandising. McKendrick suggests that the Duchess actually made pregnancy fashionable(82).

12. Hollingsworth, "Demography of the British Peerage," 30.

13. Stone, *Family, Sex, and Marriage,* passim; and Randolph Trumbach, *The Rise of the Egalitarian Family.*

14. Richard W. and Dorothy C. Wertz, *Lying-in.*

15. Edmund Burke and Thomas Paine, *Reflections on the Revolution in France and The Rights of Man*, 110.

16. David Spring, "Aristocracy, Social Structure, and Religion in the Early Victorian Period," 265.

17. That English aristocrats have both names and titles and that titles may change during the course of a lifetime has been a source of much confusion to English historians and their long-suffering readers. To eliminate this confusion as much as possible, I shall refer to individu-

als by the highest title to which they succeeded rather than by several different titles. In cases where two women ultimately bore the same title—generally women and their daughters-in-law—the ultimate title will go to the elder woman. Thus Lady Holland always refers to Elizabeth, wife of the third Baron Holland. Her daughter-in-law Augusta, though ultimately also Lady Holland, will, for the sake of clarity, be referred to consistently as Lady Augusta Fox. The only two exceptions to this rule will be for the unique case of the Sutherland title. Elizabeth (1765–1839) was Countess of Sutherland in her own right and was known by that title throughout much of her life, although a few months before her husband's death in 1833 he was made Duke of Sutherland, after which she was generally known as the Duchess-Countess of Sutherland. I prefer to eschew that clumsy title and will consistently refer to her as the Countess of Sutherland, thus saving the title of Duchess of Sutherland for her daughter-in-law Harriet (1806–1868), who as Queen Victoria's close friend and her Mistress of the Robes, was well known by the title of Duchess of Sutherland.

18. Stone, *Family, Sex, and Marriage*, 329–330, 668.

19. Ibid., 668. It is curious that Stone's examples of increasing formality after 1830 all come from the untitled characters of Jane Austen. One possibility is that the middle class was more reluctant to change to the informal mode of address. I suggest, however, that the Bennetts and the Collinses of Jane Austen used the formal mode of address in what was a self-conscious attempt to imitate their social betters, unaware that the aristocracy was itself changing precisely to distinguish itself from the stuffy middle-class habits of formality. The propensity of an upper class to use impenetrable nicknames is seen nowadays among the American "preppy" class, famous for its use of nicknames like "Muffin" and "Binkie."

20. For Lord Gower's (as he was then styled) reference to his wife, see his letter to his stepmother, Lady Stafford, of June 8, 1792, in Granville MSS PRO 30/29/5/4, Public Records Office. For the Stafford reference, see the correspondence of the first Duke of Sutherland with his parents in Granville MSS PRO 30/29/5, as above; also see Countess Castalia Granville, *Lord Granville Leveson-Gower*, vol. 1, passim. For the Napier reference, see Countess of Ilchester and Lord Stavordale, *The Life and Letters of Lady Sarah Lennox, 1745–1826*, 478.

21. See for instance, her letters of October 24 and 28, 1813, Morley

Papers, Add. MSS 48236 in the British Museum; Diaries of James, first Earl of Verulam, Gorhambury MSS D/EV F44–F50, Hertfordshire County Record Office; Marquess of Anglesey, *One-Leg*, 89–91, passim. Earl of Scarborough to his father-in-law, Andrew Robert Drummond, July 21, 1862, Drummond of Cadland MSS B5/21/26. Lady Susan Rivers to her mother, Harriet, Countess Granville, [February 1835], Granville MSS PRO 30/29/17/2; Lady Cecilia Ridley to her mother, Lady Wensleydale, [January 1842], in Viscountess Ridley, *Cecilia*, 81. Henrietta Maria, Lady Stanley of Alderley, to her husband, August 7, 1851, in Nancy Mitford, *Stanleys of Alderley*, 12.

22. Lady Harriet Cavendish to her sister Georgiana, Lady Morpeth, September 10, 1803, quoted in Sir George Leveson-Gower and Iris Palmer, *Hary-O*, 57; Earl Jermyn to his brother-in-law, Andrew Robert Drummond, [February] 1832, Drummond of Cadland MSS B5/14/6; and Lord Robert Manners to Andrew Robert Drummond, April 3, 1832, Drummond of Cadland MSS A6/28/2; Earl of Ilchester, *Chronicles of Holland House, 1820–1900*, 251, 323; see *Hary-O*, passim, and the Granville MSS PRO 30/29.

23. Diary of Elizabeth, Duchess of Grafton, entries of April 16, May 24–27, July 8, 1805 (among others) in Grafton MSS Acc. 2683 W7, West Suffolk Records Office; Granville MSS PRO 30/29/5; Marquess of Anglesey, *The Capel Letters*, 94. See for instance a letter dated April 16, 1858 in Fulford, *Dearest Child*, 93 passim.

24. Sir Galbraith Lowry Cole to the Countess of Malmesbury, April 25, 1824, Lowry Cole MSS PRO 30/43/32, Public Records Office; Lady Augusta Fox to Lord Holland, June 29, 1833, Holland House Papers, Add. MSS 51779.

25. Leveson-Gower and Palmer, *Hary-O*, 198; see for instance, the Granville MSS in which Lord Leveson (second Earl Granville, the noted foreign secretary) refers to his sisters by their pet names, but a first cousin is called "The Duchess of Sutherland." Lord Leveson to Earl Granville, May 9, 1838, Granville MSS PRO 30/29/6/4.

26. *Times* (of London), February 19, and April 13, 1839.
27. *Times* (of London), October 19 and 23, 1839.
28. *Times* (of London), September 18, 1869.
29. *Times* (of London), February 21, 1895.
30. Harriet, Lady Bessborough, to her lover, Lord Granville Leve-

son-Gower, March 30, 1806, quoted in Earl of Bessborough, *Georgiana*, 281.

31. See Judith Schneid Lewis, "Maternal Health in the English Aristocracy, 1790–1840: Myths and Realities," 97–114.

CHAPTER I. LOVE AND MARRIAGE

1. Oakley, "A Case of Maternity," 623.
2. Stone, *Family, Sex and Marriage*, 136.
3. Earl of Bessborough, *Lady Bessborough and Her Family Circle*, 31–32.
4. Lees H. Gronow, *The Reminiscences and Recollections of Captain Gronow* 1:31.
5. Ibid., 32.
6. Ibid., 31.
7. Arthur Calder-Marshall, *The Two Duchesses*, 32
8. Ibid., 133.
9. Ibid.
10. Ibid., 134–135.
11. Blanche was grandmother to the famous Mitford sisters of the twentieth century and to Clementine Hozier, who married Winston Churchill. Blanche's sister Kate was the mother of Bertrand Russell.
12. Mitford, *Stanleys of Alderley*, 8.
13. Ibid.
14. Ibid., 7.
15. Ibid., 9–10.
16. Ibid., 10.
17. Ibid., 13–14.
18. Ibid., 15.
19. Ibid., 9, 13; See also 8, 10–11, 25.
20. Calder-Marshall, *Two Duchesses*, 17–18.
21. Ibid., 12–16.
22. Malcolm Elwin, *The Noels and the Milbankes*, 43.
23. Bessborough, *Lady Bessborough and Her Family Circle*, 138.
24. Leveson-Gower and Palmer, *Hary-O*, 139.

25. Ibid., 185
26. Ibid., 55, 86, 87.
27. He is described as the "handsomest man in England" throughout the correspondence in Granville, *Lord Granville Leveson-Gower,* not only by the enamored Lady Bessborough, but also by his best friend George Canning. The Regency courtesan Harriette Wilson once inquired of the Duke of Leinster who was the "best worth having," and he told her that Lord Granville was "the most desirable man I ever saw." Harriette, however, after contriving to meet him, was disappointed. See Harriette Wilson, *Memoirs of Harriette Wilson,* 234–244. For his whist-playing, see the entry for him in the *DNB.*
28. Leveson-Gower and Palmer, *Hary-O,* 323.
29. Ibid., xiii.
30. Hector Bolitho and Derek Peel, *The Drummonds of Charing Cross,* 104.
31. Wilbur Devereux Jones, *Lord Derby and Victorian Conservatism,* 269. Far from marrying their daughters to a poor curate, the Clarendons actually married their eldest to a son of the Derbys, who became sixteenth Earl.
32. The Manners-Drummond match provides a fascinating view of British snobbery. The only thing that distinguished their married life from others was that Andrew spent his time away from home at the bank, while men of the landed classes more frequently spent their time in Parliament, at the races, or in whorehouses. Banks, however, were considered more objectionable than any of these alternatives.
33. David Thomas, "The Social Origins of Marriage Partners of the British Peerage in the Eighteenth and Nineteenth Centuries," 109.
34. Trumbach, *Rise of Egalitarian Family,* 291.
35. John Stuart Mill, "The Subjection of Women," 201.
36. For instance, Lord Granville proposed to Lady Harriet Cavendish on November 14 and they were married on December 24, 1809. William Lamb proposed to Caroline Ponsonby on May 2 and they were married on June 3, 1805. Bessborough, *Lady Bessborough and Her Family Circle,* 129, 198.
37. Hon. Henry Fox to Dr. Francis, May 15, 1762, in Ilchester and Stavordale, *Lady Sarah Lennox,* 120.
38. Calder-Marshall, *Two Duchesses,* 18.
39. Georgiana, Lady Morpeth, to her sister Harriet, Countess Gran-

ville (then styled Lady Harriet Leveson-Gower), December 25, 1809, Granville MSS PRO 30/29/17/5.

40. Gervas Huxley, *Lady Elizabeth and the Grosvenors*; 1; Earl of Clarendon to the Duchess of Manchester, February 4, 1868, in A. L. Kennedy, *My Dear Duchess*, 244.
41. Mitford, *Stanleys of Alderley*, 15-16.
42. Gervas Huxley, *Victorian Duke*, 65.
43. Ibid.
44. Ibid., 66.
45. Trumbach, *Rise of the Egalitarian Family*, 81.
46. Iris Butler, *The Eldest Brother*, 472.
47. Huxley, *Lady Elizabeth and the Grosvenors*, 12.
48. Ibid., 2.
49. Ibid.
50. Ibid., 14–15.
51. Carola Oman, *The Gascoyne Heiress*, 112.
52. Granville, *Lord Granville Leveson-Gower* 1:313.
53. Marquess of Kildare (later first Duke of Leinster) to his wife, April 13, 1762, in Brian Fitzgerald, *Correspondence of Emilia Mary (Lennox) Fitzgerald, Duchess of Leinster* 1:117.
54. Diary of Francis Hugh Seymour, the future fifth Marquess of Hertford, January 5, 1835, Seymour of Ragley MSS CR 114A/644, Warwickshire County Record Office.
55. Mrs. Stanley to Mr. Stanley (as they were then styled), November 10, 1846, in Nancy Mitford, *The Ladies of Alderley*, 119.
56. Gronow, *Captain Gronow* 1:33.
57. Ilchester, *Chronicles of Holland House*, 315.
58. According to article 26 of the "First Commissioner appointed by her Majesty to enquire into the Law of Divorce, and more particularly, into the Mode of obtaining divorces a *vinculo matrimonii*." (London: HMSO, 1853), the number of successful divorce bills for the entire country was as follows: between 1715–1774, 60, or 1 annually; 1775–1799, 74, or 3 annually; 1800–1852, 110, or 2 annually.
59. J.A. Hume, *The Letters and Journals of Lady Mary Coke* 3:52.
60. Stone, *Family, Sex, and Marriage*, 502.
61. See the accounts of Calder-Marshall, *Two Duchesses*, 25; Lord David Cecil, *The Young Melbourne*, 33; and Tresham Lever, *The Letters of Lady Palmerston*, 6n.

62. She wrote a fascinating if sensationalistic account of the fate of Mme. de Souza, the wife of the Portuguese ambassador to Paris, who died trying to conceal the birth of a lover's child. "By the by," the Countess wrote parenthetically to her mother-in-law, "we should do quite differently in England on such an occasion, for instead of so fair and honest a method of proceeding, the child w^d have been a Souza and declared as much in broad day light without any scruple to the prejudice of its brothers and sisters." Paris, January 20, 1792, Granville MSS PRO 30/29/5/4.

63. Duchess to Lady Elizabeth Foster, August 19, 1783 in Bessborough, *Georgiana*, 62.

64. Lady Harriet Cavendish to her sister, Lady Morpeth, December 21, 1807, in Leveson-Gower and Palmer, *Hary-O*, 273–274.

65. Home, *Lady Mary Coke* 3:28.

66. Anglesey, *One-Leg*, 256.

67. Ilchester, *Chronicles of Holland House*, 174–175.

68. Hyacinthe, Lady Hatherton, to Gerald Wellesley, Hatherton MSS D260M/F/5/27/59, Staffordshire Record Office.

69. Butler, *The Eldest Brother*, 486, 495.

70. Ilchester and Stavordale, *Lady Sarah Lennox*, 332–333. Lord William was a brother of Lord George Gordon, notorious for leading the anti-Catholic Gordon Riots in 1780.

71. Journal of Elizabeth, Lady Holland, June 19, 1799, Holland House Papers, Add. MSS 51928.

72. "Note on Eliza Courtney," Appendix, in Bessborough, *Georgiana*.

73. Leveson-Gower and Palmer, *Hary-O*, xiii.

74. Dorothy M. Stuart, *Dearest Bess*, 163.

75. Diary of Elizabeth, Lady Holland, [1794], Holland House Papers, Add. MSS 51927. The handsome young lover of the time was probably the twenty-one-year-old Lord Morpeth, who later became the husband of Lady Georgiana Cavendish.

76. Trumbach, *Rise of the Egalitarian Family*, 156.

77. Ilchester and Stavordale, *Lady Sarah Lennox*, 66–67, 116.

78. Marquis of Kildare to the Marchioness, April 20, 1762, in Fitzgerald, *Emily, Duchess of Leinster* 1:119.

79. Journal of Elizabeth, Lady Holland, [May 1794], Holland House Papers, Add. MSS 51927.

80. Journal of Elizabeth, Lady Holland, November 1, 1797, Holland House Papers, Add. MSS 51928.
81. Anglesey, *One-Leg*, 100.
82. Ibid., 96.
83. Hume, *Lady Mary Coke*, November 17, 1771, 3:481.
84. *Hansard's Parliamentary Debates*, 3d series, vol. 142, col. 1974 (June 26, 1856), and vol. 145, col. 783 (May 25, 1857).
85. Lady Harriet Cavendish to Countess Dowager Spencer, August 20, 1807, in Leveson-Gower and Palmer, *Hary-O*, 207.
86. Lady Harriet Cavendish to her mother Georgiana, the Duchess of Devonshire, September 1804, in ibid., 106.
87. Quoted by Lady Harriet in a letter to her sister, Lady Morpeth, November 30, 1806, in ibid., 177.
88. Ibid., 130.
89. Lady Cecilia Ridley to her mother, then Lady Parke, January 1842, in Ridley, *Cecilia*, 83.
90. Lady Mahon to her mother, the Countess of Chatham, April 24, 1780, Hoare (Pitt) MSS PRO 30/70/5/#358, Public Records Office; Lady Mahon was the daughter of Pitt the Elder (Lord Chatham), and sister of Pitt the younger, the two famous Prime Ministers. Lady Mahon had three daughters, the second being Lady Hester Stanhope, the famous traveler and eccentric.
91. See for instance, entries for January 1, 1804, February 1803, and February 13, 1805 for relations with her daughter-in-law. See May 5 and 13, 1804, for her step-daughter-in-law. Diaries of Elizabeth, Duchess of Grafton (second wife of the third Duke), Grafton MSS Acc. 2683, W5[1803], W6[1804], W7[1805].
92. Ibid, July 8, 1805.
93. Countess of Carlisle to Lady Gower (as Lady Stafford was then styled), Spa, August 27, 1772, Granville MSS PRO 30/29/4/2; Lord Hugh to Lady Horatia Seymour, August 9, 1793, Seymour of Ragley MSS CR114A/364.
94. Bessborough, *Lady Bessborough and Her Family Circle*, 182.
95. Harriet, Countess Gower (as the Duchess of Sutherland was then styled), and Georgiana, Lady Dover, to her sister Lady Caroline Lascelles, December 19, 1831, quoted in Lady Maud Leconfield, *Three Howard Sisters*, 225–229. Similarly Georgiana, Lady Dover, to Lady Caroline Lascelles, December 3, 1832, 253.

96. Huxley, *Victorian Duke*, 67.
97. Marina Warner, *Queen Victoria's Sketchbook*, 161.
98. Francis Bamford and the Duke of Wellington, *The Journal of Mrs. Arbuthnot* 1:196.
99. Elizabeth, Duchess of Rutland, to her son-in-law, Andrew Robert Drummond, April 11, 1824, Drummond of Cadland MSS B5/20/1.
100. See the correspondence between Lady Mary and Lady Elizabeth Drummond, especially letters of January 5 and January 23, 1823, and January 10, 1827, Drummond of Cadland B6/29/8/1 and B6/29/41.
101. Ilchester, *Chronicles of Holland House*, 156–158.
102. Lady Augusta Fox to Lady Holland, Holland House Papers, Add. MSS 51799.
103. Lady Augusta Fox to Lady Holland, October 28, 1836, Holland House Papers, Add. MSS 51779.
104. See for instance, Ridley, *Cecilia*, 83 (1842); Anglesey, *Capel Letters*, passim; and of course the correspondence between Lady Morpeth and Lady Granville.
105. Mitford, *Stanleys of Alderley*, 17.
106. According to Hollingsworth, over 75 percent of the aristocratic women in the birth cohorts under discussion were married. Hollingsworth, "Demography of the British Peerage," 19.

CHAPTER II. THE NAME OF MOTHER

1. Frederick, Earl Jermyn, to his brother-in-law, Andrew Robert Drummond, 5 October 1832, Drummond of Cadland MSS B5/15/10.
2. Stone, *Family, Sex and Marriage*, 88.
3. Duke of Rutland to Andrew Robert Drummond, November 28, 1822, Drummond of Cadland MSS A6/17/1.
4. For discussions of the Infant Custody Bill, see James O. Hoge and Clarke Olney, *The Letters of Caroline Norton to Lord Melbourne*. Opposition to the Infant Custody Bill is discussed in the introduction. (14). See also James O. Hoge and Jane Marcus, *Selected Writings of Caroline Norton*.
5. "A Plain Letter to the Lord Chancellor on the Infant Custody Bill," by Pearce Stevenson, Esq. [Caroline Norton], in Hoge and Marcus, *Selected Writings of Caroline Norton*, 5–11.

6. Ibid., 3.
7. Gen. Pitt to Lady Gower, August 25, 1772, Granville MSS PRO 30/29/4/3.
8. Hume, *Lady Mary Coke* 4:108.
9. Bessborough, *Georgiana*, 162.
10. Quoted in H. Montgomery Hyde, *The Londonderrys*, 62. This forbidding dowager was the daughter of Frances Anne, Marchioness of Londonderry, of our study.
11. Trumbach, *Rise of the Egalitarian Family*, 220.
12. Duchess of Devonshire to Lord Granville Leveson-Gower, March 1, 1805, in Granville, *Lord Granville Leveson-Gower* 2:34. Similarly, see Lewis, "Maternal Health in the English Aristocracy," 101, 108–109.
13. See, for example, Hyacinthe, Lady Hatherton, to her brother Gerald Wellesley, February 2, 1813, in Hatherton MSS D260 M/F/5 27/59. Perhaps more surprisingly, even so radical a couple as Lord and Lady Amberley (the parents of Bertrand Russell, well known for their support of birth control) were delighted that Kate Amberley gave birth within a year of marriage. See Bertrand and Patricia Russell, *The Amberley Papers* 1:400 (entry for July 13, 1865).
14. Edith, Marchioness of Londonderry, *Frances Anne*, 61.
15. Mitford, *Stanleys of Alderley*, 229.
16. Londonderry, *Frances Anne*, 60.
17. Calder-Marshall, *Two Duchesses*, 32; Duchess to Thomas Coutts, September 23, 1789, in Bessborough, *Georgiana*, 162; letter of Lady Elizabeth Foster to a Parisian banker, May 27, 1790, Hervey MSS Acc. 941/58/1, West Suffolk Records Office.
18. Countess of Sutherland to Lady Stafford, [September] 1786, Granville Papers PRO 30/29/5/3.
19. Quoted in Elisabeth Badinter, *Mother Love*, 166.
20. Christian Augustus Struve, *A Familiar Treatise on the Physical Education of Children*, 211.
21. Ibid., 121.
22. Cynthia White, *Women's Magazines*, 42.
23. L. M. S., "Economy," in *British Mother's Magazine*, April 1855, 85–87. Quoted in J. A. and Olive Banks, *Feminism and Family Planning in Victorian England*, 62.
24. Lady Holland was the mother of Henry Webster and Henry Fox,

fourth Lord of Holland. Lady Elizabeth Foster was the mother of Augustus Foster and Augustus Clifford, her illegitimate son by the Duke of Devonshire. The Victorian search for new names led to such atrocities as Cyril, Aldred, Osbert, and that quintessential Victorian name, Algernon.

25. Ilchester and Stavordale, *Lady Sarah Lennox*, 395.

26. Frances, Lady Morley (Lady Boringdon, as she was then styled), to her sister-in-law, Theresa Villiers, May 7, 1810, and December 30, 1812, Morley Papers, Add. MSS 48233 and 48235. Similarly, see also George Russell to his uncle, Lord Jersey, August 1822, Jersey MSS Acc. 1138/319, Middlesex County Records Office (Lady Jersey had just given birth to a first daughter after eighteen months of marriage); Georgiana Ellis to Caroline Lascelles, January 22, 1828, in Leconfield, *Three Howard Sisters*, 103; Katherine, Lady Jermyn, to Andrew Robert Drummond, November 5, 1838, Drummond of Cadland MSS B 5/14/13; John Bailey, *The Diary of Lady Frederick Cavendish*, 28

27. Gerald Wellesley to Hyacinthe, Lady Hatherton, April 1815, Hatherton MSS D260 M/F/5 27/59.

28. Ilchester and Stavordale, *Lady Sarah Lennox*, 344.

29. Lady Harriet Cavendish to her grandmother, Dowager Countess Spencer, August 8, 1807, in Leveson-Gower and Palmer, *Hary-O*, 24.

30. Stone, *Family, Sex, and Marriage*, 397-398.

31. William Buchan, *Domestic Medicine*, 2. This book sold over one hundred thousand copies. A memorial to Buchan in Westminster Abbey notes that he is the author of *Domestic Medicine*. For his influence on aristocratic women, see Lewis, "Maternal Health in the English Aristocracy." 108.

32. Duchess to her mother, October 27, 1793, in Bessborough, *Georgiana*, 203. The Duke also had his mistress, Lady Elizabeth Foster, living at Devonshire House with the family.

33. Lady Stanley of Alderley to her husband (they were then only Mr. and Mrs.), September 22, 1846, in Mitford, *Ladies of Alderley*, 115.

34. Queen Victoria to the Princess Royal, Osborne, May 31, 1861, in Fulford, *Dearest Child*, 335-336.

35. Diary of James Walter Grimston, first Earl of Verulam, entry for February 29, 1820, Gorhambury MSS D/EV F45, Hertfordshire County Records Office.

36. Hyacinthe, Lady Hatherton, to her brother, Gerald Wellesley, February 27, 1818, (she was then simply Mrs. Littleton), Hatherton MSS D260 M/F/5 25/59. Lady Augusta Fox to Lady Holland, Paris, September 27, 1833, Holland House Papers, Add. MSS 51779.
37. Lord Morley to his sister, Mrs.Villiers, 16 March 1818, Morley Papers, Add. MSS 48232.
38. Cecil Woodham-Smith, *Queen Victoria*, 398.
39. Letters of Lady Harriet Cavendish to the Duchess of Devonshire, September 1804, in Leveson-Gower and Palmer. *Hary-O*, 98, 100, 102.
40. Lady Frances Cole to Countess of Malmesbury, August 24, 1824, Lowry Cole MSS PRO 30/43/32.
41. Marquess of Wellesley to E. J. Littleton (as Lord Hatherton was then styled), October 15, 1813, Hatherton MSS D260 M/F/5/27/1. Lady Augusta Fox to Lady Holland, June 19, 1833, Holland House Papers, Add. MSS 51779.
42. See Ilchester, *Chronicles of Holland House*, 401, 435. Marie Fox, as the child was named, married Prince Louis Liechtenstein of Austria in 1872 in a Catholic ceremony presided over by Cardinal Manning.
43. Struve, *Physical Education of Children*, 170.
44. Quoted in Maurice Quinlan, *Victorian Prelude*, 67.
45. Ilchester and Stavordale, *Lady Sarah Lennox*, 612.
46. Fulford, *Dearest Child*, 115.
47. Leconfield, *Three Howard Sisters*, 216. Similarly, see Londonderry, *Frances Anne*, 56; Gerald Wellesley to his sister, Lady Hatherton (then Mrs. Littleton), April 1815, Hatherton MSS D260 M/F/5 27/59.
48. Emily Brontë, *Wuthering Heights*, 140–141.
49. See, for instance, Bessborough, *Georgiana*, 187; and Ilchester and Stavordale, *Lady Sarah Lennox*, 382.
50. Earl of Jersey (Villiers) MSS Acc. 510/275a and 510/282.
51. Woodham-Smith, *Queen Victoria*, 398.
52. Fulford, *Dearest Child*, 182.
53. Frances, Lady Morley (then styled Lady Boringdon), to her sister-in-law, Mrs. Villiers, April 6, 1810, Morley Papers, Add. MSS 48233. Similarly, see letter of Lady Augusta Fox to Lady Holland, [1833], Holland House Papers, Add. MSS 51799; and Ridley, *Cecilia*, 148.
54. Kennedy, *Dear Duchess*, 95.

55. Leveson-Gower and Palmer, *Hary-O*, 129.
56. Assessments of Augustus's problem vary from epilepsy to profound retardation. In Philip Zeigler's account, he appears to have been aphasic as well. Ziegler, *Melbourne*, 73–79.
57. Leveson-Gower and Palmer, *Hary-O*, 223.
58. This phrase, of course, gave Martha Vicinus the title for her excellent collection of articles in women's history.
59. Badinter, *Mother Love*, 235–236.
60. Leconfield, *Three Howard Sisters*, 75.
61. Lady Augusta Fox to her father-in-law, Lord Holland, July 23, [1835], Holland House Papers, Add MSS. 51779.
62. Fulford, *Dearest Child*, 182. Similarly, the Queen wrote a year later, "When I think of a merry, happy free young girl and look at the ailing aching state a young wife is generally doomed to—which you can't deny is the penalty of marriage" 254.
63. This theme has been developed, in different ways, by Peter T. Cominos in "Innocent Femina Sensualis in Unconscious Conflict," and by J. H. Plumb, "The New World of the Child in Eighteenth-Century England."
64. Pornography is not a subject that comes within the rubric of this book. However, readers of Stephen Marcus's study of Victorian pornography entitled *The Other Victorians* will recognize the social origins of the Victorian fascination with the defloration of virgins.
65. Fulford, *Dearest Child*, 254.
66. Queen Victoria to the Princess Royal, December 18, 1861, in Roger Fulford, *Dearest Mama*, 23.
67. Granville, *Lord Leveson-Gower* 2:79 [June 1805].
68. Earl of Bessborough, *Lady Charlotte Guest*, 67.
69. Richard Bootle-Wilbraham to Lord Stanley (as the fourteenth Earl of Derby was then styled), January 17, 1841, Derby/Gathorne-Hardy Papers MSS 28/1/4.
70. Lady Frances Cole to her mother, the Countess of Malmesbury, May 10, 1826, Lowry Cole MSS PRO 30/43/32.
71. Lady Louisa Connelly to Lady Sarah Napier, February 15, 1782, Bunbury MSS E18/750/2, vol. 15, West Suffolk Records Office.
72. Lord Morley to Hon. Mrs. Villiers, October 22, 1809, Morley Papers, Add. MSS 48227.

Notes for Pages 82–88

73. Diaries of the Earl of Verulam, entries for November 25, and December 1 and 13, 1819, Gorhambury MSS D/EV F44.
74. Ibid., entry for 2 August 1822, D/EV F46.
75. Ibid., entry for 6 May 1821, D/EV F46.
76. James Y. Simpson, "Discovery of a New Anesthetic Agent," 934–937.
77. Woodham-Smith, *Queen Victoria*, 528.
78. Frederick Prescott, *The Control of Pain*, 31.
79. James Y. Simpson, *Obstetric Memoirs and Contributions*, 64.

CHAPTER III. THE ARISTOCRATIC ACCOUCHEUR

1. Knighton, Sir William, *Memoirs of Sir William Knighton, Baronet, G. C. H.* 1:58-57. Hereafter cited as *Memoirs*.
2. Christopher Hibbert, George IV: Regent and King, 227n.
3. "Summary of the Report . . . [on] Remuneration of Labour in Great Britain" 495.
4. Jean Donnison, *Midwives and Medical Men*, quoting Philip Thicknesse, "Man-Midwifery Analyzed," [1765], and Shorter, *Women's Bodies*, 143.
5. Sir George Clark, A History of the *Royal College of Physicians* of London 2:588-589.
6. *Lancet*, March 17, 1827, 768–769.
7. Ibid., (March 3, 1827, 701–702.
8. The first man-midwife to be knighted was David Hamilton (1663–1721), who attended Queen Anne and was knighted by her. Sir David also attended Caroline, Princess of Wales. According to the *DNB* entry for him, Hamilton acquired a fortune of £80,000, which he lost in the South Sea Bubble. Sir Richard Manningham (1690–1759) gained widespread fame in the exposure of Mary Tofts, who had claimed she gave birth to rabbits. See Irving S. Cutter and Henry R. Viets, *A Short History of Midwifery*, 15; and "Richard Manningham, " *DNB*. Sir Richard was the accoucheur who was too busy to take on the case of Sterne's fictional Mrs. Shandy.
9. Sir Hans Sloane's baronetcy of 1716 was the second conferred on a physician. Clark, *Royal College of Physicians*, p. 489n.

10. See Randolph Trumbach, "The Aristocratic Family in England, *1690–1780*," 25, 38.

11. Upper-class women offered their financial support to the new lying-in institutions. Susan, Countess of Harrowby (1772–1838), was a "Donor and Subscriber" to the British Ladies Lying-In Hospital, where the Duchess of Argyll was a patron. The account book belonging to Lady Grimston for the year 1781 reveals that she made generous contributions on a quarterly basis to the "Lying-in Charity." See Donnison, *Midwives and Medical Men*, 52, 232–233; and Gorhambury MSS D/EV F39.

12. Cutter and Viets, *A Short History of Midwifery*, 19–20. By comparison, a midwifery text of 1678 advised that babies who emerged "in a disorderly manner" were to be pushed back into the womb by the midwife (7).

13. Ibid., 31.

14. Ibid., 28.

15. Ibid. 36, 41, 100–101, 105, 108.

16. Historical demographer Thomas McKeown believes that during the end of the eighteenth century, the "only change in obstetric practice likely to have contributed to a reduction of maternal or infant mortality was an improvement in the hygiene of delivery." See McKeown, *The Modern Rise of Population*, 106. See also Stone, *Family, Sex and Marriage*, 72.

17. Harvey Graham, *Eternal Eve*, 360. On the occasion of Fielding Ould's knighthood in 1759, the following ditty made the rounds of Dublin:

> Sir Fielding Ould is made a knight;
> He should have been a lord by right;
> For then each lady's prayer would be—
> Oh Lord, good Lord, deliver me!

Quoted by Herbert Thoms, *Our Obstetric Heritage*, 64. For more on Sir Fielding, (1710–1789), see also Cutter and Viets, *A Short History of Midwifery*, 22–23; and "Fielding Ould," in *DNB*.

18. Cutter and Viets, *A Short History of Midwifery*, 15; and Clark, *Royal College of Physicians* 2:500.

19. Cutter and Viets, *A Short History of Midwifery*, 36.

20. Judy Barrett Litoff makes this point in *American Midwives, 1860 to the Present*, 8–9.
21. H. Laing Gordon, *Sir James Young Simpson and Chloroform (1811–1870)*, 57. In 1852 the Royal College of Surgeons was authorized to examine persons for a Licentiate in Midwifery. It was not until 1886, however, that licensed medical practitioners were required to be qualified in mid-wifery, as well as in medicine and surgery. Munro Kerr, R. W. Johnstone, and Miles H. Philips, *Historical Review of British Obstetrics and Gynaecology 1800–1950*, 333.
22. Knighton, 1:11-12.
23. Ibid., 14.
24. Ibid., 79–80.
25. W. J. Reader, *Professional Men*, 19.
26. Knighton, *Memoirs* 1:72. Under the new definition, gentlemanliness became a quality that everyone understood but that was nevertheless hard to define. As a result, whether or not an individual was truly a gentleman became a subjective judgment. Harriette Wilson, the famous Regency courtesan, had the opportunity to inspect the gentlemanliness of a large number of individuals, and she offered the following discussion on the subject:

> There are in fact various kinds of gentlemen. A man is a gentleman, according to Berkeley Craven's definition of the word, who has no visible means of gaining his livelihood; others have called Lord Deerhurst and Lord Barrymore and Lord Stair gentlemen, because they are Lords; and the system at White's Club, the members of which are all choice gentlemen of course, is and ever has been never to blackball any man who ties a good knot in his handkerchief, keeps his hands out of his breeches-pockets, and says nothing. For my part, I confess I like a man who can talk and contribute to the amusement of whatever society he may be placed in: and that is the reason I am always glad to find myself in the company of Lord Hertford, not-withstanding he is so often blackballed at White's. *Memoirs of Harriette Wilson* 1:196

27. Knighton, *Memoirs* 1:12.
28. Thomas Denman, *Memoir of My Own Life*, Croft Papers, 1779.
29. Richard Croft to Mrs. Denman, May 9 and 22, 1790, Croft Papers, Lot 1.

30. Richard Croft to Mrs. Denman, July 7, 1790, Croft Papers, Lot 1.
31. Reader, *Professional Men*, 37.
32. Bransby B. Cooper, *The Life of Sir Astley Cooper, Bart.* 1:273.
33. Richard Croft to Mrs. Denman, May 22, 1790, Croft Papers, Lot. 1.
34. Ibid., May 17, 1790.
35. Given this structure in which patients determined the value of services received, income from private practice sometimes seems to have been more like gifts of favor, or even tips, than real fees. In 1813, after performing an operation for "the stone" on a West India merchant named Hyatt, Sir Astley Cooper began to take his leave. Suddenly Hyatt threw a nightcap at him. It proved to contain a check for a thousand guineas. Cooper, *Sir Astley Cooper* 2:159.
36. Ibid., 159.
37. Clark, *Royal College of Physicians*, 500
38. Cutter and Viets, *A Short History of Midwifery*, 28.
39. Graham, *Eternal Eve*, 190.
40. See for instance I. S. L. Loudon, "A Doctor's Cash Book," 255.
41. Biographical information on the five accoucheurs, except where otherwise noted, comes from the following sources: Denman: *DNB*; William Munk, *The Roll of the Royal College of Physicians of London* 3:333–334; Thoms, *Our Obstetric Heritage*, 66; "Memoir of Sir Richard Croft," *Times*, February 16, 1818, 3; Sir Joseph Arnould, *Life of Thomas, First Lord Denman* 1:2; *Gentleman's Magazine*, March 1818, 277. For Croft: "Memoir of Sir Richard Croft," op. cit.; *DNB*; *Gentleman's Magazine*, op. cit.; *Times*, February 14, 16, and 18, 1818. For Clarke: *DNB*; *Medical Times and Gazette* 36 (September 12, 1857): 282. For Knighton: *DNB*; Munk *Royal College of Physicians* 3:39–40; Hibbert, *George IV*, 223–227. For Locock: *DNB*; "Obituary of Sir Charles Locock, Bart.", *Lancet*, July 31, 1875, 184. The "Memoir of Sir Richard Croft," which appeared in the *Times* on February 16, 1818, a few days after Croft's death, contained several untruths about Denman, some of which were rebutted in the *Gentleman's Magazine* the next month (see above). The inference was that Denman's origins were even more lowly than in fact they were. The *Times* attributed all of Denman's success to Hunter's intervention in 1783, and suggested that earlier in his career Denman kept shop as an apothecary and

operated a boarding house. He did, of course, lodge two of Hunter's pupils (namely, Croft and Baillie), which was a common practice among established medical men, encouraging a master-disciple relationship. Nor did Denman, as far as I can tell, ever engage in retail trade as an apothecary. Furthermore, Denman had a flourishing career well before 1783.

42. Ca. 1796 Knighton wrote of his education in London: "The operations performed here are executed in the most masterly manner. Cline, whom I attend in anatomy, and Cooper in surgery, are men of the first abilities." (*Memoirs* 1:15).

43. Harold Perkin, *The Origins of Modern English Society*, 38, 44–45, 49.

44. Knighton, *Memoirs* 1:59.

45. Richard Croft to Mrs. Denman, June 6 and July 20, 1790, Croft Papers, Lot 1.

46. Her two daughters were Harriet, Countess Granville, and Georgiana, Countess of Carlisle. Her niece, Lady Caroline Lamb, and a niece by marriage, Maria, Lady Duncannon, also were attended by Croft. By 1818, when Croft died, these four women had experienced twenty-three births and four miscarriages. Lady Carlisle had, previous to Princess Charlotte's death, already engaged Croft to attend at her eleventh confinement, which was to take place in May 1818. Letter of Georgiana, Lady Morpeth, November 8, 1817, Croft Papers, Lot 4.

47. Sir Benjamin C. Brodie, *Autobiography of the Late Sir Benjamin C. Brodie, Bart.*, 126. Hereafter cited as Brodie, *Autobiography*.

48. Accounts differ as to the origins of the Wellesley-Knighton connection. One account suggests that Moll only became a patient of Knighton's in London (Hibbert, *George IV*, 224), whereas another suggests that Knighton knew Moll in Plymouth. See A. Aspinall, "George IV and Sir William Knighton." According to Aspinall, "whilst at Plymouth" Knighton "contracted an intimacy with a woman known by the name of Poll Raffles, who subsequently became one of the Marquess of Wellesley's numerous mistresses," a phrase that makes the tantalizing suggestion that the original relationship between Knighton and Moll was not of a professional nature. See Aspinall, 57. Wellesley's biographer, however, traces Knighton's relationship directly to the Marquess himself. "Knighton," Iris Butler has written, "Did hang about the Wellesley seraglio at Ramsgate in 1808–09 and Hyacinthe [Lady

Wellesley] gives veiled hints of his usefullness to her husband's concubines." Knighton "owed his start up the ladder to the Marquess and is part of Wellesley's mysterious connection with the County of Devonshire." See Butler, *The Eldest Brother*, 413, 414. According to Butler, it was not Moll Raffles, but a Miss Lesley who was to accompany Wellesley to Spain and required Knighton's attention (Butler, 402). This is curious in the light of other evidence that Wellesley hired Knighton only to please Moll. Hibbert, 224; and Aspinall, 57. Knighton's memoirs, edited by his wife, are understandably hazy on this point, but Lady Knighton does say that the "kind patronage and influence of a limited number of persons of rank and consequence, to whom Dr. Knighton's ability had become known during his residence in Devonshire, tended essentially to his success," which suggests that Knighton knew Wellesley at Plymouth. Knighton, *Memoirs* 1:80.

49. Richard Croft to Mrs. Denman, April 23, 1790, Croft Papers, Lot 1.

50. Russell C. Maulitz, "Metropolitan Medicine and the Man-Midwife," 30.

51. Ibid., 34.

52. Harriet, Duchess of Sutherland (then Countess Gower), to her sister, Lady Caroline Lascelles, December 28, 1832, in Leconfield, *Three Howard Sisters*, 256.

53. *Lancet*, July 31, 1875, 184.

54. Aspinall, "George IV and Knighton," 65.

55. Knighton, *Memoirs* 1:72–73.

56. Ibid., 2:185.

57. Brodie, *Autobiography*, 146.

58. M. Jeanne Peterson, *The Medical Profession in Mid-Victorian London*, 106.

59. Lady Morley (Lady Boringdon, as she was then styled) to Hon. Mrs. Villiers, January 15, 1814, Morley Papers, Add. MSS 48236.

60. In addition to those references cited below on this point, Norman D. Jewson, "Medical Knowledge and the Patronage System in Eighteenth-Century England," 8, passim, especially 374–375; and Noel and José Parry, *The Rise of the Medical Profession*, especially 29.

61. Peterson, *Medical Profession in Mid-Victorian London*, 55.

62. Shortt, "Physicians, Science and Status," 60, 63.

63. James Grieg, *The Farington Diary*, 225.

64. Lady Harriet Cavendish to her sister, Georgiana Lady Morpeth, August 26, 1802, in Leveson-Gower and Palmer, *Hary-O*, 28.

65. Elizabeth, Countess of Bristol, to her husband, fifth Earl, and later, first Marquess, October 8 [1816] Hervey MSS 941/56/76.

66. Cooper, *Sir Astley Cooper* 1:297.

67. Thomas W. Laqueur, "The Queen Caroline Affair," 448. It was Denman who, at the end of a rousing speech to close Caroline's defense, added the unfortunate phrase "Go and sin no more." This soon appeared in ditty form on the streets of London as:

> Most gracious Queen, we thee implore,
> Go Away, and sin no more.
> But if the effort prove too great
> Go away at any rate.

68. *Chronicles of Holland House*, 100.

69. On Clarke's appointment as physician to Queen Adelaide on the accession of William IV. *Lancet*, April 17, 1830, 87.

70. Croft to Mrs. Denman, May 9, 1790, Croft Papers, Lot 1.

71. Croft to Mrs. Denman [May 22, 1790], Croft Papers, Lot 1.

72. Croft to Mrs. Denman, Saturday noon [undated, April or May 1790], Croft Papers, Lot 1.

73. Ibid.

74. Margaret Croft to Mrs. Denman, July 18, 1790, Croft Papers, Lot 1.

75. Richard Croft to Mrs. Denman, May 14, 1790, Croft Papers, Lot 1.

76. Richard Croft to Mrs. Denman, n. d., Croft Papers, Lot 1.

77. Richard Croft to Mrs. Denman, May 9 [1790], Croft Papers, Lot 1.

78. Richard Croft to Mrs. Denman, April 25, 1790, Croft Papers, Lot 1.

79. Richard Croft to Mrs. Denman, [May 24, 1790], Croft Papers, Lot 1.

80. Calder-Marshall, *Two Duchesses*, 106n.

81. The cup and saucer remain in the care of Croft's descendent, Richard Page Croft, the owner of the manuscript collection, who pointed them out to me and explained their history.

82. Croft to Dr. Denman, Wednesday morning [June 9, 1790], Croft Papers, Lot 1.

83. Dowager Lady Spencer to her daughter Harriet, Lady Bessborough, June 4, 1807 in Bessborough, *Lady Bessborough and Her Family Circle*, 160. See also Frances, Countess of Morley, to her sister-in-law, the Hon. Theresa Villiers, April 23, 1814, Morley Papers, Add. MSS 48237; Princess Charlotte to Richard Croft, August 29, 1817, Croft Papers, Lot 2; Ridley, *Cecilia*, 93; Earl Jermyn to Andrew Robert Drummond, February 1832, Drummond of Cadland MSS B5/14/6; Georgiana, Lady Dover, to Lady Caroline Lascelles, December 16, 1831, in Leconfield, *Three Howard Sisters*, 288.

84. Richard Croft to Mrs. Denman, n. d., Croft Papers, Lot 1.

85. Lady Clanwilliam to Emma, Countess of Derby (then Lady Stanley), January 29, 1841, Derby/Gathorne-Hardy MSS 28/1/12. Lady Derby's husband was, of course, the great Victorian Conservative Prime Minister.

86. Elizabeth Longford, "Queen Victoria's Doctors," 78.

87. A. M. W. Stirling, *The Letter-Bag of Elizabeth Spencer-Stanhope* 1:114.

88. The letters of Princess Charlotte to Sir Richard Croft during her pregnancy in 1817 form lot 2 of the Croft Papers.

89. Norman Himes, *Medical History of Contraception*, 125.

90. Sir Charles Mansfield Clarke, "Notes on the Theory and Practice of Midwifery, and of the Diseases of Women and Children," unpaginated, Library of the Wellcome Institute for the History of Medicine.

91. Sonia Keppel, *The Sovereign Lady*, 73.

92. Denman, *Introduction to the Practice of Midwifery*, 246; Clarke, "Theory and Practice of Midwifery." Dr. Andrew Thynne, "Notes of Lectures on Midwifery, taken down by Page Nichol Scott," 94–96, Library of the Wellcome Institute for the History of Medicine. Thynne was first lecturer in midwifery at St. Bartholomew's Hospital.

93. Wood, "Fashionable Diseases," 33.

94. Regina Morantz, "The Lady and Her Physician," 48.

95. Sophia Curzon to Aunt Mary Noel, January 1, 1782, in Elwin, *Noels and Milbankes*, 187.

96. Longford, "Queen Victoria's Doctors," 76.

97. Denman, *Introduction*, 263.

98. Longford, "Queen Victoria's Doctors," 76.

99. Typically, fees were based on the patient's rank as well as on the medical service performed. S. W. F. Holloway has made the suggestion that physicians set charges in direct proportion to the cost of their patient's house rental. Childbirth cost five guineas, he estimated, in families whose homes were valued at above £100. However, upper-class incomes varied widely, particularly among the very few with very large incomes, and these are the people with whom we are concerned. How would such a system operate for those whose homes were valued at several thousand, or hundreds of thousands of pounds, and who had several homes? See S. W. F. Holloway, "Medical Education in England, 1830–1858," 309.

100. Thea Johnston Holme, *Prinny's Daughter*, 5.

101. Longford, "Queen Victoria's Doctors," 86. Royalty could pay incredibly high medical fees. According to John Brooke, George III's biographer, the King's physicians (including Croft's friend and brother-in-law, Matthew Baillie) received thirty guineas each a visit plus expenses, even when they made several visits a week. The total medical expenses for George III's prolonged illness were enormous. In 1812 Lord Liverpool was told that the previous year's medical expenses for the King totaled £33,998. When the King died, the total medical expenses were estimated at £271,691 18s.—possibly the most expensive illness in history. See John Brooke, *King George III*, 285.

102. Hibbert, *George IV*, 224. Because the embassy proved to be of shorter duration than expected, and because Wellesley was unable to pay the entire sum upon which Knighton had counted, a compromise was reached by way of introducing Knighton to the Prince of Wales. Aspinall, "George IV and Knighton," 57. Knighton appears to have extracted a good deal from Wellesley, since Knighton had received £3,000 before leaving England, for a trip that lasted only three months (Aspinall, 58n). According to Iris Butler, Knighton also received a guinea a day from the government, but she is incorrect when she states that Knighton did receive the full £5,000. See Butler, *The Eldest Brother*, 416. That Wellesley paid Knighton what proved to be £1,000 a month and still felt that he owed Knighton something (and therefore the introduction to the Prince) indicates that Knighton must have rendered some extraordinarily valuable service during the mission abroad, although to this day no one knows what it was. The incident, therefore, testifies to Knighton's discretion as well as to his greed. By comparison, Sir Astley

Cooper was kept on a £600 a year retainer by a wealthy city man, but of course Cooper had many other patients. Cooper, *Sir Astley Cooper* 2:157.
103. Hibbert, *George IV*, 227n.
104. *Medical Times and Gazette* 36 (September 12, 1857): 282.
105. *DNB* entry for Sir Charles Locock.
106. Cooper, *Sir Astley Cooper* 2:408.
107. Ibid. 157–158.
108. Letters of June 18, 1823, and December 4, 1825, quoted in Maulitz, "Metropolitan Medicine and the Man-Midwife," 34, 40.
109. Cooper, *Sir Astley Cooper* 2:461.
110. Knighton *Memoirs* 2:91. At another point, Knighton wrote, "With respect to my practice, my progress surpasses what I expected, and kind fortune seems to have laid fast hold of me. . . . But stop—I feel no security, as something new may arise, the least expected perhaps, and turn the scales" (1:74–75).
111. Brodie, *Autobiography*, 116–117.
112. Ibid., 126.
113. Cooper, *Sir Astley Cooper* 2:233.
114. Ibid., 1: 228–229.
115. Jane Austen, *Pride and Prejudice*, 366.
116. Brodie, *Autobiography*, 108–109; Knighton, *Memoirs* 2:182.
117. Thomas, "Social Origins of Marriage Partners," 107–108.
118. Bamford and Wellington, *Journal of Mrs. Arbuthnot* 1:186.
119. Ibid., 1:245. Knighton's patients included Liverpool's own sister, Charlotte, Countess of Verulam, who had been attended by Knighton as late as the summer of 1822.
120. Quoted in Aspinall, "George IV and Knighton," 66–68.
121. See Hibbert, *George IV*; Aspinall, "George IV and Knighton," 81; also Brodie, *Autobiography*, 125.
122. Knighton's Memoirs 2:8.
123. See for instance, Dorothy M. Stuart, *Daughter of England*, 308, 312; Holme, *Prinny's Daughter*; and T. H. Green, *Memoirs of Her Late Royal Highness Princess Charlotte Augusta of Wales*.
124. See Calder-Marshall, *Two Duchesses*, 176; also *Times* (London), February 16, 1818, and *Gentleman's Magazine*, March 1818.
125. The spurious issue himself, who by now was the sixth Duke of

Devonshire, gave credence to these stories by his failure to marry. Of the three principals, only Lady Elizabeth Foster (whom the Duke had married after the Duchess's death) was still alive. She, however, was in Rome, digging up antiquities and flirting with Cardinal Consalvi. It was said she had converted to Catholicism and had confessed the story of the switched babies to a priest, who let the story get out. However, it could hardly have been coincidental that the rumor surfaced immediately after Princess Charlotte's death, supposedly at Croft's hands. Additional credence was given to the story because the sixth Duke, alone of the Duchess Georgiana's children, was devoted to Lady Elizabeth, and came to Rome to be with her on her deathbed in 1824. The Duchess's daughters Lady Georgiana (later Lady Morpeth) and Lady Harriet Cavendish hated Lady Elizabeth—they felt, quite rightly, that she had usurped their mother's place. The kernel of truth behind the rumor was the fact that both the Duchess Georgiana and Lady Elizabeth Foster had given birth to the Duke's children in August 1785. But both of the children were girls—Lady Harriet Cavendish and Caroline St. Jules, who was to marry George Lamb. The story of the switched babies was so intriguing that it continued to circulate for about a century. See Calder-Marshall, *Two Duchesses*, 176.

126. Letter of Robert Gardiner to Lady Croft, July 14, 1818, Lady Croft Memorandum Book, Croft Papers.

127. See for instance, the *Lancet* of August 8, 1829, 592.

128. See the *Lancet*, March 3, 1827, 701–702, and March 17, 1827, 768–769.

129. *Times* (London), September 10, 1857, 5.

130. Ibid., July 26, 1857, 5.

131. Peterson, *Medical Profession in Mid-Victorian London*, 3–4.

132. Gordon, *Sir James Young Simpson*, 75.

CHAPTER IV. PREGNANCY

1. Mary Noel to Lady Judith Milbanke, October 12, 1791, in Elwin, *Noels and Milbankes*, 393. Lady Judith had suffered miscarriages in 1777 and 1782.

2. Granville, *Lord Granville Leveson-Gower* 1:71.
3. Diary of her mother, Elizabeth, Duchess of Grafton, Grafton MSS Acc. 2683 W7; Lord Morley to Hon. Mrs. Villiers, May 4, 1810, Morley Papers, Add. MSS 48228; Diary of Lord Verulam, Gorhambury MSS D/EV F46.
4. Bessborough, *Lady Charlotte Guest*, 30. For a variety of reasons Lady Charlotte felt that she was not accepted into the high circles to which she was entitled by birth. She was a daughter of the ninth Earl of Lindsay, who died when she was a small child. Her mother then married a country clergyman named Pegus, whom Lady Charlotte detested. She blamed this marriage and her mother's continued residence in the country for her family's lack of standing. Lady Charlotte's own marriage to John (Merthyr) Guest was a curious one. She was not enough of a snob to refrain from marrying "trade," but enough of a snob to want acceptance for herself, husband, and children in the highest circles of the landed aristocracy. Her efforts were eventually successful. The Guests bought an estate in Dorset, Canfield; her husband was granted a baronetcy (though not a peerage as she had hoped); but her eldest son was raised to the peerage as Viscount Wimborne. Several of her children married into the highest ranks of the peerage.
5. Leconfield, *Three Howard Sisters*, 205.
6. Bessborough, *Lady Charlotte Guest*, 111.
7. Russell and Russell, *Amberley Papers* 1:352, 357.
8. Lady Morley to Hon. Mrs. Villiers, November 4, 13 and December 19, 1809, Morley Papers, Add. MSS 48233. Compare the wife's sober account of this accident with her husband's melodramatic and nearly hysterical seven-page letter of November 3, 1809. Also Add. MSS 48233.
9. Earl of Banbury to his sisters, [1802], Banbury/Knollys MSS 1M44/116/10, Hampshire Record Office.
10. Lady Morley to Hon. Mrs. Villiers, February 8, 1810, Morley Papers, Add. MSS 48233.
11. Lady Holland's Journal, [Autumn 1795], Holland House Papers, Add. MSS 51927.
12. Lady Granville to her aunt, Lady Bessborough, August 28, 1810, in Granville, *Lord Granville Leveson-Gower* 2:361.
13. Leconfield, *Three Howard Sisters*, 41.

14. Lady Frances Cole to her parents, Earl and Countess of Malmesbury, June 13, 1826, Lowry Cole MSS PRO 30/43/52.
15. Lady Holland's Journal, February 10, 1793, Holland House Papers, Add. MSS 51927.
16. Londonderry, *Frances Anne*, 103.
17. Russell and Russell, *Amberley Papers*, 351 and 357.
18. Fulford, *Dearest Mama*, June 15, 1858, 115. Caroline Grosvenor and Charles Beilby, *The First Lady Wharncliffe and Her Family, 1779–1856*, 2:327.
19. Susan, Lady Harrowby, to her brother, Lord Granville, October 14, 1807, Granville MSS PRO 30/29/6/4.
20. In the springs of 1807 and 1808 Lady Jersey wrote letters to her husband, saying farewell in case she died in childbirth, which in both cases she expected imminently. The sixth Earl of Jersey was born in April 1808, but neither Hollingsworth nor any of the peerage directories record the birth of a child to her in 1807. She was so far advanced in pregnancy when she wrote the letter that she could not have miscarried, so either she gave birth to a stillborn child or it died in early infancy. She eventually had seven children, although she did not have a daughter until 1822, more than eighteen years after her marriage. Her third daughter and last child was born in 1828—twenty-four years after marriage. Lady Jersey died in 1867 at the age of eighty-two. See Earl of Jersey (Villiers) MSS Acc. 1128.
21. Jewson, "Medical Knowledge and the Patronage System," 369–386.
22. William Moss, *Essay on . . . the Treatment and Diseases of Pregnant and Lying-in Women*, 356–358; Thynne, "Notes of Lectures on Midwifery," 84.
23. Lady Morley to Hon. Mrs. Villiers, May 7, 1810, Morley Papers, Add. MSS 48233.
24. Lady Morley to Hon. Mrs. Villiers, May 18, 1810, Morley Papers, Add. MSS 48233. Lady Morley was in her ninth month of pregnancy.
25. Untitled 1817 statement by Sir Richard Croft on the management of Princess Charlotte's pregnancy, Croft Papers, Lot 3. Hereafter cited as "Untitled Statement." Something of a mythology has developed over the death of Princess Charlotte, in which Croft is cast as the villain.

Dorothy M. Stuart, the Princess's biographer, has written that "wine and meat were forbidden" the Princess during her pregnancy, which contradicts Croft's own statement. See Stuart, *Daughter of England*, 327.

26. Moss, *Treatment of Diseases of Pregnant and Lying-in Women*, 365.

27. Sir Archibald Macdonald to his stepmother-in-law, Lady Stafford, September 26, 1787, Granville MSS PRO 30/29/4/6; Earl of Banbury to his sisters, January 1810, Banbury/Knollys MSS 1M44/129/1–2.

28. Lady Morley to Hon. Mrs. Villiers, October 10, 1813, Morley Papers, Add. MSS 48236.

29. Croft, "Untitled Statement."

30. Denman, *Introduction*, 233.

31. Moss, *Treatment and Diseases of Pregnant and Lying-in Women*; Thomas Bull, *Hints to Mothers for the Management of Health during Pregnancy*, 26 and 407.

32. Susan, Lady Rivers, to her mother, Harriet, Countess Granville, February 1835, Granville MSS PRO 30/29/17/2. Although Lady Rivers expected the baby in February, it did not arrive until May 28.

33. Richard Croft to Mrs. Denman, May 9, 1790, Croft Papers, Lot 1.

34. Denman, *Introduction*, 234.

35. Lady Holland's Journal, [November 1798], Holland House Papers, Add. MSS 51928.

36. Earl of Banbury to his sisters, April 7 and 10, 1810, Banbury/Knollys MSS 1M44/129/12.

37. Diary of Charlotte, Countess of Verulam, Gorhambury MSS D/EV F78; Diary of James, Earl of Verulam, Gorhambury MSS D/EV F47.

38. Lady Augusta Fox to Lady Holland, September 24, 1838, Holland House Papers, Add. MSS 51928.

39. Bull, *Hints to Mothers*, 28.

40. Butler, *The Eldest Brother*, 487.

41. The only exception to this pattern is the mysterious case of Lady Judith Milbanke. She was the only one in the group with delayed fertility who married late—at the age of twenty-six. She had a miscarriage a

year after marriage, another five years later, and then did not become pregnant again for ten years. On that occasion her pregnancy was successful, and she gave birth at the age of forty-one to Lord Byron's future wife.

42. Bessborough, *Georgiana*, 52. Of course a contributing factor to Georgiana's relative infertility must surely have been her intermittent and unsatisfactory sexual relationship with the Duke.

43. In one of the first medical lectures to appear in the *Lancet*, the prominent surgeon John Abernethy expressed the belief that menstruation served to mitigate sexual desire in the female by relieving "uterine irritation" and thus preventing "that strong degree of desire, which would render the part indecent." *Lancet* 2, no. 186 (March 24, 1827):789. For other contemporary beliefs concerning menstruation. see Thynne, "Notes of Lectures on Midwifery," 95; Denman, *Introduction*, 172; and Clarke, "Theory and Practice of Midwifery." For diagnosis of pregnancy, see Denman, 264. Patricia Branca chides the accoucheurs for not using the Jaquemeier test for diagnosing pregnancy, developed in France in 1836. It required doctors to recognize the color changes in the vagina and cervix consequent on pregnancy. However, there is no evidence that this knowledge was disseminated among British accoucheurs. They would have had to have a great deal of experience in the examination of pregnant and nonpregnant women before this test would become useful. See Branca, *Silent Sisterhood*, 83.

44. Bessborough, *Georgiana*, 53, 126, 144–145. M. Calonne was concerned because the Duchess had borrowed large sums from him. She felt that only the birth of a son would give her the emotional leverage to lay her debts before the Duke, or as she put it in a letter to Calonne, "Si je suis grosse je ne hesiterais pas a tous dire au Duc, puis que la naissance d'un fils serait probablement la fin de tous nos embarasses." Ibid., 145.

45. Lady Augusta Fox to Lady Holland, September 27, 1833, Holland House Papers, Add. MSS 51779.

46. Lady Augusta Fox to Lady Holland, n.d., Holland House Papers, Add. MSS 51779.

47. Lady Holland to Lady Augusta Fox, September 10, 1834, Holland House Papers, Add. MSS 51779.

48. Lady Augusta Fox to Lady Holland, October 15, 1834, Holland

House Papers, Add. MSS 51779. According to Sonia Keppel's account, the Foxes had a very happy marriage despite their childlessness. Keppel, *Sovereign Lady*, chap. 29., "Strained Relations."

49. Lady Augusta Fox to Lady Holland, October 20, 1835, and November 7, 1835, Holland House Papers, Add. MSS 51779.

50. Lady Holland to Lady Augusta Fox, July 1835, and April 1, 1836, Holland House Papers, Add. MSS 51779.

51. Lady Augusta Fox to Lady Holland, August 27, 1836, Holland House Papers, Add. MSS 51779.

52. Lady Holland to Lady Augusta Fox, November 10, 1836, Holland House Papers, Add. MSS 51779. The mysterious displaced uterus probably referred not to the wandering womb of days of yore, but simply to the retroverted or otherwise malpositioned uterus—a common condition, though one more likely to cause miscarriages than infertility.

53. Lady Augusta Fox to Lord Holland, November 5, 1836, Holland House Papers, Add. MSS 51779.

54. Denman, *Introduction* 225; Thynne, "Notes of Lectures on Midwifery," 86; Clarke, "Theory and Practice of Midwifery" and Edward Rigby, *Memoranda for Practitioners in Midwifery*, 13. Rigby was a lecturer on midwifery at St. Thomas's Hospital and assistant physician to the General Lying-in Hospital.

55. Thomas Denman, *Aphorisms on the Application and Use of the Forcepts and Vectis*, 75. The Japanese thought morning sickness was caused by the suppression of the menstrual flow and so was inevitable. See H. Lalung, *L'accouchement à travers les âges et les peuples*, 29.

56. Lady Morley to Hon. Mrs. Villiers, November 4, 1813, Morley Papers, Add. MSS 48236.

57. Mitford, *Stanleys of Alderley*, 42.

58. Denman, *Introduction*, 234; Thynne, "Notes of Lectures on Midwifery," 86; Moss, *Treatment and Diseases of Pregnant and Lying-in Women*, 350–351.

59. Lady Morley to Hon. Mrs. Villiers, November 14, 1813, Morley Papers, Add. MSS 48236; Lady Frances Cole's Recipe Book, Lowry Cole MSS PRO 30/43/119/2.

60. Denman, *Introduction*, 245.

61. Susan, Marchioness of Stafford, to her son, Lord Granville, March 15, 1786, in Granville, *Lord Granville Leveson-Gower* 1:6; Lady Morley to Mrs. Villiers, November 21, 1813, Add. MSS. 48236;

Lady Frances Cole's Recipe Book, Lowry Cole MSS PRO 30/43/119/2.
62. Denman, *Introduction*, 245.
63. Diary of Lord Verulam, November 7, 1822, Gorhambury MSS D/EV F44.
64. Queen Victoria to the Princess Royal, December 22, 1858, in Fulford, *Dearest Child*, 152. The Princess was born in 1840.
65. Denman, *Aphorisms*, 74.
66. Buchan, *Domestic Medicine*, 222.
67. Michael Ryan, *Lectures on Population, Marriage, and Divorce*, 63; Rigby, *Memoranda for Practitioners*, 15–16; and Denman, *Introduction*, 466.
68. Ilchester and Stavordale, *Lady Sarah Lennox* 2:51.
69. Lady Morley to Hon. Mrs. Villiers, December 14 and 21, 1812, Morley Papers, Add. MSS 48235.
70. Denman, *Introduction*, 469; Clarke, "Theory and Practice of Midwifery"; Thynne, "Notes of Lectures on Midwifery," 100; and Rigby, *Memoranda for Practitioners*, 17.
71. Londonderry, *Frances Anne*, 68.
72. Lady Morley to Hon. Mrs. Villiers, November 15 to December 26, 1812; and Lord Morley to Hon. Mrs. Villiers, December 28, 1812; Morley Papers, Add. MSS 48235. "Erroneous sofa" was, of course, a direct translation of the French expression for miscarriage, *fausse couche*, an expression often used by fashionable Englishwomen.
73. Lady Holland to Lady Augusta Fox, September 22, 1838, Holland House Papers, Add. MSS 51779.
74. Lady Augusta Fox to Lady Holland, September 24, 1838, Holland House Papers, Add. MSS 51779.
75. Londonderry, *Frances Anne*, 123.

CHAPTER V. THE CONFINEMENT: CHILDBIRTH

1. Hyacinthe, Lady Hatherton, to Gerald Wellesley, October 13 and November 5, 1813, Hatherton MSS D260 M/F/5/27/59.
2. Londonderry, *Frances Anne*, 60.
3. Ida Macalpine and Richard Hunter, *George III and the Mad-Business*, 243.

4. This was true even as late as 1842. See Bull, *Hints to Mothers*, 10.

5. Denman, *Introduction*, 311–312.

6. Arnold van Gennep, *The Rites of Passage*, xiii, passim.

7. Ibid., x, where van Gennep emphasized "the relationship between actual spatial passage and the change in social position, expressed in such ritualization of movements from one status to another as an "opening of the doors."

8. Van Gennep quotes (10) Frazer and Crawley on this. See also Margaret Mead and Niles Newton, "Cultural Patterning of Perinatal Behavior."

9. Hume, *Lady Mary Coke*, 3:119.

10. See, for instance, Elwin, *Noels and Milbankes*, 85, 342; and Hume, *Lady Mary Coke* 4:167.

11. [London], January 24 [1804], Banbury/Knollys MSS 1M44/117/3.

12. Leconfield, *Three Howard Sisters*, 230.

13. See for instance, Elwin, *Noels and Milbankes*, 406–417; Mitford, *Ladies of Alderley*, 57.

14. Lord Worcester to his mother, the Duchess of Beaufort, March 7, 1816, Granville MSS PRO 30/29/6/4.

15. Lady Mary Drummond to her daughter-in-law, Lady Elizabeth Drummond, January 5, 1832, Drummond of Cadland MSS B6/29/7; and Andrew Robert Drummond to his wife, Lady Elizabeth, February 1823, Drummond of Cadland MSS, autograph volume.

16. Londonderry, *Frances Anne*, 71.

17. Leconfield, *Three Howard Sisters*, 64.

18. Londonderry, *Frances Anne*, 71.

19. Woodham-Smith, *Queen Victoria*, 26.

20. Lady Morley to Mrs. Villiers, June 9, 1810, Morley Papers, Add. MSS 48233.

21. Diary of the Earl of Verulam, December 19 and 27, 1822, Gorhambury MSS D/EV F46 and D/EV F49, respectively.

22. Leconfield, *Three Howard Sisters*, 206.

23. Lady Morley to Mrs. Villiers, December 12, 1812, Morley Papers, Add. MSS 48238.

24. Huxley, *Victorian Duke*, 67.

25. Isabella Beeton, *The Book of Household Management*, 1055–1057.

26. Jean E. Donnison, "The Development of the Profession of Midwife in England, 1750–1902," 99.

27. Andrew Robert Drummond to Lady Elizabeth Drummond, March 1839, Drummond of Cadland MSS, autograph volume. Hospital training was not always a recommendation. In 1778 Sophia Curzon wrote to her aunt, "Lady Scarsdale wishes me to desire you to enquire out for a whet Nurse as she very much desires I would have somebody out of the country, as she says that Ford once recommended a Nurse to Lady Milsintown who came out of an Hospital and that she turned out to be dirty and everything that was dreadful, which she says is most likely to be the case again as the Doctors always recommend people out of the Hospital." See Elwin, *Noels and Milbankes*, 120. Lady Scarsdale was Sophia Curzon's mother-in-law.

28. Harriet Cavendish to her sister Georgiana, Lady Carlisle, November 8, 1806, in Leveson-Gower and Palmer, *Hary-O*, 157.

29. Leconfield, *Three Howard Sisters*, 86n.; Princess Charlotte to Richard Croft, August 18, 1817, Croft Papers, Lot 2; Leconfield, 86, 135, 250–252.

30. Leconfield, *Three Howard Sisters*, 135.

31. Ibid., 252.

32. Diary of Charlotte, Countess of Verulam, Gorhambury MSS D/EV F78; Diary of the Earl of Verulam, December 7, 1822, Gorhambury MSS D/EV F46; Leconfield, *Three Howard Sisters*, 68.

33. Letter of October 9, 1813, Weigall MSS U1371 C11, Kent Archives Office.

34. Lord Granville to Lady Bessborough, September 23, 1812 "at three o'clock in the morning," Granville MSS PRO 30-29/6/8; Lowry Cole MSS PRO 30/43/32; Lady Cecilia Ridley to her mother, Lady Parke, in Ridley, *Cecilia*, 167; Lady Frances Cole to her mother, Countess of Malmesbury, April 17, 1824, Lowry Cole MSS PRO 30/43/32.

35. Ilchester and Stavordale, *Lady Sarah Lennox* 2:21; Louisa Connolly to Lady Sarah Napier, August 8, 1872, Bunbury MSS 18/750/2, vol. 16.

36. Anglesey, *Capel Letters*, 113. Lady Caroline was a daughter of the Earl of Uxbridge, and her husband was the second son of the Earl of

Essex. They had been forced to move to Brussels out of economic necessity, since, as younger children themselves, they had great difficulty in supporting so large a brood.

37. Londonderry, *Frances Anne*, 58.
38. Lady Rivers to her mother, Lady Granville, February 1835, March 4, 1835, March 1835, April 1835, Granville MSS PRO 30/29/17/2.
39. Lady Rivers to her mother, Lady Granville, February 20, 1835, Granville MSS PRO 30/29/17/2.
40. Ridley, *Cecilia*, 125.
41. Diary of Elizabeth, Lady Holland, January 31, 1799, Holland House Papers, Add. MSS 51928.
42. Ibid.
43. Leveson-Gower and Palmer, *Hary-O*, 243. For her other daughter-in-law, Lady de Mauley, see Granville, *Lord Granville Leveson-Gower* 2:533.
44. Bessborough, *Lady Charlotte Guest*, 23.
45. Sir Galbraith Lowry Cole to "Mama" (the Countess of Malmesbury), April 25, 1824, Lowry Cole MSS PRO 30/43/32.
46. Stuart, *Dearest Bess*, diary entry for September 4, 1785. This is the child, named Caroline St. Jules, who was given £30,000 on her marriage to George Lamb, the younger son of Lord Melbourne (and younger brother of the future Prime Minister). Lady Elizabeth also gave birth to a son by the Duke, named Augustus Clifford, in 1788. Both children remained close to their legitimate Devonshire half-siblings throughout their adult lives.
47. Iris Palmer, *The Face without a Frown*, 76.
48. Leconfield, *Three Howard Sisters*, 225n.
49. Jack Dewhurst, *Royal Confinements*, 106.
50. Lot 2 of the Croft Papers contains the correspondence between Princess Charlotte and Richard Croft during her last pregnancy. Lot 3, the "New Croft Papers," contains Croft's notebook of Princess Charlotte's labor. For criticism of the royal family for their failure to be with Charlotte, see Hon. Mrs. Hugh Wyndham, *Correspondence of Sarah Spencer, Lady Lyttleton*, 200; the Morley Papers; and the contemporary pamphlet by Green, *Memoirs of Her Late Royal Highness*.
51. Longford, "Queen Victoria's Doctors," 76. Similarly, see Woodham-Smith, *Queen Victoria*, 216.

52. Warner, *Queen Victoria's Sketchbook*, 106–107.
53. Denman, *Introduction*, 320.
54. Mead and Newton, "Cultural Patterning," 209; Clarke, "Theory and Practice of Midwifery"; Thynne, "Notes of Lectures on Midwifery," 48–50.
55. Clarke, "Theory and Practice of Midwifery."
56. Thynne, "Notes of Lectures on Midwifery," 199–200.
57. Denman, *Introduction*, 331.
58. Ibid., 223. For modern studies on the relationship of psychological preparation and labor efficiency, see Sheila Kitzinger, *The Experience of Childbirth*, 148–149; and Pauline Shereshefsky and Leon Yarrow, *Psychological Aspects of a First Pregnancy and Early Postnatal Adaptation*, 19–20.
59. Thynne, "Notes of Lectures on Midwifery," 15; Clarke, "Theory and Practice of Midwifery."
60. Clarke, "Theory and Practice of Midwifery."
61. Buchan, *Domestic Medicine*, 224.
62. Denman, *Introduction*, 329.
63. Clarke, "Theory and Practice of Midwifery."
64. Given the conditions under which childbirth occurred, this may have been the most appropriate position for delivery. According to one modern textbook (1975), the Sims position is best for home deliveries, providing the maximum of comfort and freedom from restraint for the patient. Significantly, the position brings bearing-down movements under control, allowing slower delivery of the head and fewer perineal injuries—goals stressed by our accoucheurs, who encouraged slow labors to reduce lacerations. However, it is not a good position for forceps deliveries—so again, as long as the accoucheurs insisted on this position, it was probably wise to avoid instrumental deliveries as much as possible. See Harry Oxorn and William Foote, *Human Labor and Birth*, 110.
65. Denman, *Introduction*, 263. The position was regarded as a bizarre one by a French commentator who thought "tres-pudique Albion" was a nation of hypocrites. See G. J. Witkowski, *Histoire des accouchements chez tous les peuples*, 534. Witkowski was on the faculty of the University of Paris; Lalung, *L'Accouchement à travers les âges*, 59.
66. In an article entitled, "What is the Natural Position of a Woman

during Labour?" which appeared in the *Medical Times and Gazette*, Rigby estimated that in a state of nature, a woman might assume a variety of positions, but that if the labor were prolonged, exhaustion would cause her to lie down before the baby was born. He reported on an experiment done by a Dr. Naegele of Heidelberg in which a "natural" specimen of motherhood (young, illiterate, healthy, and unmarried) was left alone in a room furnished with a bed, sofa, and a labor chair. She took the pains in a variety of positions, generally standing up, but ultimately gave birth on her left side. However, in a larger experiment conducted in Posen, one hundred cases of concealed parturition were observed. Here, half the women gave birth in positions that Rigby termed "unusual." Of these, thirty gave birth while standing, eighteen while squatting, and two kneeling. See Edward Rigby, "What Is the Natural Position of a Woman during Labour?" 345–346.

67. Dr. McIvor, "Remarks Connected with Midwifery," *London Medical Gazette*, 611–613.

68. Denman, *Introduction*, 371.

69. Thynne, "Notes of Lectures on Midwifery," 194.

70. Denman, *Introduction*, vii.

71. Palmer Findley, *Priests of Lucina*, 323. The forty years probably covers the approximate period of 1775–1815 or 1780–1820. By comparison, modern obstetricians recommend that the use of forceps should be considered if there has been a "Lack of advancement in the presence of good uterine contractions for 2 hours" in a primipara (a woman who has not given birth before, such as Princess Charlotte), and one hour in a multipara. Forceps should only be used when the pelvis is of adequate size, there is no soft tissue obstruction, the cervix is completely dilated and retracted, the membranes have ruptured, and the bowel and bladder emptied—conditions that Denman would also have met before using forceps. See Oxorn and Foote, *Human Labor and Birth*, 281, 283. Also E. Stewart Taylor, *Beck's Obstetrical Practice*, 534.

72. Denman, *Introduction*, 272.

73. Thynne, "Notes of Lectures on Midwifery," 173.

74. Denman, *Introduction*, 274.

75. Richard Croft to Mrs. Denman, May 14, 1790, Croft Papers, Lot 1.

76. Clarke, "Theory and Practice of Midwifery"; Thynne, "Notes of Lectures on Midwifery," 181; Denman, *Aphorisms*, 13. Hollywood

melodrama not withstanding, husbands were never given the choice between the lives of their wives or their children.

77. Thynne, "Notes of Lectures on Midwifery," 196; Clarke, "Theory and Practice of Midwifery."

78. Clarke, "Theory and Practice of Midwifery"; Thynne, "Notes of Lectures on Midwifery," 196; Denman, *Aphorisms*, 16. The student who took down Clarke's lectures underlined this point with great emphasis.

79. John Greene Crosse, "Obstetrical Case Books for 1819, and 1833–1843" MS 1916, 1:16, Library of the Wellcome Institute Library for the History of Medicine.

80. Earl of Banbury to the Misses Knollys, September or October 1800, Banbury/Knollys MSS 1M44/115/6.

81. Denman, *Introduction*, 295; Thynne, "Notes of Lectures on Midwifery," 152.

82. Robert Robertson, "Observations on the Third Stage of Labour," 541–543.

83. A corrected draft of the history of Princess Charlotte's labor, in unknown handwriting, Croft Papers, Lot 3.

84. Postscript by Dr. John Sims to the statement written by the three doctors (Sims, Croft, and Baillie) for the members of the royal family, Croft Papers, Lot 3.

85. Lady Holland's Journal, January 31, 1799, Holland House Papers, Add. MSS 51928.

86. Corrected draft of the history of Charlotte's labor, in an unknown handwriting, Croft Papers, Lot 3.

87. The details of the birth are repeated in several reports that compose Lot 3 of the Croft Papers. The most detailed description of the third stage appears in a statement dated and signed by Croft, endorsed "afterbirth."

88. Ibid.

89. Ibid.

90. A corrected draft of the history of Princess Charlotte's labor, in unknown handwriting, Croft Papers, Lot 3.

91. Ibid., and "The History of the Princess's Labor" in Croft's handwriting, Croft Papers, Lot 3.

92. The shock Priscilla, Countess of Westmoreland, received upon hearing the news of the Princess's death was said to be responsible for

the birth of a stillborn daughter about two weeks later. "Memoir of Priscilla, Countess of Westmoreland," Weigall MSS U1371 F18/1. The shock was also held responsible for the premature labor and death of the Countess of Albemarle. See Green, *Memoirs of Her Late Royal Highness*, 389. However, we learn from another source that the forty-two-year-old Lady Albemarle had already given birth to fifteen children, which may also have contributed to her death. See *Gentleman's Magazine*, December 1817, 568.

93. Green pointed out, however, that court etiquette prevented an authenticated account of any "illustrious female's" autopsy from being made public. He cited the Duchess of Devonshire's death in 1806 as an example. *Memoirs of Her Late Royal Highness*, 540.

94. H. Harvey Evers, "Presidential Address," 485–495.

95. Sir Eardley Holland, "The Princess Charlotte of Wales: A Triple Obstetric Tragedy," 905–919.

96. Macalpine and Hunter, *Mad-Business*, 246.

97. See the letters Princess Charlotte wrote to Croft during her pregnancy, Croft Papers, Lot 2. Thanks to Katheryn Renney, R.N.P., of the U.S.P.H.S. Hospital in Baltimore, for a helpful discussion of this case. Symptoms of preeclampsia that the Princess exhibited included puffiness or edema, florid complexion accompanied by dizzy spells (which could indicate a rise in blood pressure), and headache. Her urinary problems might indicate the presence of albumin although that of course was not analyzed. We are not, however, ruling out the possibility that she died as a result of postpartum hemorrhage and shock, as her death certainly fits the clinical picture of shock. Oxorn and Foote describe the features of postpartum hemorrhage: the pulse becomes rapid and weak, blood pressure falls, the patient turns pale and cold, and there is shortness of breath, air hunger, sweating, and finally coma and death. Women can, indeed, go into shock from the exhaustion of a prolonged labor, without having necessarily hemorrhaged, which might have been the case with the Princess Charlotte. See Oxorn and Foote, *Human Labor and Birth*, 397.

98. Green, *Memoirs of Her Late Royal Highness*, 407.

99. Lady Morley to Hon. Mrs. Villiers, November 16, 1817, Morley Papers, Add. MSS 48241.

100. Grosvenor and Beilby, *First Lady Wharncliffe* 1:228.

101. Sir Anthony Carlisle, in an open letter to the Right Hon. Robert Peel, *Lancet* 2, no. 183, March 3, 1827:701–702.
102. Quoted by Holland, "Triple Obstetric Tragedy," 916.
103. Mead and Newton, "Cultural Patterning," 222.
104. Suitor, "Husbands' Participation," 286. One wonders if the doctor who found the husband's presence at a confinement "indelicate" thought it equally indelicate of the husband to have gotten his wife pregnant in the first place.
105. *Lancet* 2, March 3, 1827: 711. According to Litoff, the use of ergot to induce uterine contractions had been introduced into the United States in 1808. *American Midwives*, 19.
106. John Craig, "On the Treatment of Women in Protracted Labours," 888–893.
107. Quoted in James Y. Simpson, "Discovery of a New Anaesthetic Agent," 933–947.
108. Bull, *Hints to Mothers*, 10.
109. Simpson, "New Anaesthetic Agent," 123.
110. Ibid., 121–122.
111. Ibid., 112–113.
112. W. Tyler Smith, "A Lecture on the Utility and Safety of the Inhalation of Ether in Obstetric Practice," 321.
113. Palmer Findley, *The Story of Childbirth*, 241.
114. Mitford, *Ladies of Alderley*, 151, 155.
115. Ibid., 215.
116. Mitford, *Stanleys of Alderley*, 309.
117. Letter of April 15, 1853, Drummond of Cadland MSS B6/78/197.

CHAPTER VI. THE CONFINEMENT: RECOVERY

1. Trumbach, *Rise of the Egalitarian Family*, esp. 197–235.
2. Buchan, *Domestic Medicine*, 227.
3. Malcolm Elwin, *Lord Byron's Wife*, 25.
4. Trumbach, *Rise of the Egalitarian Family*, 184–185.
5. Ibid., 223.
6. Stone, *Family, Sex, and Marriage*, 430–431.

7. Trumbach, *Rise of the Egalitarian Family*, 185.
8. Hume, *Lady Mary Coke* 4:85.
9. Moss, *Treatment and Diseases of Pregnant and Lying-in Women*, 433, 15.
10. Lady Bessborough to Lord Granville, in Granville, *Lord Granville Leveson-Gower* 2:434.
11. Lady Louisa Connolly to Lady Sarah Napier, August 30, 1782, Bunbury MSS E18/750/2, vol. 16; Countess of Sutherland to Lady Stafford, August 29, 1786, Granville MSS PRO 30/29/5/3.
12. Duchess of Rutland to Lady Elizabeth Drummond, August 25, 1825, Drummond of Cadland MSS B6/79/1/56; Mitford, *Ladies of Alderley*, 242.
13. Trumbach, *Rise of the Egalitarian Family*, 185, 185n.; Countess of Sutherland to Lady Stafford, August 29, 1786, Granville MSS PRO 30/29/5/3.
14. Georgiana, Lady Morpeth (later, Lady Carlisle), to her sister, Harriet, Lady Granville (then Lady Harriet Leveson-Gower), December 25, 1809, Granville MSS PRO 30/29/17/5.
15. Leconfield, *Three Howard Sisters*, 225–230. Blanche, Lady Burlington's husband, was William Cavendish, a distant cousin of hers, and the heir apparent of her uncle, the sixth Duke of Devonshire. The Duke was very fond of the young couple. Her husband succeeded to the title as seventh Duke after her death.
16. Leconfiled, *Three Howard Sisters*, 230; Lord Leveson (the future second Earl Granville, the Victorian foreign secretary), to his father, Lord Granville, November 24, 1840, Granville MSS PRO 30/29/6/4.
17. Lady Hatherton to Gerald Wellesley, November 5, 1813, Hatherton MSS D260 M/F/5/27/59; Huxley, *Lady Elizabeth and the Grosvenors*, 22.
18. Richard Croft to Mrs. Denman, Friday morning, May 28, 1790. Croft Papers, Lot 2; Oman, *Gascoyne Heiress*, 114; Leconfield, *Three Howard Sisters*, 232; Diary of Charlotte, Countess of Verulam, September 1813, Gorhambury MSS D/EV F78; Diary of James, first Earl of Verulam, January 9, 1823, Gorhambury MSS DEV F48.
19. Leconfield, *Three Howard Sisters*, 130.
20. Mitford, *Stanleys of Alderley*, 81.
21. Lady Louisa Macdonald to Lady Stafford, August 24, 1787, Granville MSS PRO 30/29/4/6.

22. Bessborough, *Lady Charlotte Guest*, 31.
23. See Enid Porter, *Cambridgeshire Customs and Folklore*, 15.
24. Shorter, *Women's Bodies*, 288–289.
25. Diary of Charlotte, Countess of Verulam, May 15, 22 and 24, 1810, Gorhambury MSS D/EV F78; April 29 and May 1, 1812, Gorhambury MSS D/EV F78. Diary of Elizabeth, Duchess of Grafton, January 21, 1787, Grafton MSS Acc. 2683, W1.
26. Bessborough, *Lady Bessborough and Her Family Circle*, 164.
27. Mabell, Countess of Airlie, *Lady Palmerston and Her Times*, 29.
28. Londonderry, *Frances Anne*, 73.
29. Oman, *Gascoyne Heiress*, 115.
30. Elizabeth Foster, *Children of the Mist*, 29. The author was named for her eighteenth-century ancestor.
31. See, for instance, Lady Mary Drummond to Lady Elizabeth Drummond, January 23 [1823], Drummond of Cadland MSS B6/29/8/1; Lady Holland to Lady Augusta Fox, September 29, 1838, Holland House Papers, Add. MSS 51779.
32. Hyde, *The Londonderrys*, 27.
33. Ashley Montagu, *Sex, Man, and Society*, 254.
34. Lord Hugh to Lady Horatia Seymour, August 13, 1793, Seymour of Ragley MSS CR114A/264. Lady Horatia was the daughter of the second Earl Waldegrave. Her husband was the fifth son of the first Marquess of Hertford. Lord Hugh and Lady Horatia died within a few months of each other in 1801.
35. Countess of Sutherland to Lady Stafford, [September] 1786, Granville MSS PRO 30/29/5/3.
36. Lord Harrowby to Lord Granville, August 13, 1805, in Granville, *Lord Granville Leveson-Gower* 2:104; Lord Granville to Lady Bessborough, December 5, 1810, in ibid., 371; Tresham Lever, *Letters of Lady Palmerston*, 29; Londonderry, *Frances Anne*, 128; Leconfield, *Three Howard Sisters*, 135; and Queen Victoria to her uncle, King Leopold of the Belgians, December 15, 1840, in John Raymond, *Queen Victoria's Early Letters*, 44.
37. Richard Croft to Mrs. Denman, Monday morn. [May 31, 1790], Croft Papers, Lot 1.
38. Richard Croft to Mrs. Denman, June 2, 1790, Croft Papers, Lot 1.

39. Lady Carlisle to Lady Granville, Christmas Day, 1809, Granville MSS PRO 30/29/17/5.

40. November 25 and 27, 1832, in Leconfield, *Three Howard Sisters*, 252.

41. Earl of Banbury to his sisters, January 1804, Banbury/Knollys MSS 1M44/117/1.

42. Earl of Banbury to his sisters, February 4 and 16, 1804, Banbury/Knollys MSS 1M44/117/5.

43. Lady Banbury (1777–1818) was the daughter of Ebenezer Blackwell, a Lombard Street banker. Her husband, the titular eighth Earl, discontinued the use of his title after an investigation and resolution of the House of Lords in 1813, when it was decided that one of his ancestors was not of legitimate birth. He was afterward known as General William Knollys. The title Viscount Knollys was eventually given to one of their descendents.

44. See, for instance, Fleetwood Churchill, *On the Diseases of Women Including the Diseases of Pregnancy and Childbed*, 543, 545. Churchill was English-born and Edinburgh-educated, but established his practice in Dublin. He was twice president of the Obstetrical Society of Dublin, and president of the Kings and Queens College of Physicians. For more on diet during the puerperium, see Thynne, "Notes of Lectures on Midwifery," 201. He told his medical students that "after delivery we generally give a light cordial, some gruel, with a few spoonsful of wine in it, or an opiate. After first labours, as they are much more *feverish*, we confine women to a low diet, as tea, chicken broth & etc. for some little time, but in succeeding ones especially if they are low and nervous, we allow them a more generous support." See also Clarke, "Theory and Practice of Midwifery." Modern advice would generally concur, but not so harshly. One widely used textbook recommends that "Diet on the first day of delivery should consist chiefly of liquids, as the patient is usually dehydrated and not hungry. By the second day she can eat what she likes." J. P. Greenhill, *Obstetrics*, 477.

45. Lord Morley to his sister, Hon. Mrs. Villiers, June 10, 1810, Morley Papers, Add. MSS 48233; Lord Leveson to his father, Lord Granville, November 24, 1840, Granville MSS PRO 30/29/6/4.

46. Ridley, *Cecilia*, 125. Mary Howard, the daughter of Lord Parke, was the sister of Lady Cecilia Ridley. Mary married a younger son of the sixth Earl of Carlisle and was the mother of the ninth Earl. She died dur-

ing this confinement, supposedly of typhoid fever. Her diet was not blamed. See also Mrs. Spencer-Stanhope to her son, John, August 16, 1824, in Stirling *Elizabeth Spencer-Stanhope* 2:80–81.

47. Leconfield, *Three Howard Sisters*, 252.
48. Stuart, *Daughter of England*, 295–296; Lady Morley to Hon. Mrs. Villiers, July 18, 1810, Morley Papers, Add. MSS 48233.
49. Stone, *Family, Sex, and Marriage*, 430–431; Trumbach, *Rise of the Egalitarian Family*, 185.
50. Stone, *Family, Sex, and Marriage*, 431.
51. Trumbach's description of the Duchess and the problems she faced in her family life are entirely apt and coincide with my own ideas about the Duchess. See *Rise of the Egalitarian Family*, esp. 219–222.
52. Ilchester and Stavordale, *Lady Sarah Lennox* 2:36.
53. Palmer, *Face without a Frown*, 90–91.
54. Leconfield, *Three Howard Sisters*, 99.
55. Earl of Banbury to his sisters, February 4, 1804, Banbury/Knollys MSS 1M44/117/5.
56. Lady Frances Cole to her mother, the Countess of Malmesbury, January 18, 1824, Lowry Cole MSS PRO 30/43/32.
57. Lady Mary Drummond to Lady Elizabeth Drummond, January 10, 1827, Drummond of Cadland MSS B6/29/41.
58. Leveson-Gower and Palmer, *Hary-O*, 209. Similarly, in 1865 the Earl and Countess of Derby openly expressed their disappointment when their daughter-in-law was unable to nurse. See Kennedy, *My Dear Duchess*, 232.
59. Lactation prevents conception by delaying the resumption of ovulation after a woman gives birth. However, this delay varies in duration from woman to woman and from pregnancy to pregnancy, so it is an unreliable and unpredictable method of birth control. For nineteenth-century knowledge of the relationship of lactation and conception, see Robert Barnes, "An Inquiry into the Relations between Menstruation, Conception, and Lactation, and the Influence of Lactation in Causing Abortion," *Lancet*, December 4, 1852. Modern demographers agree that lactation causes an increase in intervals between births. Potter has estimated that the average interval between first and second births is eighteen months in nonlactating mothers and twenty-seven months in those who do nurse. See R.G. Potter, "Birth Intervals," 155.

60. Leveson-Gower and Palmer, *Hary-O*, 117.
61. Elwin, *Noels and Milbankes*, 120; Kennedy, *My Dear Duchess*, 232.
62. Trumbach, *Rise of the Egalitarian Family*, 220.
63. Nursing postponed the next pregnancy but could not really prevent the birth of a large family. Among those who nursed some or all of their children were Harriet, Duchess of Sutherland (eleven children in twenty-five years) and Susan, Lady Rivers (thirteen children in twenty-one years).
64. See the Diaries of the Earl of Verulam, Gorhambury MSS D/EV F44–F50, esp. D/EV F44 and D/EV F49.
65. The Duchess was upset after reading Dr. Michael Underwood's book on the diseases of children in which he stated that nervous women ought not breast-feed. Underwood had sent the Duchess his book, possibly with an eye to her patronage. See Richard Croft to Mrs. Denman, Monday morning, [May 31] 1790, Croft Papers, Lot 1.
66. See Buchan, *Domestic Medicine*, 1.
67. Lord Jermyn to Lady Elizabeth Drummond, July 11, 1835, Drummond of Cadland MSS B6/50/87.
68. Raymond, *Queen Victoria's Early Letters*, 74.
69. P. Pitt to Lord Gower, October 1772, Granville MSS PRO 30/29/4/3; Londonderry, *Frances Anne*, 128; and Huxley, *Lady Elizabeth and the Grosvenors*, 29.
70. Diary of the Earl of Verulam, December 9 and 13, 1822, Gorhambury MSS D/EV F46.
71. Diary of Francis Hugh Seymour, future fifth Marquess of Hertford, entry for November 3, 1835, Seymour of Ragley MSS CR 114A/G 44. Lady Catherine married John Foster Barham, M.P., in 1834. He died in 1838. In 1838 she married George, fourth Earl of Clarendon, the Liberal statesman, and had four sons and four daughters.
72. Queen Victoria to the Princess Royal, March 9, 1859, in Fulford, *Dearest Child*, 165.
73. Bessborough, *Lady Charlotte Guest*, 65, 68.
74. Lady Holland's Journal, December 14, 1809, Holland House Papers, Add. MSS 51937.
75. The word *confined* in the sense of *gave birth to* first appeared in the 1770s, when *lay-in* and *brought to bed* were the most popular terms for birth. The use of the terms *confined* and *confinement* increased in

popularity throughout the last three decades of the eighteenth century, finally outpacing the two older expressions during the first decade of the nineteenth century, according to the literary evidence used in preparing this book. During the years 1800 to 1809, *confined* was used in 33 percent of the expressions for birth. Its popularity continued to grow, while that of *lay-in* and *brought to bed* continued to diminish. During the teens, *confined* was used in 58 percent of the expressions; in the 1820s, 59 percent; in the 1830s and 1840s, 53 percent. *Brought to bed* and *lay-in* gradually became archaisms, although older people continued to use these expressions even in the middle of the nineteenth century. The term *accouchement*, like *confined* and *lay-in*, could mean both the actual birth and the period of recovery that followed. It was first used by members of the group in question (and their correspondents) during the 1790s, and was used by someone in every decade at least until the 1850s, but it never achieved great popularity. Similarly, the term *delivered* was used at least once in every decade between the 1770s and 1840s. My findings are similar to that of the *Oxford English Dictionary*, which traces the word *confinement* (in the sense in which it is used here) only back as far as 1772, making it a relatively modern term. *Lying-in*, by contrast, is traced back as far as 1440.

76. Countess of Sutherland to her mother-in-law, Lady Stafford, Paris, March 2, 1792, Granville MSS PRO 30/29/5/4.

IN CONCLUSION

1. Hyde, *The Londonderrys*, 38.
2. Ibid., 29. In addition to Seaham Hall, the Londonderrys owned her ancestral home, Wynyard Park (also in Durham, nearer the coal fields); his ancestral home, Mt. Stewart; Holdernesse House, which they purchased in London in 1822 (later called Londonderry House); Garron Tower, which Lady Londonderry built on the Antrim estate she had inherited from her mother; and of course, her "hameau" at Rosebank.
3. Ibid., 52–53.
4. Mark Girouard, *Life in the English Country House*, 214, 228.
5. Keppel, *Sovereign Lady*, 277.
6. Ibid., 275.

7. Calder-Marshall, *Two Duchesses*, 59.
8. Hyde, *The Londonderrys*, 52–53.
9. Trumbach, *Rise of the Egalitarian Family*, 224–235.
10. Badinter, *Mother Love*, 316.
11. Peter Gay, *The Bourgeois Experience* 1:174.
12. Countess of Sutherland to Lady Stafford, Paris, May 25, 1792, Granville MSS PRO 30/29/5/4.
13. Fitzgerald, *Emily, Duchess of Leinster* 1:159. Her newly conceived twelfth child would grow to be the great Irish national hero, Lord Edward Fitzgerald.
14. Mitford, *Ladies of Alderley*, 142–143.
15. Mitford, *Stanleys of Alderley*, 27.
16. Gay, *Bourgeois Experience*, 207.

Bibliography

MANUSCRIPTS

PRIVATE COLLECTIONS

Croft Papers. Owned by Richard Page Croft, Esq., of Ware, Herts.
Derby/Gathorne-Hardy Papers. Owned by Richard Hobbs, Esq., and deposited in the Parker Library, Corpus Christi College, Cambridge.
Drummond of Cadland MSS. Owned by Maldwin Drummond, J.P., of Cadland Estate, Fawley, Hants.

PUBLIC COLLECTIONS

British Museum, London

   Holland House Papers. Add. MSS 51926–51940 and 51779.
   Morley Papers. Add. MSS 48218–48301.

Hampshire Record Office, Winchester

   Banbury/Knollys MSS 1M44.

Hertfordshire County Record Office, Hertford

   Gorhambury MSS D/EV.

Kent Archives Office, Maidstone

   Weigall MSS U1371.

Middlesex County Records Office, London

   Earl of Jersey (Villiers) MSS Acc. 510 and 1138.

Public Records Office, London

    Lowry Cole MSS PRO 30/43.
    Granville MSS PRO 30/29.
    Hoare (Pitt) MSS PRO 30/70.

Staffordshire Record Office, Stafford

    Hatherton MSS D260

Warwickshire County Record Office, Warwick

    Seymour of Ragley MSS CR114A.

Wellcome Institute for the History of Medicine, London

    Clarke, Sir Charles Mansfield. "Notes on the Theory and Practice of Midwifery, and of the Diseases of Women and Children." MSS 858, ca. 1820.
    Crosse, John Greene. "Obstetrical Case Books for 1819, 1825, and 1833–1843." MSS 1916, 1917.
    Thynne, Andrew. "Notes of Lectures on Midwifery, taken down by Page Nichol Scott." MSS 4788, ca. 1807.

West Suffolk Record Office, Bury St. Edmonds

    Bunbury MSS E 18/750/2.
    Grafton MSS Acc. 2683.
    Hervey MSS Acc. 941.

PERIODICALS

Annual Register
Gentleman's Magazine
Lancet
London Medical Gazette
Medical Times and Gazette
North American Review
Pamphleteer
Times (of London)
Transactions of the Royal Society

Bibliography

Books and Journal Articles

Adburgham, Alison. *Shops and Shopping: Where, and in What Manner, the Well-Dressed Englishwoman Brought Her Clothes, 1800–1914*. London: George Allen & Unwin, 1964.

Airlie, Mabell, Countess of. *Lady Palmerston and Her Times*. London: Hodder & Stoughton, 1922.

Anglesey, Marquess of (ed.). *The Capel Letters: Being the Correspondence of Lady Caroline Capel and Her Daughters, 1814–1817*. London: Jonathan Cape, 1955.

———. *One-Leg: The Life and Letters of Henry William Paget, First Marquess of Anglesey*. London: Jonathan Cape, 1961.

Ansell, Charles. *On the Rate of Mortality at Early Periods of Life, the Age at Marriage, the Number of Children to a Marriage, the Length of a Generation, and other Statistics of Families in the Upper and Professional Classes*. London: National Life Assurance Co., 1874.

Arnould, Sir Joseph. *Life of Thomas, First Lord Denman*. Boston: Estes & Lauriat, 1874.

Aspinall, A. "George IV and Sir William Knighton." *English Historical Review* 55, no. 217, January 1940.

Austen, Jane. *Pride and Prejudice*. London: Penguin Books, 1980.

Badinter, Elisabeth. *Mother Love*. New York: Macmillan, 1981.

Bailey, John (ed.). *The Diary of Lady Frederick Cavendish*. New York: Frederick A. Stokes & Co., 1927.

Bamford, Francis, and the Duke of Wellington (eds.). *The Journal of Mrs. Arbuthnot, 1820–1832*. London: Macmillan & Co., 1950.

Banks, J. A., and Olive Banks. *Feminism and Family Planning in Victorian England*. New York: Schocken Books, 1964.

Barker-Benfield, G. J. *The Horrors of the Half-Known Life: Male Attitudes toward Women and Sexuality in Nineteenth-Century America*. New York: Harper & Row, 1976.

Beeton, Isabella. *The Book of Household Management*. 2d ed. London: Ward, Lock, & Tyler, 1869.

Bessborough, Earl of (ed.). *Georgiana: Extracts from the Correspondence of Georgiana, Duchess of Devonshire*. London: John Murray, 1955.

———. *Lady Bessborough and Her Family Circle*. London: John Murray, 1940.

―――. *Lady Charlotte Guest: Extracts from her Journal, 1833–52.* London: John Murray, 1950.
Bolitho, Hector, and Derek Peel. *The Drummonds of Charing Cross.* London: George Allen & Unwin, 1967.
Branca, Patricia. *Silent Sisterhood: Middle-Class Women in the Victorian Home.* London: Croom Helm, 1975.
Brodie, Sir Benjamin C. *Autobiography of the Late Sir Benjamin C. Brodie, Bart.* 2d ed. London: Longmans, Green, & Co., 1865.
Brontë, Emily. *Wuthering Heights.* New York: Washington Square Press, 1960.
Brooke, John. *King George III.* New York: McGraw-Hill, 1972.
Buchan, William. *Domestic Medicine.* London: T. Dolby, Brittania Press, 1772.
Bull, Thomas. *Hints to Mothers for the Management of Health During the Period of Pregnancy, and in the Lying-in Chamber; with an exposure of popular errors in connexion with those subjects.* 2d ed. New York: Wiley & Putnam, 1842.
Burke, Edmund, and Thomas Paine. *Reflections on the Revolution in France and The Rights of Man.* New York: Dolphin Books, 1961.
Butler, Iris. *The Eldest Brother: The Marquess Wellesley, the Duke of Wellington's Eldest Brother.* London: Hodder & Stoughton, 1973.
Calder-Marshall, Arthur. *The Two Duchesses.* New York: Harper & Row, 1978.
Cecil, David, Lord. *The Young Melbourne.* New York: Bobbs-Merrill, 1939.
Churchill, Fleetwood. *On the Diseases of Women Including the Diseases of Pregnancy and Childbed.* A New American Edition, with Notes and editions by D. Francis Condie, M.S. Philadelphia: Blanchard & Lea, 1852.
Clark, Sir George. *A History of the Royal College of Physicians of London.* 3 vols. Oxford: Clarendon Press, for the Royal College, 1966.
Cominos, Peter T. "Innocent Femina Sensualis in Unconscious Conflict." In Martha Vicinus, ed., *Suffer and Be Still: Women in the Victorian Age.* Bloomington: Indiana University Press, 1972.
Cooper, Bransby B. *The Life of Sir Astley Cooper, Bart.* 2 vols. London: John W. Parker, 1843.
Craig, John. "On the Treatment of Women in Protracted Labours." *London Medical Gazette* 45, May 17, 1850: pp. 888–893.

Creston, Dormer. *The Regent and His Daughter*. London: Thornton Butterworth, 1932.
Cutter, Irving S., and Henry R. Viets. *A Short History of Midwifery*. Philadelphia and London: W. B. Saunders, 1964.
Denman, Thomas. *Aphorisms on the Application and Use of the Forceps and Vectis*. Philadelphia: Benjamin Johnson, 1803.
———. *Introduction to the Practice of Midwifery*. From the last London edition. With notes and emendations by John W. Francis. New York: E. Bliss and E. White, 1821.
Dewees, William P. *A Treatise on the Diseases of Females*. Philadelphia: Carey & Lea, 1826.
Dewhurst, Jack. *Royal Confinements: A Gynaecological History of Britain's Royal Family*. New York: St. Martin's, 1980.
Dictionary of National Biography [DNB]. London: Oxford University Press.
Donegan, Jane B. *Women and Men Midwives: Medicine, Morality, and Misogyny in Early America*. Westport, Conn.: Greenwood Press, 1978.
Donnison, Jean E. "The Development of the Profession of Midwife in England, 1750–1902." Ph.D. diss., Department of Economics, London School of Economics, 1974.
———. *Midwives and Medical Men: A History of Inter-Professional Rivalries and Women's Rights*. New York: Schocken Books, 1977.
Elwin, Malcolm. *Lord Byron's Wife*. New York: Harcourt, Brace, & World, 1962.
———. (ed.). *The Noels and the Milbankes: Their Letters for Twenty-five Years, 1767–1792*. London: Macdonald & Co., 1967.
Evers, H. Harvey. "Presidential Address." Delivered to the North of England Obstetrical and Gynaecological Society. *Journal of Obstetrics and Gynaecology of the British Empire*. 58, December 1950: pp. 485–495.
Findley, Palmer. *Priests of Lucina: The Story of Obstetrics*. Boston: Little, Brown, & Co., 1939.
———. *The Story of Childbirth*. Garden City, N. Y.: Doubleday, Doran and Co., 1933.
Fitzgerald, Brian (ed). *Correspondence of Emilia Mary (Lennox) Fitzgerald, Duchess of Leinster, 1731–1814*. Dublin: Stationary Office, 1949.

Forbes, Thomas Roger. *The Midwife and the Witch*. New Haven: Yale University Press, 1966.

Foster, Elizabeth. *Children of the Mist: A True and Informal Account of an Eighteenth-Century Scandal*. London: Hutchinson, 1960.

Fulford, Roger (ed.). *Dearest Child: Letters between Queen Victoria and the Crown Princess of Prussia, 1858–1861*. London: Evans Brothers, 1964.

———. *Your Dear Letter: Private Correspondence of Queen Victoria and the Crown Princess of Prussia, 1865–1871*. New York: Charles Scribners' Sons, 1971.

Gay, Peter, *The Bourgeois Experience: Victoria to Freud: Vol. I, Education of the Senses*. New York: Oxford University Press, 1984.

Girouard, Mark. *Life in the English Country House: A Social and Architectural History*. New Haven: Yale University Press, 1978.

Gordon, H. Laing. *Sir James Young Simpson and Chloroform (1811–1870)*. New York: Longmans, Green & Co., 1897.

Gordon, Linda. *Women's Body, Women's Right: A Social History of Brith Control in America*. New York: Grossman Publishers, 1976.

Graham, Harvey. *Eternal Eve: The Mysteries of Birth and the Customs That Surround It*. London: Hutchinson & Co., 1960.

Granville, Castalia, Countess (ed.). *Lord Granville Leveson-Gower: Private Correspondence, 1781 to 1821*. 2 vols. London: John Murray, 1916.

Green, Thomas. *Memoirs of Her Late Royal Highness Princess Charlotte Augusta of Wales, and of Saxe-Coburg*. London: Caxton Press, 1818.

Greenhill, J. P. *Obstetrics*. 13th ed. Philadelphia and London: W. B. Saunders & Co., 1965.

Greig, James (ed.). *The Farington Diary*. London: Hutchinson & Co., 1925–1928.

Gronow, Lees H. *The Reminiscences and Recollections of Captain Gronow, 1810–1860*. 2 vols. London: John C. Nimmo, 1900.

Grosvenor, Caroline, and Charles Beilby (eds). *The First Lady Wharncliffe and Her Family, 1779–1856*. 2 vols. London: Wm. Heinemann, Ltd., 1927.

Haller, John S., and Robin Haller. *The Physician and Sexuality in Victorian America*. Urbana: University of Illinois, 1974.

Hansard's Parliamentary Debates. 3d series. Vol. 142, col. 1974 (June 26, 1856); vol. 145, col. 783 (May 25, 1857).

Hibbert, Christopher. *George IV: Regent and King.* New York: Harper & Row, 1973.

Himes, Norman. *Medical History of Contraception.* New York: Gamut Press, 1963.

Hoge, James O., and Jane Marcus (eds.). *Selected Writings of Caroline Norton.* Delmar, N.Y.: Scholars' Facsimililes and Reprints, 1978.

Hoge, James O., and Clarke Olney (eds). *The Letters of Caroline Norton to Lord Melbourne.* Columbus: Ohio State University Press, 1974.

Holland, Sir Eardley. "The Princess Charlotte of Wales: A Triple Obstetric Tragedy." *Journal of Obstetrics and Gynaecology of the British Empire* 58, December 1951: pp. 905–919.

Hollingsworth, T. H. "A Demographic Study of the British Ducal Families." *Population Studies* 11, July 1957.

———. "The Demography of the British Peerage." Supplement to *Population Studies* 18, no. 2, 1964.

Holloway, S. W. F. "Medical Education in England, 1830–1858. *History* 49, 1964: pp. 299–324.

Holme, Thea Johnston. *Prinny's Daughter: A Life of Princess Charlotte of Wales.* London: Hamish Hamilton, 1976.

Hume, J. A. (ed.). *The Letters and Journals of Lady Mary Coke.* 4 vols. London: Kingsmead Reprints, 1970.

Huxley, Gervas. *Lady Elizabeth and the Grosvenors: Life in a Whig Family, 1822–1839.* London: Oxford University Press, 1965.

———. *Victorian Duke: The Life of Hugh Lupus Grosvenor, First Duke of Westminster.* London: Oxford University Press, 1967.

Hyde, H. Montgomery. *The Londonderrys: A Family Portrait.* London: Hamish Hamilton, 1979.

Ilchester, Countess of, and Lord Stavordale (eds.). *The Life and Letters of Lady Sarah Lennox, 1745–1826.* 2 vols. London: John Murray, 1902.

Ilchester, Earl of. *Chronicles of Holland House, 1820–1900.* New York: E. P. Dutton, 1938.

——— (ed.). *Elizabeth, Lady Holland, to her Son, 1821–45.* London: John Murray, 1946.

Jewson, Norman D. "Medical Knowledge and the Patronage System in Eighteenth-Century England." *Sociology* 8, no. 3, September 1974: pp. 369–386.

Jones, Wilbur Devereux. *Lord Derby and Victorian Conservatism.* Athens: University of Georgia Press, 1956.

Kennedy, A. L. (ed.). *My Dear Duchess: Social and Political Letters to the Duchess of Manchester.* London: John Murray, 1956.

Keppel, Sonia. *The Sovereign Lady: A Life of Elizabeth Vassall, 3rd Lady Holland, with Her Family.* London: Hamish Hamilton, 1974.

Kerr, Munro, R. W. Johnstone, and Miles H. Philips. *Historical Review of British Obstetrics and Gynaecology, 1800–1950.* Edinburgh and London: E. & S. Livingstone, Ltd., 1954.

Kitzinger, Sheila. *The Experience of Childbirth.* 3d ed. Baltimore: Penguin Books, 1972.

Knighton, Sir William. Memoirs of Sir William Knighton, Baronet, G.C.H., Keeper of the Privy Purse during the Reign of His Majesty George IV including his correspondence with many Distinguished Personages. Edited by Lady Knighton. 2 vols. London: Richard Bentley, 1838.

de Lalung, H. *L'Accouchement à travers les âges et les peuples.* Paris: Cortial, 1939.

Laqueur, Thomas W. "The Queen Caroline Affair: Politics as Art in the Reign of George IV." *Journal of Modern History* 54, no. 3, September 1982.

Leconfield, Maud, Lady (ed.). *Three Howard Sisters: Selections from the Writings of Lady Caroline Lascelles, Lady Dover, and Countess Gower, 1825–1833.* London: John Murray, 1955.

Lever, Tresham (ed.). *The Letters of Lady Palmerston.* London: John Murray, 1957.

Leveson-Gower, Sir George, and Iris Palmer (eds.). *Hary-O: The Letters of Lady Harriet Cavendish, 1796–1809.* London: John Murray, 1940.

Lewis, Judith Schneid. "Maternal Health in the English Aristocracy, 1790–1840: Myths and Realities." *Journal of Social History* 17 no. 1, Fall 1983: pp. 97–114.

Litoff, Judy Barrett. *American Midwives, 1860 to the Present.* Westport, Conn.: Greenwood Press, 1978.

Londonderry, Edith, Marchioness of (ed.). *Frances Anne: The Life and Times of Frances Anne, Marchioness of Londonderry, and Her Husband Charles, Third Marquess of Londonderry.* London: Macmillan & Co., 1958.

Longford, Elizabeth. "Queen Victoria's Doctors." In Martin Gilbert, ed., *A Century of Conflict, 1850–1950.* New York: Atheneum, 1967.

Loudon, I. S. L. "A Doctor's Cash Book: The Economy of General Practice in the 1830's." *Medical History* 27, July 1983: pp. 249–268.

Macalpine, Ida, and Richard Hunter. *George III and the Mad-Business.* London: Allen Lane, 1969.

McKendrick, Neil. "Josiah Wedgewood and the Commercialization of the Potteries." In Neil McKendrick, John Brewer, and J. H. Plumb, eds., *The Birth of a Consumer Society: The Commercialization of Eighteenth-Century England.* Bloomington: Indiana University Press, 1982.

McKeown, Thomas. *The Modern Rise of Population.* London: Edward Arnold, 1976.

Marcus, Stephen. *The Other Victorians.* New York: Basic Books, 1966.

Maulitz, Russell C. "Metropolitan Medicine and the Man-Midwife: The Early Life and Letters of Charles Locock." *Medical History* 26, 1982: pp. 25–46.

Mead, Margaret, and Niles Newton. "Cultural Patterning of Perinatal Behavior." In Stephen Richardson and Alan Guttmacher, eds., *Childbearing: Its Social and Psychological Aspects.* Baltimore: Williams & Wilkins Co., 1967.

Mill, John Stuart. "The Subjection of Women." In Alice Rossi, ed., *The Feminist Papers.* New York: Bantam Books, 1980.

Mitford, Nancy (ed.). *The Ladies of Alderley: Being the Letters Between Maria Josepha, Lady Stanley of Alderley, and her Daughter-in-Law, Henrietta Maria Stanley, during the years 1841–1850.* London: Hamish Hamilton, 1967.

———. *The Stanleys of Alderley: Their Letters between 1851–1865.* London: Hamish Hamilton, 1968.

Montagu, Ashley. *Sex, Man, and Society.* New York: Tower Publications, 1969.

Morantz, Regina. "The Lady and Her Physician." In Mary S. Hartman and Lois Banner, eds., *Clio's Consciousness Raised: New Perspectives on the History of Women*. New York: Harper Colophon Books, 1974.

Moss, William. *An Essay on the Management, Nursing, and Diseases of Children from the Birth; and on the Treatment and Diseases of Pregnant and Lying-in Women, with Remarks on the Domestic Practice of Medicine. The Whole Designed for Domestic Use and Purposely adapted for Female Comprehension, in a Manner perfectly consistent with the Delicacy of the Sex; and Suited to the Medical Student and Younger Practitioner.* Egham, England: C. Boult, 1974.

Munk, William. *The Roll of the Royal College of Physicians of London.* 3 vols. 2d ed. London: The College, 1878.

National Research Council Committee on Maternal Nutrition. *Maternal Nutrition and the Course of Pregnancy.* Washington, D.C.: National Academy of Sciences, 1970.

Oakley, Ann. "A Case of Maternity: Paradigms of Women as Maternity Cases." *Signs* 4, 1979: pp. 607–631.

Oman, Carola (ed.). *The Gascoyne Heiress: The Life and Diaries of Frances Mary Gascoyne-Cecil, Marchioness of Salisbury, 1802–1839.* London: Hodder & Stoughton, 1968.

Oxorn, Harry, and William Foote. *Human Labor and Birth.* 3d ed. New York: Appleton-Century-Crofts, 1975.

Palmer, Iris. *The Face without a Frown: Georgiana, Duchess of Devonshire.* London: F. Muller, 1947.

Parry, Noel, and José Parry. *The Rise of the Medical Profession: A Study of Collective Social Mobility.* London: Croom Helm, 1976.

Perkin, Harold. *The Origins of Modern English Society, 1780–1880.* London: Routledge & Kegan Paul, 1969.

Peterson, M. Jeanne. *The Medical Profession in Mid-Victorian London.* Berkeley: University of California Press, 1978.

Plumb, J. H. "The New World of the Child in Eighteenth-Century England." *Past and Present* 67, May 1975.

Porter, Enid. *Cambridgeshire Customs and Folklore.* London: Routledge and Kegan Paul, 1969.

Potter, R. G. "Birth Intervals: Structure and Change." *Population Studies* 17, part 2, 1963: pp. 156–166.

Prescott, Frederick. *The Control of Pain.* London: English Universities Press, Ltd., 1964.

Quinlan, Maurice. *Victorian Prelude: A History of English Manners, 1700–1830*. New York: Columbia University Press, 1941.
Raymond, John (ed.). *Queen Victoria's Early Letters*. Rev. ed. London: B. T. Batsford, Ltd., 1963.
Reader, W. J. *Professional Men: The Rise of the Professional Classes in Nineteenth-Century England*. London: Weidenfeld & Nicolson, 1966.
Ridley, Viscountess (ed.). *Cecilia: The Life and Letters of Cecilia Ridley, 1819–1845*. London: Rupert Hart-Davies, 1958.
Rigby, Edward. *Memoranda for Practitioners in Midwifery*. New York: L. W. Ransom, 1840.
———. "What Is the Natural Position of a Woman during Labour?" *Medical Times and Gazette* 36, October 3, 1857: pp. 345–346.
Robertson, Robert. "Observations on the Third Stage of Labour." *London Medical Gazette*, December 31, 1841: pp. 541–543.
Rosenberg, Charles, and Carroll Smith-Rosenberg. "The Female Animal: Medical and Biological Views of Woman and Her Role in Nineteenth-Century America." *Journal of American History* 60, no. 2, September 1973: pp. 332–356.
Russell, Bertrand, and Patricia Russell (eds.). *The Amberley Papers: The Letters and Diaries of Lord and Lady Amberley*. 2 vols. London: Leonard and Virginia Woolf, 1937.
Ryan, Michael. *Lectures on Population, Marriage and Divorce, As Questions of State Medicine, Comprising an Account of the Causes and Treatment of Impotence and Sterility, Etc*. Delivered at the Medical Theater, Hatton Garden. London: Renshaw & Rush, 1831.
Scholten, Catherine M. "On the Importance of the Obstetrical Art: Changing Customs of Childbirth in America, 1760–1825." *William & Mary Quarterly*, 3d series, 34, no. 3, July 1977.
Shereshefsky, Pauline, and Leon Yarrow (eds.). *Psychological Aspects of a First Pregnancy and Early Postnatal Adaptation*. New York: Raven Press, 1973.
Shorter, Edward. *A History of Women's Bodies*. New York: Basic Books, 1982.
Shortt, S. E. D. "Physicians, Science, and Status: Issues in the Professionalization of Anglo-American Medicine in the Nineteenth Century." *Medical History* 27, January 1983: pp. 51–68.

Simpson, James Y. "Discovery of a New Anesthetic Agent, More Efficient than Sulphuric Ether." *London Medical Gazette*, November 26, 1847: pp. 934–937.

———. *Obstetric Memoirs and Contributions*. 2 vols. Edinburgh, 1855.

Smith, W. Tyler. "A Lecture on the Utility and Safety of the Inhalation of Ether in Obstetric Practice." *Lancet*, March 27, 1847.

Spring, David. "Aristocracy, Social Structure, and Religion in the Early Victorian Period." *Victorian Studies* 6, no. 3, March 1963.

Stirling, A. M. W. (ed.). *The Letter-Bag of Lady Elizabeth Spencer-Stanhope, 1806–1873*. 2 vols. London: John Lane, 1913.

Stone, Lawrence. *The Family, Sex, and Marriage in England, 1500–1800*. New York: Harper & Row, 1977.

———. "Marriage among the English Nobility in the Sixteenth and Seventeenth Centuries." *Comparative Studies in Society and History* 3, no. 2, 1961.

Struve, Christian Augustus. *A Familiar Treatise on the Physical Education of Children*. Translated from the German, and with Three Lectures by A. F. M. Willich, M.D. London: Murray & Highley, 1801.

Stuart, Dorothy M. *Daughter of England*. London: Macmillan & Co., Ltd., 1951.

———. *Dearest Bess: The Life and Times of Lady Elizabeth Foster, Afterwards Duchess of Devonshire*. London: Methuen & Co., 1955.

Suitor, Jill. "Husbands' Participation in Childbirth: A Nineteenth Century Phenomenon." *Journal of Family History* 6, 1981.

"Summary of the Report of the Select Committee Appointed to Inquire into the Causes Which Have Led to the Extensive Reduction in the Remuneration of Labour in Great Britain." *Pamphleteer* 23, no. 46.

Taylor, E. Stewart. *Beck's Obstetrical Practice*. 9th ed. Baltimore: Williams & Wilkins Co., 1971.

Thomas, David, "The Social Origins of Marriage Partners of the British Peerage in the Eighteenth and Nineteenth Centuries." *Population Studies* 26, 1972: pp. 99–111.

Thompson, F. M. L. *English Landed Society in the Nineteenth Century*. London: Routledge and Kegan Paul, 1963.

Thoms, Herbert. *Our Obstetric Heritage: The Story of Safe Childbirth*. Hamden, Conn.: Shoe String Press, 1960.

Trumbach, Randolph E. "The Aristocratic Family in England, 1690–1780." Ph. D. diss., Department of History, Johns Hopkins University, 1972.

———. *The Rise of the Egalitarian Family: Aristocratic Kinship and Domestic Relations.* New York: Academic Press, 1978.

Turberville, Arthur S. *The House of Lords in the Age of Reform, 1784–1837.* London: Faber & Faber, 1958.

van Gennep, Arnold. *The Rites of Passage.* Chicago: University of Chicago Press, 1960.

Warner, Marina. *Queen Victoria's Sketchbook.* New York: Crown, 1979.

Wertz, Richard C., and Dorothy Wertz. *Lying-in: A History of Childbirth in America.* New York: Free Press, 1977.

White, Cynthia. *Women's Magazines: 1693–1968.* London: Michael Joseph, 1970.

Wilson, Harriette. *The Memoirs of Harriette Wilson, Written by Herself.* 2 vols. London: Eveleigh Nash, 1909.

Witkowski, G. J. *Histoire des accouchements chez tous les peuples.* Paris: G. Stenheil, 1887.

Wood, Ann Douglas. "The Fashionable Diseases: Women's Complaints and Their Treatment in Nineteenth-Century America." *Journal of Interdisciplinary History* 4, Summer 1973.

Woodham-Smith, Cecil. *Queen Victoria.* New York: Alfred A. Knopf, 1972.

Wyndham, Hon. Mrs. Hugh (ed.). *Correspondence of Sarah Spencer, Lady Lyttleton, 1787–1870.* London: John Murray, 1912.

Ziegler, Philip. *Melbourne: A Biography of William Lamb, 2nd Viscount Melbourne.* London: Collins, 1976.

Index

Abdy, Lady Anne. *See* Bentick, Lady Anne
Abortion, 230
Accoucheurs, 2–4, 17, 130, 221, 222–223; career paths of, 90–91; 94–101; gentlemanliness of, 87, 91–93, 102–105, 107, 113, 117, 119–120; patronage of, 96–103, 117–121, 267n102; payment of, 92–94, 106, 108, 113–115, 119, 262n35, 265n81, 267n102; relations with clients, 8–9, 92–93, 105–115, 117–119, 173–176. *See also* Clarke, Sir Charles Mansfield; Croft, Sir Richard; Denman, Thomas; Knighton, Sir William; Locock, Sir Charles
Adultery, 38–44, 84, 227–228; perceived sinfulness of, 46–47; relationships with illegitimate children, men and women compared, 28, 39, 43-44, 169, 252n62. *See also* Divorce
Airlie, Blanche, Countess of (Hon. Blanche Stanley), 140, 200, 230, 233, 249n11; childhood and family setting, 23; courtship, 23–25, 31; wedding, 33
Airlie, David, seventh Earl of, 23–25, 33
Albert, Prince Consort, 68–69, 75, 79, 113, 128, 173, 188, 242
Almack's, 19–20, 35, 235, 238

Amberley, Kate, Lady, 125, 128, 255n13
Anesthesia, 16, 58, 72–73, 83–84, 189–192, 231
Arbuthnot, Mrs. (Maria), 117–118
Argyll, Elizabeth, Duchess of: 162
Aspinall, A., 101
Austen, Jane, 23, 117, 247n19

Badinter, Elizabeth, 77–78, 226
Baillie, Matthew, 97–98, 183, 184, 267n101
Banbury, Charlotte, Countess of, 132, 134, 148, 181, 233; and breastfeeding, 210; ill after birth of sixth child, 207–208; phlebotomized, 134; rides during pregnancy, 126
Banbury, William, titular eighth Earl of (General William Knollys), 286n43; compares town and country confinements, 158; concern for wife's health, 181, 207–208
Barham, Lady Catherine, 214–215
Beaufort, Charlotte, Duchess: 123, 233
Beeton, Isabella, 163
Bentick, Lady Anne, 42, 69, 135–136, 233
Bessborough, Harriet, Countess of, 15, 18, 25, 27, 28, 39–40, 44, 46, 47, 53, 80, 109, 168, 196, 200, 234, 250n27
Birth control. *See* contraception

305

Boys, preference for birth of, 60–61, 65–66
Breast-feeding, 193, 194–195, 209–213, 217, 230, 287n59, 288n63, 288n65
Bristol, Elizabeth, Countess of, 104
Brodie, Sir Benjamin, 95, 98, 99, 102, 105, 116
Brontë, Emily, 74
Buccleuch, Duchess of, 195
Buchan, William, 62, 67, 143, 176, 194, 195, 256n31
Burges, Hon. Elizabeth Bland, 148, 234
Burke, Edmund, 9
Burlington, Blanche, Countess of, 53, 74, 158, 164, 171–172, 198, 199–200, 234
Byron, George Gordon, Lord, 77, 139, 239, 240

Calder-Marshall, Arthur, 61, 108
Capel, Lady Caroline, 12, 81–82, 166, 168, 234, 277–278n36
Carlisle, Sir Anthony, 87, 187
Carlisle, Caroline, Countess of and Frederick, fifth Earl of, 49–50; 53, 104, 224, 240
Carlisle, Georgiana, Countess of. *See* Morpeth, Georgiana, Viscountess
Carlyle, Jane Welsh, 24, 33
Carlyle, Thomas, 231
Caroline, Princess of Wales (and Queen of England), 172, 234
Caudle, 193, 194, 198–199, 217
Cavendish, Lady Blanche. *See* Burlington, Blanche, Countess of
Cavendish, Lady Harriet. *See* Granville, Harriet, Countess

Charlotte, Princess, 7, 16, 113, 193, 234; attendants at confinement, 164, 172; death in childbirth, 100, 116, 118, 149, 154–155, 182–187, 282n97; impact of her death, 7, 16, 118–119, 154, 173–174, 179, 186–187, 269n125, 281–282n92; prenatal care of, 131–132, 132–133, 271–272n25
Childbirth: positions assumed for, 177–178, 279n64, 279–280n66; words used to describe, 71–72, 216, 288–289n75. *See also* Pregnancy, words used to describe
Christening, 193, 202–205
Churchill, Frances, Lady, 12, 52, 124, 235
Churching, 193, 201–202, 226
Clarendon, George, fifth Earl of, 29, 33, 76, 211, 250n31
Clarke, Sir Charles Mansfield, 88, 106, 112, 114, 144, 207–208; career, 94–95, 98, 100, 101, 110, 111, 120, 121; on management of the delivery, 177, 180, 181; on management of patients in labor, 174–175, 176
Clarke, John, 89, 95
Coke, Lady Mary, 40, 47, 60, 157, 158, 195
Cole, Lady Frances, 12, 70, 81–82; 127, 141–142, 166, 235; breast-feeding, 210; christening of child, 203; gives birth during hurricane, 169
Contraception, 84, 111, 212, 219, 225, 228–231, 287n59
Cooper, Sir Astley, 93–94, 95, 104, 114–115, 116–117, 262n35, 263n42, 267n102–103

Index

Coventry, Lady Augusta. *See* Fox, Lady Augusta
Cowper, Emily, Countess, 14, 20, 164, 203, 205, 235
Croft, Margaret Denman, Lady, 92, 97–98, 99, 105, 106–108, 119
Croft, Sir Richard, 94–95, 105, 111, 121, 164, 196; administers prenatal care, 131–133; character of: 106–107, 116, 118–119; and Devonshires, 92–93, 97–99, 103, 106–109, 117, 118–119, 133, 179–180, 206–207, 263n46, 265n81, 269n125; management of Princess Charlotte's case, 131–132, 132–133, 172, 182–187, 271–272n25; postpartum care, 206–207; suicide of, 100, 116, 118–119, 184, 186, 269n125; use of instruments during delivery, 179–180
Curzon, Hon. Sophia, 112, 211, 235, 277n27

Denman, Thomas, 89, 92, 94, 95, 98, 107, 109, 112, 113, 114, 121, 133–134, 140–143, 144, 187, 191, 262–263n41; attends Duchess of Devonshire, 97, 99, 133, 136, 171; and Cavendish family, 94–95, 96–97, 99, 105; compares health of lower- and upper-class women, 133, 155; on management of patients in labor, 174–176; on miscarriage, 143–144; on the third stage of labor (delivery of the placenta), 182, 184; on the use of forceps, 178–179
Denman, Thomas (the younger, Lord Chief Justice), 105, 114, 265n67

Derby, Edward, fourteenth Earl of, 29–30, 235
Derby, Emma, Countess of, 29, 81, 109–110, 235
Devonshire, Georgiana, Duchess of, 8, 12, 15, 21, 39, 50, 70, 92–93, 97, 104, 119, 133, 222, 236, 240, 246n11; christenings of children, 202, 203–204; confinement of, 199, 206–207; difficulty conceiving, 136–137; gives birth, 170–171; marriage to the Duke, 21, 26, 32, 36, 44, 60, 69, 169, 224, 226, 269n125, 273n42, 273n44; nursing, 61, 209–210, 211–213, 288n65; relationship with her children, 12, 21, 44, 67–68, 69; relationship with in-laws, 61, 203–204, 211–212; rewarded for bearing son, 61. *See also* Croft, Sir Richard, and Denman, Thomas
Devonshire, William, fifth Duke of, 20, 21, 22, 26, 32, 36, 44, 60, 61, 93, 106–108, 117, 119, 137, 169, 170–171, 224, 236, 269n125
Diet: postpartum, 193, 208–209, 216, 217, 286n44; prenatal, 131–132, 147–148. *See also* Prenatal care
Disraeli, Benjamin, 220, 224–225
Divorce, 38–48, 337–338, 351n58; Divorce Act of 1857, 20, 48, 227–228; legal procedure, 40–41, 48, 227–228; social consequences of, 41–44
Domesticity, 2–4, 8–13, 55–56, 58–60, 121, 155–156, 172–173, 195, 202, 213, 223–231; conflicts between roles of wife and mother, 67–69; and divorce, 38–48; im-

Domesticity (continued)
pact on women, 2, 17, 25, 31, 57–58, 58–60, 62, 63, 67–71, 76, 78–84, 151–152, 227–231; marriage strategies, 18–31, 55; privatization, 4, 9, 16, 38, 40, 53, 55, 58, 159, 215, 223, 227; relationship of nuclear family to extended kin, 2, 9, 12–13, 48–55, 138–139, 146–147, 150–152, 170–173, 229–230. See also Marriage

Douglas, Ann. See Wood, Ann Douglas

Dover, Georgiana, Lady, 67, 158, 161, 164–165, 172

Dowries, 18, 34–35, 44, 278n46

Drummond, Andrew Robert, 29, 159, 163, 197, 210, 236, 241, 250n32

Drummond, Lady Elizabeth, 12, 213, 236; confinement, 197; decision to marry, 28–29, 30; nursing, 210; preparation for childbirth, 159–160, 163; relationships with parents and in-laws compared, 30, 53–54

Duncannon, John, fourth Viscount, 27, 28, 50, 236

Duncannon, Harriet, Viscountess. See Bessborough, Harriet, Countess of

Duncannon, Maria, Viscountess, 77, 236; attempts nursing, 210; confinement, 181–182, 196; courtship, 27; fertility, 124; on pregnancy, 168; relationships with parents and in-laws compared, 50, 53

Ellis, Sarah Stickney, 73, 77
Evers, Harvey, 185, 186

Fane, Lady Maria. See Duncannon, Maria Viscountess

Farquhar, Sir Walter, 103–104

Fatherhood, 44, 67–69

Fertility, 6, 8, 36, 122–124, 152, 221

Forceps, 88–89, 178–181, 182–183, 185, 189, 191, 279n64, 280n71

Foster, Lady Elizabeth, 32, 44, 106–107, 108, 119, 169–170, 203, 236, 269n125, 278n46

Fox, Lady Augusta, 12, 134–135, 223, 236, 247n17; anxious to be a mother, 70–71, 76, 137–139; on marriage, 78; miscarriage, 137, 146–147; relationships with mother and mother-in-law compared, 54; stillbirths, 137

Fox, Henry, fourth Lord Holland, 12, 54, 137–139, 223–224

Fox, Marie (adopted daughter of Henry and Lady Augusta Fox), 71, 257n42

Fox, Mary (Lady Lilford, sister of Henry, fourth Lord Holland), 224

Funerals, 13–14

General Medical Act (1858), 87, 120

Gentlemanliness, 87, 91–93, 102–105; 107, 113, 117, 119–120, 261n26

George IV (earlier known as Prince of Wales and Prince Regent), 7, 39, 85, 101, 102, 103–104, 116, 117–118, 172, 203, 234, 236, 240, 267n102

George III, 36, 45, 185, 187, 267n101

Girouard, Mark, 222

Gooch, Robert, 99–100, 115

Gower, Lord. See Sutherland, second Duke of

Grafton, Elizabeth, Duchess of, 12, 158, 237; churched, 201; relationships with daughters and daughters-in-law compared, 52
Granville, Granville Leveson-Gower, first Earl, 28, 32, 36, 39–40, 44, 198, 205, 234, 237, 250n27
Granville, Harriet, Countess (Lady Harriet Cavendish), 12, 32, 44, 76, 104, 164, 237, 269n125; decision to marry, 27–28; recovers from childbirth, 205; relationship with sister, 32, 49, 50, 66–67, 70, 166, 198; travels during pregnancy, 127
Griffiths, Mrs. (monthly nurse), 164, 196
Guest, Lady Charlotte, 237; character, 80–81, 270n4; conduct during pregnancy, 124–125; gives birth, 168–169; recovery after birth, 200, 215; social position of, 270n4

Harrowby, Susan, Countess of, 128–129, 205, 237–238, 260n11
Hatherton, Hyacinthe, Lady, 42, 199, 238; childbirth, 153–154, 155, 165; courtship and marriage, 34, 69
Holland, Augusta, Lady. See Fox, Lady Augusta
Holland, Sir Eardley, 185
Holland, Elizabeth, Lady, 12, 44, 50, 65, 137, 238, 247n17; Childbirth: 75–76, 111, 168, 183; divorced from Sir Godfrey Webster, 41–42, 43, 45–46, 111; marriage to Sir Godfrey, 45–46; pregnancy, 126–127, 134, 150; recovery after birth, 215–216; relationship with her children, 43, 54, 146–147

Holland, Henry, fourth Lord. See Fox, Henry, fourth Lord Holland
Holland, Henry, third Lord (husband of Elizabeth, Lady Holland), 12, 41–42, 43, 105, 111, 117, 137, 238
Hollingsworth, T. H., 5–6
Hunter, William, 89, 95, 97, 98, 179
Husbands, presence of at births, 170–173, 188

Illegitimacy, 28, 39, 43–44, 169, 252n62
Infant Custody Act (1839), 59
Infertility, 6, 76, 135–139, 147, 148–149, 272–273n41, 273n42

James I (James VI of Scotland), 83
Jermyn, Frederick, Earl (second Marquess of Bristol), 57, 77, 213, 238
Jermyn, Katherine, Countess, 12, 57, 213, 238
Jersey, Sarah, Countess of, 61, 74–75, 128–129, 238, 271n20

Kent, Victoria, Duchess of, 160, 242
Knighton, Sir William, 88, 94–95, 99, 102, 110, 121, 134; ambitions, 85, 97; anxiety, 115–116, 268n110; education, 90–92, 95, 263n42; and George IV, 85, 101, 102, 105, 111, 117–118, 172, 267n102; and Marquess Wellesley, 98, 101, 111, 114, 263–264n48, 267n102

Lamb, Lady Caroline, 52–53, 77, 202, 203, 239
Lancet, 106, 119, 188, 189, 190
Lascelles, Lady Caroline, 67, 68, 239
Leinster, Emily Duchess of, 65, 239; extraordinary fertility of, 36–37,

Index

Leinster, Emily Duchess of, (cont.) 123–124, 136; relationship with husband, 36–37; resignation to her twelfth pregnancy, 229
Leinster, James, first Duke of, 36–37, 45
Lennox, Lady Sarah, *See* Napier, Lady Sarah
Leopold, Prince of Saxe-Coburg (husband of Princess Charlotte and future king of the Belgians), 172, 234–235
Liverpool, Robert, second Earl of, 118, 268n119
Locock, Sir Charles, 88, 138–139, 191, 207; career, 94–95, 98, 109–110, 114, 120, 121; early years, 99–100, 115; and Queen Victoria, 112–113, 128, 142, 173
Londonderry, Frances Anne, Marchioness of, 160, 205, 239; character, wealth and social position of, 204, 219–220, 222, 224–225, 289n2; christenings of children, 203, 204; fears miscarriage, 144; postpartum depression, 214; pregnancy, 128, 166–167; rewarded for birth of son, 61; travels during pregnancy, 150, 160
London, significance of giving birth in, 155, 156–160, 194
Lying-in hospitals, 88, 89, 163, 221, 260n11

Macalpine, Ida, and Hunter, Richard, 154–155, 185
Mahon, Hester, Lady, 51
Mainwaring, Emma, 191
Manningham, Richard, 87, 88, 89, 178, 259n8

Marriage, 2, 17, 44–47, 48, 226–227, 254n106; companionate, 25, 31, 35–36, 55–56, 67–69, 214–215; negative attitudes towards: 38, 67–69, 78–79, 214–215, 227, 258n62; as source of sexual satisfaction, 36–37, 167; strategies for, 18–31, 35, 55; togetherness, 37–38, 214–215
Mead, Margaret, 187
Medical fees, 92–94, 106, 108, 113–115, 119, 262n35, 267n99, 267n101, 267–268n102
Melbourne, Elizabeth, Viscountess: 39, 46, 47, 52–53, 172, 239–240
Menstrual cycle, 82–83, 136, 273n43
Midwives, 17, 83, 85, 86, 90, 105, 120, 151, 178, 221
Milbanke, Lady Judith, 122, 148, 194, 210, 211, 240, 269n1, 272–273n41
Mill, John Stuart, 31
Miscarriages, 65, 77, 135, 142–147, 148–149, 152
Modesty, 111–113, 177–178
Morantz, Regina, 112
Morley, Frances, Countess of, 11, 103, 240; miscarriages, 140, 144–146; pregnancy, 75–76, 82, 124, 125–126, 131, 132–133, 140–141, 150–151; prepares for confinement, 161; recovery after birth, 208, 209; wants a daughter, 65, 70
Morley, John, first Earl of, 11, 82, 146, 229, 230
Morning sickness, 140–141, 149, 223
Morpeth, George, sixth Viscount (and sixth Earl of Carlisle), 21–23, 24, 39, 252n75

Index

Morpeth, Georgiana, Viscountess, 32, 240; childhood and family setting, 20–21, 108, 202, 209–210, 269n125; and her children, 66–67, 164; confinements, 198, 207, 263n46; courtship, 21–23, 25; relations with in-laws, 49–50, 52, 166, 198; use of wet-nurses, 211
Mortality, 223, 260n16; infant, 6, 148; maternal, 182–187
Moss, William, 133, 195–196, 207

Naming practices, significance of, 10–11, 55, 58, 64–65, 223, 247n19; use of and choice of first names, 58, 64–65, 255–256n24; use of names rather than titles, 11–13, 55; nicknames, 11–13, 247n19
Napier, Lady Sarah (Lady Sarah Lennox), 11, 72, 209, 240; and her children, 66; confinement, 166, 197; divorce and remarriage, 40–41, 42–43, 45–46, 82, 135; marriage to Sir Charles Bunbury, 32, 45, 135, 226; miscarriage, 143–144; wants a daughter, 65
Nature, reliance on during childbirth, 154–155, 173–174, 178–179, 187; role of in defining health, 129, 132, 135, 136, 149–150, 151–152, 221–223
Newton, Niles, 187
Noel, Mary, 122, 210
Norton, Caroline, 59
Nurses, monthly, 162–165, 173; wet, 163, 172, 195, 209, 211, 212, 213, 217, 277n27
Nursing. *See* Breast-feeding

Oakley, Anne, 3, 17
Obstetric Society, 87, 120, 187
Obstetricians. *See* Accoucheurs
Opiates, use of, 141–142, 144, 184, 206–207, 216
Ould, Sir Fielding, 88, 89, 260n17

Palmerston, Emily Viscountess. *See* Cowper, Emily, Countess
Patronage. *See* Accoucheurs
Pelvic exams, 112–113, 177
Perkin, Harold, 96
Peterson, Jeanne, 103, 120
Physicians, Royal College of, 85, 87, 91
Pornography, 258n64
Postmaturity, 166–167, 186
Postpartum depression, 213–216
Pregnancy, words used to describe, 71–72. *See also* Childbirth
Prematurity, 165–166
Prenatal care, 147–151; diet, 131–132, 144; exercise, 122, 125–126, 132–133; lowering system, 130–135, 144; phlebotomy, 130, 133–135, 141, 144, 146, 176. *See also* Nature
Primogeniture, 5, 9–10, 49; eldest sons, 9, 58, 64; younger sons, 10, 64

Regent Prince. *See* George IV
Ridley, Lady Cecilia, 12, 51, 166, 240
Rigby, Edward, 177, 222, 280n66
Rivers, Susan, Lady, 11–12, 133, 167, 241, 288n63
Romanticism, 24–26, 31, 46, 209, 219–223, 224, 231; *See also* Nature
Russell, Lord John, 128

Rutland, John, fifth Duke of, and Elizabeth, Duchess of, 12, 29, 53–54, 58, 191, 197, 213, 236, 238

St. Jules, Caroline (Hon. Mrs. George Lamb), 44, 107, 269n125, 278n46
Salisbury, Frances, Marchioness of, 14, 35, 199, 203, 214, 241
Scarborough, Frederica, Countess of, 11, 210, 241
Seymour-Conway, Lady Horatia, 52, 204–205, 241
Shorter, Edward, 2, 201
Simpson, Sir James Young, 72, 83–84, 88, 121, 189, 190
Smellie, William, 89, 94, 95
Spas, 132, 136–137, 150
Spencer, Georgiana, first Countess of (Dowager), 21, 26, 93, 98, 106–108, 170, 202, 236
Spring, David, 10
Stafford, Susan, Marchioness of, 11, 12, 36, 52, 60, 123, 214, 241
Stanley of Alderley, Henrietta Maria, Lady, 14, 23, 61, 241–242; has abortion, 230; and anesthesia, 191; and her children, 23–25; and her husband, 37, 68; and her mother-in-law, 54–55
Stanley, Blanche. *See* Airlie, Blanche, Countess of
Stillbirth, 6, 137, 149, 183
Stone, Lawrence, 2, 8, 11, 18, 58, 67, 156, 195, 209, 247n19
Struve, Christian Augustus, 62, 71, 73
Stuart-Wortley, Lady Caroline, 186
Stuart-Wortley, Lady Emmeline, 213
Sutherland, Elizabeth, Countess of, 5, 11, 12, 39, 141, 242, 247n17; attitude towards children, 62, 66; and birth control, 228–229; christening of heir, 205; confinements, 197–198, 216; uses wet nurses, 211, wealth and position of, 5, 13
Sutherland, George, second Duke of (husband of Harriet, Duchess of Sutherland), 11, 33, 34, 161–162, 171, 242
Sutherland, Harriet, Duchess of, 33, 34, 100, 101, 127, 160, 164, 165, 171, 200, 205, 242, 247n17; ill after birth of sixth child, 207, 208–209; nurses her infant, 210, 288n63; relationships with sisters, 74, 164–165

Thomas, David, 30
Thynne, Andrew, 103, 112, 132, 140, 175, 178–179, 180–181
Trumbach, Randolph, 8, 11, 30, 34, 156, 194–195, 196, 197, 209, 217

Underwood, Michael, 113, 172, 288n65

Vanderbilt, Consuelo, Duchess of Marlborough, 60
Van Gennep, Arnold, 156, 276n7
Verulam, Charlotte, Countess of, 242, 268n119; christening of children, 202–203; confinements, 161, 165, 200, 201; nursing behavior, 82, 212, 230; pregnancies, 82–83, 124, 134, 142, 230; relationship with husband, 69, 82–83, 214–215, 230
Verulam, James, first Earl of, 11, 69, 82–83, 142, 161, 214, 229–230, 242
Victoria, Crown Princess of Prussia, 12, 53, 70, 75, 78–79, 142

Index

Victoria, Queen, 7, 33, 80, 99, 101, 110, 160, 242; and Albert, 68–69, 75, 79, 173, 188; and anesthesia, 83–84, 189, 191; attitudes towards childbearing, 1, 53, 72, 75, 112–113, 173, 215; and her daughter, 12, 53, 70, 75, 142; on marriage, 78–79, 227, 258n62; on maternal nursing, 211; postpartum depression, 213; pregnancy of, 125, 128, 142; recovery, 198, 205, 208

Virginity, 79, 226–227, 258n64

Waterloo, Battle of, 8, 94, 120, 166
Webster, Elizabeth, Lady. See Holland, Elizabeth, Lady
Weddings, 32–34, 47
Wellesley, Hyacinthe. See Hatherton, Hyacinthe, Lady
Wellesley, Lady Charlotte (Marchioness of Anglesey), 11, 41, 46–47
Wellesley-Pole, Catherine, 165–166
Wellesley, Richard, Marquess, father of Lady Hatherton and Lady Anne Bentick, 34, 42, 70, 136, 233 238; patron of Sir William Knighton, 98, 101, 114, 263–264n48, 267n102
Wertz, Richard W. and Dorothy C., 9
Westminster, Constance, Duchess of, 53, 243; marriage, 33–34; preparations for childbirth, 162, 165
Westminster, Elizabeth, Marchioness of, 211, 243; confinements, 199, 215; courtship, 35; depressed after birth of eighth daughter, 214; marriage, 32, 34–35
Westmoreland, Pricilla, Countess of, 243, 281–182n92
White, Charles, 89
Wilson, Harriette, 250n27; 261n26
Wollstonecraft, Mary, 69
Wood, Ann Douglas, 112